MILITARY FORCES IN 21st CENTURY
PEACE OPERATIONS

This book explains why neither military nor civilian agencies can act alone in managing modern conflicts and why joint civil-military efforts are needed. As the record of peace operations interventions over nearly a decade and a half since the end of the Cold War demonstrates that the international community is doing badly at creating civil-military partnerships, the author argues that those efforts must be deliberately planned from the outset of an operation and cannot be added on as afterthoughts when all else has failed.

As the divisive issues are neither simply structural nor organizational but predominantly cultural, they involve attitudes, beliefs, perceptions – positive and negative, partly true and partly false. The solutions to the problems and misunderstandings involve changing attitudes, moving beyond prejudices and replacing competition with cooperation. James V. Arbuckle proposes that the principal mechanisms for resolving these issues will be common *and concurrent* civil-military training and education.

James V. Arbuckle served thirty-six years as an infantryman in Canada and in Germany, and with UNFICYP and UNPROFOR. He is a member of the Faculty of the Lester B. Pearson Canadian International Peacekeeping Training Centre, and was from 1999 to 2003 working with the OSCE. He now lives in Austria.

CONTEMPORARY SECURITY STUDIES

MILITARY FORCES IN 21ST CENTURY PEACE OPERATIONS

No job for a soldier?

James V. Arbuckle

Routledge
Taylor & Francis Group

LONDON AND NEW YORK

First published 2006
by Routledge
2 Park Square, Milton Park, Abingdon, Oxon OX14 4RN

Simultaneously published in the USA and Canada
by Routledge
270 Madison Ave, New York, NY 10016

Routledge is an imprint of the Taylor & Francis Group,
an informa business

Transferred to Digital Printing 2009

© 2006 James V. Arbuckle

Typeset in Times New Roman by
Newgen Imaging Systems (P) Ltd, Chennai, India

British Library Cataloguing in Publication Data
A catalogue record for this book is available from the British Library

Library of Congress Cataloging in Publication Data
A catalog record for this book has been requested

ISBN10: 0–415–39370–1 (hbk)
ISBN10: 0–415–54498–X (pbk)
ISBN10: 0–203–96939–1 (ebk)

ISBN13: 978–0–415–39370–6 (hbk)
ISBN13: 978–0–415–54498–6 (pbk)
ISBN13: 978–0–203–96939–7 (ebk)

This book is dedicated to Senator (Lieutenant-General Ret'd)
Romeo Dallaire, O.C.,C.M.M.,M.S.C.,C.D.
A hero to all, save only to himself;
Never without honour – EVER.

CONTENTS

CONTENTS

Part I

PEACE IN THE MODERN WORLD

We have finished the job; what shall we do with the tools?
(Emperor Haile Selassie
of Abyssinia, 1941)

1

PREFACE

In 1995, I was one of four facilitators on a course at the Lester B. Pearson Canadian International Peacekeeping Training Centre in Nova Scotia. Of about thirty participants on the course, perhaps one-third were Canadian military, the rest were international military and civilians. One day, in the course of a lecture on coordinating mechanisms in multi-agency operations, the lecturer, a serving Canadian officer, informed us that he had under his command in Bosnia-Herzegovina 'a light armoured squadron re-roled as recce'. I was one of less than ten persons in that room who had the slightest idea what all that meant – which was, at any rate, of little importance to the subject at hand. Everyone else – military and civilians – was baffled, alienated, and to some degree angered by the arrogance and the opacity of the jargon.

I knew then that a book like this needed to be written, but it took me five years to realize that I would have to write it.

This book presents some views of the interrelationships of military and civilian agencies in modern peace operations. It is written for those in the military who may be sceptical about their armies' suitability for peace operations, on the grounds that such operations degrade their capability to fight and win the nation's wars. These are not always soldiers. Winston Churchill, sometimes a soldier, said that 'Those who can win a war well can rarely make a good peace and those who could make a good peace could never have won the war'.[1] This book has also been written for those who may be sceptical about any army's suitability either for humanitarian relief or for conflict resolution; these may believe that armed forces are more frequently a part of the problem than of any solution. This second group is usually, but not always, civilians. As Condaleeza Rice said in 2000: 'The military is a special instrument. It is meant to be. It is not a civilian police force. And it is most certainly not intended to build a civilian society'.[2]

Ironically, the two groups often seem to agree: it's no job for a soldier. Thus, when the Commander of US Forces in Afghanistan said, 'Job one is close with and destroy those who would destroy us. Nation building is not in my charter',[3] one could scarcely quibble with his interpretation of US policy – even if building an army without reference to the state which it was to serve might sound like the recipe for a *Reichswehr*. However, just over one year later, back in the

3

United States and in a new command, that same officer was quoted as having said that 'Afghanistan's recovery from war and economic stagnation is in danger unless the international community takes bolder steps in the rebuilding efforts...security...would improve if the nation's economy received foreign assistance for big projects like roads'.[4]

So there is really a third group for whom this book is written, and it includes all those of us who see both –' or many – sides of this very important question. Instead of the 'No, but –' groups, they might form the 'Yes, but –' group.

I hope that, after reading this book, that third group will be much the larger.

Jamie Arbuckle, Vienna, 2003 and Cambridge, 2004

Acknowledgements

I have many to thank, and absolutely none to blame, for this book. I want to thank the Lester B. Pearson Canadian International Peacekeeping Training Centre for getting me started on re-thinking my experiences in critical modes I could not otherwise have imagined: especially Alex, Ben, David, Dorothy and Pam, helped with their advice, support and friendship. I am forever grateful to Stephanie, Jason and Joshua who actually lived a good deal of what I have written. My editor, Donald Halstead, more than anyone, convinced me that the manuscript had a book in it, and despite his busy schedule stayed with me through several revisions, until it was so. The final form of this book owes much to those anonymous reviewers who provided such substantial and constructive criticism. Above all, I must thank my partner, critic, editor-in-chief and wife, Dr Ingrid Lehmann, without whom I would never have realized this need, nor seen it through. My greatest debt, however, is to the soldiers of all ranks, past, present and future, of The Royal Canadian Regiment, which has for almost my entire adult life been more than my profession, and far more than my career – it has been my home, and in a sense it still is.

2

INTRODUCTION

Our army is composed of the scum of the earth.
(The Duke of Wellington, 1831)

Obedient, sober, mute, and nameless like mud, that is the army of
the future, my Prince.
(Ismail Kadare, *Three Elegies for Kosovo*, 1998)

Peacekeeping operations have not *come a long way since their modern inception in the aftermath of the Second World War*, nor have they come very far since their supposed renaissance in the aftermath of the Cold War. Doctrinally and conceptually, it seems as if more than a half-century of peacekeeping, just like more than a decade of peace enforcement, had all been crammed into a past so recent as to prevent any analysis, let alone any learning from that far from brief experience. We are now into that heretofore nearly unimaginable twenty-first century, repeating questions, carrying forward misperceptions, re-making mistakes that have been with us throughout the last half of the previous century. For all our talk of lessons learned, that book is always and everywhere dwarfed by the book of lessons *not* learned.

The major difficulty which has haunted us this past half-century or so has been the failure of military and civilian agencies to develop reliable and efficacious relationships in crises which clearly and repeatedly call for them to do that above all else. There is no lack of evidence that this failure is serious and frequent, but there has been little durable work on finding and installing remedies. The history of twentieth century peacekeeping will be of inching our way forward, repeating mistakes endlessly even when we know better, losing our way so frequently as to give rise to serious questioning about whether this is even progress at all. For all our seeming understanding of the conflicts which dominate our lives, which threaten our societies, we might be Easter Islanders.

As the twenty-first century opens, the coalition invasion and occupation of Iraq in 2004, which is scarcely a peacekeeping operation in its goals or in its effects, nevertheless illustrates the essential themes of this work. The superpower (with its dwindling array) was very quickly bogged down in insuperable difficulties, having wagered against all advice that a military solution would be *the* solution, that a single power could achieve almost alone what it judged that the international community could not (or would not) do, and that international agencies, especially non-governmental organizations (NGOs), would be of little use. Then, belatedly and amid growing domestic and re-awakened international scepticism, the international community, specifically the United Nations, was urged to assume an important post-war role. At about that same time, the US Secretary of Defence and a British former Secretary-General of the North Atlantic Treaty Organization (NATO) also made fresh demands on NATO to 'renew' that regional organization by assuming further responsibilities in Iraq and in Afghanistan.

The Iraq situation thus re-affirms, even if by default, a few things which many knew all along:

- Neither military nor civilian agencies can act effectively alone in managing modern conflicts.
- Joint civil-military efforts are needed, and those efforts must be deliberately planned from the outset of an operation; they cannot be added on as afterthoughts when all else has failed.
- The record of such interventions over nearly a decade and a half since the end of the Cold War demonstrates that we are doing badly at creating civil-military partnerships, and that we are not getting better.

However the issues of international and inter-organizational cooperation may be managed or mismanaged at the strategic level, at the operational and the tactical level the divisive issues are not simply structural nor organizational, they are predominantly cultural. They involve attitudes, beliefs, perceptions – positive and negative, partly true and partly false. The solutions to the problems and misunderstandings which thus arise will involve changing attitudes, moving beyond prejudices, replacing competition with cooperation. The principal mechanisms for resolving these issues will be common *and concurrent* civil-military training and education.

Of course, there may be structural impediments to better inter-agency cooperation, and there may be structural remedies. For one example, the creation of Civil-Military Operations Coordination Centres (CMOCC) in missions where civil-military cooperation was considered critical, was a success that has now so many fathers that it is a little difficult to tell just where it began. One of the earliest of these was established in Somalia (UNOSOM I) in 1993, when the Special Representative of the Secretary-General (SRSG) directed his Civil Affairs Officer to find some way of coordinating critical information among the military and the civilian agencies in the area. (Michael C. Williams says the UNOSOM CMOCC was copied from an earlier UNPROFOR-UNHCR model.[1]) The CMOCC of the United Nations Mission in Haiti (UNMIH) was housed in a hangar at the airport, and was like a trade fair: one entered the hangar to find an information desk, a diagram of the Centre's layout, and around the hangar were the booths of all the organizations and agencies who wished to be there. The area was secure and you could drink the water. Each day there were completely open briefings which might be attended by almost anyone who had any business there at all. At those briefings one might hear the most frank and intimate details of such issues as road and bridge states, demining, and health and security issues. The CMOCC of the United Nations Mission in Kosovo (UNMIK) was much the same. However, the NGO participation in the UNMIK CMOCC was minimal, most of them disdaining even the most informal contact with what they considered a military organization.

Organizational barriers to cooperation are more complex. In 1992 a much-discussed issue for the United Nations Protection Force in the former Yusoslavia (UNPROFOR) concerned the Pink Zones, those areas in Croatia which were pre-dominantly Serb, but were outside the Protected Areas that were the basis of the UN mandate in Croatia. The common wisdom then was that UNPROFOR would never go into the Pink Zones, but it was nevertheless clear that the United Nations would either enter the Pink Zones or watch them blow up in their faces. The European Community Monitors (ECM), who were active in the Pink Zones, were invited to take up a desk in the UNPROFOR Operations Centre. The arrangement lasted about two weeks, until the Chief Operations Officer of UNPROFOR and the ECM Sector Chief learned of this unauthorized crossing of lines, and the arrangement was abruptly terminated. Less than six weeks later UNPROFOR, acting in great haste and with some serious information gaps, occupied the Pink Zones (see Chapter 17).

But organization charts need not be the cattle runs they sometimes become. The Four Pillars of the UNMIK do *not* include the Kosovo Force (KFOR), which is only briefly referred to in the enabling United Nations Security Council Resolution (UNSCR) 1244 (S/1999/661, 9 June 1999) as 'the international security presence'. Nevertheless, the cooperation between the international civilian and military agencies in Kosovo is as close and effective as I have seen (see also Chapter 6). The CMOCC that many NGO's would not set foot in was entirely provided by KFOR – the space was rented, staffed, organized by them and then made freely available to all.

Organizational and structural barriers do exist, and sometimes organizational and structural remedies may alleviate the problems they cause. However, those barriers exist and will continue to arise because at its root the problem is attitudinal and cultural, and will only be remedied by addressing it as such. Adding layers to organizations often has little to do with solving problems, and proposals which cost money are easily defeated or postponed. We are all well aware of the dangers of bureaucratic layering, we know how infrequently more layers solve problems and we know too well how easy it is to defeat anything which does not already have a budget line. The CMOCC was a success in most missions where it was established in no small part just because it cost nothing – the personnel were already there in some position or another, and this was merely one way for them to do their jobs. The infrastructure was minimal and the cost must have been next to nothing. No one in New York or Washington or Brussels had to be asked if this might be done.

This attitudinal aspect of the problem is especially acute in humanitarian peace operations, and it is this aspect of the spectrum of peacekeeping operations on which this book will largely but not exclusively concentrate. The authors of the report of *The International Commission on Intervention and State Sovereignty* have written of

> the very strong opposition expressed by humanitarian agencies, humanitarian organizations and humanitarian workers towards any militarization of the word 'humanitarian'; whatever the motives of those engaging in the intervention, it is anathema for the humanitarian relief and assistance sector to have this word *appropriated* to describe any kind of military action.[2]

Nevertheless, as will be shown, humanitarian intervention often must be accompanied, and has sometimes been preceded, by a military intervention. The recent history of Kosovo, in particular the experience of the Organization for Security and Cooperation in Europe (OSCE) there, as well as that of the NGO community, illustrates this.

Those NGOs who expressed their humanitarian disdain for the military by staying away from the UNMIK CMOCC, had in fact been forced to withdraw into Macedonia and Albania in the spring of 1999, largely because of the seriously deteriorating security situation. The internationals, then principally the OSCE, left as well – and, by then, so had nearly 90% of the Kosovar Albanian population. The internationals and the NGOs were able to return to Kosovo by the end of that summer only because by then the KFOR was there too. Most important, so were the refugees – in addition to those 75,000 who had been assisted to return by the UNHCR, there had occurred 'massive "spontaneous returns" ' of Kosovar Albanians 'who have come back without the assistance of the international community.... Just ninety days after the conclusion of the fighting, some 800,000 Kosovar Albanians had returned home..., before the international community could set up its operations, clear land mines and deliver critical supplies'.[3] It seemed not to matter to the 'beneficiaries' that 'their' operation had been 'militarized' – they were home, and that was all that mattered to them.

It is very clear that it is the military–NGO interface which is the most difficult in peace operations, and this is especially true of humanitarian operations. And it is here that the antithetical attitudes and cultures are most clearly manifest. The problems arise in part due to growth: just as peace operations of all kinds increased ten-fold in the 1990s, so did NGOs experience their own exponential growth in numbers and types of organizations. In 1995 the UN estimated that there were 29,000 international NGOs; five years later there were more than 2 million in the United States alone. In the USSR there were none; in Russia in 2000 there were 65,000. In Kenya, 240 new NGOs are created each year.[4] Thomas Weiss has described the resulting situation in the following words:

> Last week, I was talking to a couple of colleagues just back from Kigali. I learned that there are at least 150 international NGOS in Kigali tripping over one another, vying for turf, looking for resources. I have described this effort as like trying to herd cats.[5]

8

Actually, Weiss' information was not quite accurate: others subsequently estimated at least twice that number of NGOs in Kigali in 1994 – but no one was quite sure. Five years later, in Kosovo, which is a box about 100 kilometres on a side, some estimated there were about 500 NGOs in the province – but no one was quite sure.

Michael C. Williams has described the changing situation and roles of the NGOs, and the problems which have attended this growth:

> The proliferation of NGOs is one of the most remarkable developments in the landscape of political and social conflict in the 1990s.... As the number of NGOs has increased so has their impact on crises. These organizations have taken on work that governments and international agencies were unable, or unwilling, to do. They have usually been the first to enter a country and the last to leave.... NGOs work at the grassroots, often with local knowledge that is superior to that of military intelligence. They are able to bypass the local political bureaucracy with which foreign military forces have to treat on a formal basis.... NGOs are by nature flexible and anti-bureaucratic, strengths that enable them to undertake work that others cannot.

That is the plus-side of the balance sheet. However, every organizational culture has its strengths and its weakness; Williams gives us both sides of the story:

> As RAND Corporation analysts Margaret Cecchine Harrell and Robert Howe put it, 'many of the people with whom the military must deal have little understanding of the military and may be actively anti-military. This is especially true of the volunteer non-governmental organizations, many of which were formed largely due to mistrust of or dissatisfaction with governmental agencies'.... David Owen found the military in Bosnia 'bitter in their denunciation of some of the NGOs who to them were a pestilential nuisance, resisting all attempts at coordination, and then complaining that they were not being properly protected'.

Williams summarizes: 'Many NGOs regard the military as out of touch with the values and members of the society they seek to protect. The military, on the other hand, can see NGOs as undisciplined and an impediment to their work'.[6]

We will return to this subject again (see Chapters 9 and 26), not to belabour the NGOs, but to explore further this most complex and vital aspect of civil-military cooperation.

Suffice it here now to reiterate that, in the twenty-first century, civilian and military agencies can no more work in isolation from one another than could armies, navies and air forces operate effectively in single service isolation in the twentieth century.

This book will suggest that the military are often their own worst advocates, fuelling prejudice and tending to justify stereotyping, presenting themselves clumsily or not at all, and seeming to fulfil pre-judgement based on apocryphal and anachronistic views.

It has been a near constant of recent humanitarian interventions that the security environment was from the outset, or soon became, the *conditio sine qua non* of the operation: either a factor in launching the operation at all, as in Kosovo, or in its sustainment, as in pre-Dayton Bosnia. Nevertheless, failure on the part of other agencies to understand the military, or to recognize them as an essential partner, tends to preclude an understanding of military goals and capabilities. Prejudice thus generally restricts the usefulness of the military, as the civilians – politicians, diplomats, international and regional organizations, NGOs – place unrealistic demands on a military force, withhold trust and respect, and marginalize their contribution.

This book has three aims. In order of priority these are:

First, to present the military culture to their civilian partners, as one characterized by traditions of study, discipline, hardihood, service and diversity, but one whose efficacy in humanitarian operations is often limited by negative perceptions in the very community they attempt to serve.

These negative perceptions of the military are of course mirrored by a traditional military disdain for civilians.

Thus the second aim of this book is to awaken the military to the need for civilian, international, regional and NGOs as fully cooperative partners in humanitarian operations.

The military are easily their own worst advocates, reinforcing negative stereotypes by their behaviour and their language, and it is here that the military have much soul searching to do, especially in respect of the received wisdom of their cultural heritage.

The third aim of this book is therefore to re-cast military roles and capabilities for the military themselves. The military culture must be a window, not a barrier; an opportunity for communications, not a substitute for them. So this book, in presenting the military to the civilians, might also be to the military as the adage on the architrave of the Temple of Apollo at Delphi: *Know thyself*.

Following this introduction, Part II will discuss the positive aspects of military culture and traditions, and describe the countervailing prejudices. It will be proposed that a more catholic appreciation of the military might foster a more comprehensive view of, and a more co-operative attitude towards, the military as a major and often vital contributor to humanitarian operations. I will described how the modern soldiers' culture can be a vehicle for change, just as those soldiers will cling to some austere values, such as their hardihood and their discipline, which are of constant value to them – and to those who may, from time to time, very badly need for them to do so.

Part III will describe in more detail how that culture has yielded a body of doctrinal principles, and how that intellectual corpus has yielded capabilities that have in turn led to formal structures and practices. Here lie the remedies to the problems, which are in reality neither organizational nor structural, but are in fact cultural. Recognition and an appreciation of cultural differences as such will suggest how they may be overcome or accommodated. For example, the insistence by the International Committee of the Red Cross (ICRC) on its twinned traditions of neutrality and confidentiality are seen by some as a refusal to name and to condemn evil – it was in breaking with this tradition that Bernard Kouchner (among others) founded Medicins Sans Frontiers (MSF). But these traditions must be seen in light of Swiss traditions and culture, and allowance must be made for them – the ICRC will approach its work non-judgementally, and it will never make public whatever negotiations and accommodations it may from time to time enter into with any parties.

Part IV will propose that the remedy to what is clearly a cultural conflict will be training and education, and will describe very briefly what is now being done, and some brave and imaginative efforts in this direction which must be rescued from bureaucratic conflicts and neglect. It will be seen that training and education can lead to the development of empathetic relationships, which can and must replace the traditionally antithetical relationships.

Part V will conclude and summarize this review of the problems of military and civilian operations.

Mathew Arnold's famous definition of culture as 'the best that has been thought and said in the world', is an echo of a more certain age. We have learned that not all aspects of culture are entirely positive, and this is especially true of the military culture. Certain aspects of the military culture such as social apartheid, a predilection for authoritarian systems and structures, and a reliance on received wisdom, have become ingrained for very good historical and social reasons, many of which are today nevertheless anachronistic. At the same time, a simplistic attitude towards neutrality, a dislike of the use of force towards any ends and in any situations is also simply outdated. In an increasingly interdependent world, and in increasingly interdependent peace operations, we can no longer afford to maintain cultural barriers, but must seek instead to find ways to communicate and to interact effectively with other cultures, as with the organizations and agencies they manifest.

The members of the military professions – the soldiers, sailors and aircrew – are like medical doctors, entertainers, athletes, in that they often select their eventual careers at an early age. Many of these would have begun a long and especially demanding apprenticeship at an age when they may not have been entirely aware of just what they had decided on. (Nineteenth-century and earlier Royal Navy officers, like two of Jane Austen's brothers, were enrolled as midshipmen in their pre-teens.) Decisions made by adolescents tend also to be highly romantic, but that romanticism often endures into maturity and beyond. Altruism, adventure, service, along with travel and a dislike of routine, characterize many in the military, and not just those in their first assignments.

It is little recognized that this is a point the military often have in common with many civilian peacekeepers – in the New Member Induction Programme at the OSCE, the class participants will often average forty years of age, or older. These middle-aged, and often older, civilian women and men, usually highly educated and widely experienced, are often headed for remote places of discomfort, danger and relatively little pay. They are thus more like the officers than either group commonly realizes.

I spent my early years wanting to be a soldier, and my middle period being one. Like many officers, I considered myself a student of my profession. My earliest service was marked by rigorous study and gruelling examinations. This produced, and still produces in most officers today, a decidedly academic attitude towards the history and the culture of the military profession, even when 'the exigencies of the service' saw to it that we pursued our researches in an environment often primitive in the extreme – in the year I wrote Lieutenant-to-Captain promotion examinations, I spent 180 days in the field.

Cohesiveness of culture and of attitudes is a strength, but it can be a weakness as well. For better or for worse, then, I will in what follows often speak from personal experience. I am well aware of the perils of reference to purely personal experience. However, if the unexamined life is worth little, the unlived examination has also its shortcomings. As Eric Hobsbawm has described in his analysis of the twentieth century:

> This book...rests on curiously uneven foundations. In addition to the wide and miscellaneous reading of a good many years,...I have drawn on the accumulated knowledge and opinions of...what the social anthropologists call a 'participant observer', or simply...an open-eyed traveller.[7]

In just that spirit of the 'open-eyed traveller', I intend to synthesize direct experience, study and research. This, then, is my epistemology: to situate my direct experiences on a wider plain where research – indirect experience – will serve to contextualize and to broaden my field of observation.

There have been others who have investigated the role of the military in modern peace operations, and I am grateful to several for their works, to which I refer in this book. These modern investigators have usually been non-military, seeking as it were to work from the outside inwards. They have sometimes not been very successful, and there are several reasons for this. In the first place, they are detected and perceived as investigators, and are either resented or misled, sometimes both. Second, there is the Heisenberg Principle: observation alters the observed, whether the experiments in Hartford which proved only that people are *always* more productive when they know they are observed,[8] or what has been called the Vance Effect, whereby 'the parties' to a conflict will *always* misbehave for distinguished visitors.[9] It has too often seemed that the outside-in approach to the military culture has so far produced little of real value: as little that will ring true to the soldiers, as will usefully instruct civilians.[10] Perhaps the military culture will only yield to working from the inside-out, as did Clausewitz, du Picq, John Masters, Sir John Hackett and S.L.A. Marshall, for just a few examples of soldiers whose pens were at least as mighty as their swords. Indeed, the fact that the military constitutes a culture not easily accessible to outsiders is scarcely a recent discovery.

This is not to say that the outsiders' views are without value, still less that outsiders have no contribution to make. Clearly, external audits have value just because they are external to the subject. To state otherwise is indeed the ad hominem argument often advanced – fallaciously or self-servingly – by the insiders, the self-appointed elite. As I will relate elsewhere, H.G. Wells accurately described aerial warfare – and its futility – at a time when there was not an air force in the world.

It might seem that this book, written by a Canadian with some NATO experience, is necessarily Western (specifically North American and European) in its orientation, especially in describing the military culture. However, my experience, at first hand and more widely still at second hand, is also with international peace operations, and these are scarcely Western constructs. For example, in UNPROFOR in 1992 I was responsible for the Operations Centre in the headquarters of the Force. Under my command were duty officers from Russia, Czechoslovakia, Poland, Kenya, France and Nigeria. As I will describe later, the United Nations rather vaguely follows some NATO doctrines, but not all, so I was concerned to see how the former Warsaw Pact (WP) and African officers would work into this. I was also concerned that former WP officers would be meeting former Soviet officers for the first time since the Cold War, and I could not imagine how their relationships could be other than fraught, to say the least.

As it happened, I had nothing to worry about on the scores of competence, nor of cooperation.

The Kenyan officer had been the Adjutant of his country's Staff College, the Nigerian had done his officer training at Royal Military Academy Sandhurst; the former Warsaw Pact officers and the Russians were scrupulously professional and highly competent, and were able to understand nearly all their fellow Slavs, a tremendous and unlooked-for capability of my group.[11] All spoke excellent English, and all had undergone Staff College training in their own countries. Never have I seen so many hatchets buried so quickly and so deeply. I realized then that I was seeing the military culture at its best: open to change, quick to adapt, pride in professional excellence, comfortable with stress and fatigue. These were, I realized for the severalth time in my career, not Western values nor culture, they were rather professional values and culture. And all had served from time to time in various military alliances and coalitions, both standing (such as NATO and the WP) and *ad hoc* (such as peace keeping operations), and were well accustomed to submerging their national cultures in a collective culture; any tendency to ethno-centrism would have long ago been left at home.

Nor did I ever experience national-cultural differences to have significant impact on collective capacities for peace operations. Most national contingents are relatively small, usually about battalion strength and, whether or not a given nation does or does not have conscription, peacekeepers are almost always volunteers who are serving beyond an initial engagement. Moreover, the officers and senior NCOs are almost always professionals and it is this professionalism which, in my experience, creates a potential for bonding within the military culture. In this culture, with all its strengths and weaknesses, units and officers and soldiers are more alike than not, and it is that military culture which tends to unite them, whatever national and/or cultural differences might otherwise be the norms.

Throughout this book we will encounter significant communication gaps and misunderstandings. This is in no small part due to the inadequacies of the contextual framework which has confounded discussions of peace operation since their inception, which for the purposes of this book is taken as the founding of the United Nations. The next chapter will therefore summarize very briefly the current contextual framework for peace operations.

3

TOWARDS A CONCEPTUAL FRAMEWORK FOR PEACE OPERATIONS

Doctrine: a set of guiding principles, carried into effective structures and roles, is a powerful tool for shaping what we aim to do, influencing how we perceive our tasks and guiding us as we fill our toolkits. Doctrine is not dogma, it is guidance and not rules, and one who designs or one who implements doctrine is not a *doctrinaire*. Doctrine is at best permissive, not restrictive: it should tell us not what we may not do, rather doctrine should guide us as to how we might do what we want or need to do. Doctrine is where principles and practice meet, and it is also where academics and practitioners meet – or they should.

Peacekeeping doctrine is notoriously imprecise, and the frequent vacuums, lacunae, duplications and misunderstandings encountered by students and practitioners of peace operations are themselves a major obstacle in a cross-cultural communications exercise which is already complex enough. Inevitably, the academic confusion is shared by the practitioners in field operations. What types of peace operations are we discussing? Or, more to the point, what sort of operation are we now *doing?* What do these terms mean: use of force, rules of engagement, command and control? – and these are military terms. How are they to be communicated to putative civilian partner agencies, when the military are themselves unclear as to what they mean by these terms? What, today, is war? What then is a war crime? And just what is a complex humanitarian emergency? What is the difference between and the relationship to one another of man-made and natural disasters? What is a state? Then what is a failed state? And, above all, *so what?* When is an armed conflict a war? And is the absence of war, peace? It's as Samuel Johnson said of the weather: it 'generates language more efficiently than knowledge'.

These are not mere semantic issues: in 1994, the US Delegation to the United Nations was at some pains to prevent the use of the term 'genocide' to describe the situation as it was then developing in Rwanda. As we know, they were generally successful in this and thus in their real aim, which was to avoid an intervention – an issue to which I shall return later, but for which the President of the United States later apologized to the people of Rwanda (see Chapter 6).[1] Even after that, the US State Department contended (or pretended to contend) that the 1948 Genocide Convention (which the United States did not sign until 1984) enables, it does not compel action, which Philip Gourevitch has rightly called 'absurd'.[2]

So we must digress here substantially, to provide some strategic and historic context for peace operations – generalizations, no matter how commonly used, have their limits. It is therefore necessary, before we enter into a more detailed discussion of military roles, functions and capabilities, to explore some of the doctrinal context or, as some would perhaps describe it, the doctrinal laxity surrounding the evolution and the present state of the art of peacekeeping operations.

Humanitarian interventions and operations

The terms 'humanitarian' and 'humanitarian operation' are, like most terms used to describe peace operations, not easily nor uniformly defined – which is of course at the root of a lot of our problems. *The Concise Encyclopedia of the United Nations* says that 'Humanitarian assistance is understood as all measures intended to relieve acute distress of groups of people'. The *Encyclopedia* quotes the United Nations Office for the Coordination of Humanitarian Assistance (OCHA) that 'complex emergencies' are humanitarian crises with multiple causes (political, military, economic, etc.) that require a broad and comprehensive assistance approach instead of separate interventions by agencies and institutions'.[3] Mark Duffield writes that the immediate post-Cold War concept of humanitarian interventions was concerned to develop 'institutional arrangements that allowed aid agencies to work in situations of ongoing conflict and to support civilians in war zones'. Today, he says, that policy has changed: 'the new humanitarianism' views 'developmental tools and initiatives' as acting to 'reduce violent conflict and prevent its recurrence'. This 'convergence of development and security', he writes, marks a shift 'from helping people...towards supporting processes'.[4]

None of these descriptions clearly distinguish between humanitarian crises which have arisen, on the one hand, from natural disasters and, on the other hand, from man-made disasters. For our purposes here, we will be considering humanitarian emergencies arising from an essentially man-made disaster such as armed conflict, but we will keep in mind that man-made and natural disasters are often linked – a natural disaster may lead to conflict over resources; armed conflict may produce critical shortages and so another dimension to an ongoing conflict.

Duffield's points about 'the new humanitarianism' are important, and we will again encounter this disagreement between those who on the one hand seek to render aid for its own sake, and those who on the other hand render aid as conditional on progress in a peace process. The disagreement is so subtle it often goes unrecognized, producing more discord than discourse.

The generations of peacekeeping

There have been since the inception of the United Nations at least two generations of peacekeeping operations. Ironically, it is what many now call the Second-Generation operations – enforcement operations – which were prescribed in the

Charter, while the operations now commonly referred to as First Generation are not provided for anywhere in the Charter.

Michael Pugh has described the generations of peace operations:

> The traditional term 'peacekeeping' had a generally-accepted definition: a multinational force, sometimes with a civilian element, mandated to administer, monitor or patrol in conflict areas in a neutral and impartial way, usually with the consent of the parties to a dispute, and nearly always under the provisions of Chapter VI of the UN Charter.[5]

Notwithstanding the reference to Chapter VI, which in fact deals with the 'Pacific Settlement of Disputes', this then is First Generation Peacekeeping: 'consensual', 'Chapter VI' as they in fact came commonly to be called, or 'traditional' peacekeeping operations. Dag Hamarskjold called these first peace missions Chapter $VI\frac{1}{2}$ Operations.[6] Terry May cites a US Defence Department leave-no-stone-unturned definition of 'traditional peacekeeping' operations as the

> deployment of a U.N., regional organization, or coalition presence in the field with the consent of the parties concerned, normally involving U.N., regional organization or coalition military forces, and/or police and civilians. Non-combat military operations (exclusive of self-defence) that are undertaken by outside forces with the consent of all major belligerent parties, designed to monitor and facilitate implementation of an existing agreement in support of diplomatic efforts to reach a political solution to the dispute.[7]

Those 'First Generation' operations were generally military operations,[8] with only one exception operating under a UN mandate, and with a Force Commander as Head of Mission. Pugh also provides us with a good description of what came next and since:

> Since the end of the Cold War the problem-solving, technicist contextualization of peace support operations has been reflected in a preoccupation with disputed labels. Attempts to redefine operations (sometimes under the enforcement provisions of Chapter VII) have spawned a host of new descriptors such as 'multi-dimensional peacekeeping' and 'peace enforcement' ... these terms have in common their occupation of an ethically sound moral ground: peace operations being desirable and humanitarianism widely approved as an ethical response to suffering. Thus 'peace support' is a positive signifier, suggesting a moral concern for order and security in the international system. Above all, these terms convey the sense that external actors are intent upon, or engage in, maintaining or creating peace.[9]

And that describes the admittedly disputatious Second Generation of peace operations: 'wider peacekeeping', 'peace enforcement'. May cites another US Defence Department description of such operations as 'aggravated peace operations'; which despite the curious modifier provides an accurate description of such operations:

> Military operations undertaken with the full consent of all major belligerent parties, but which are complicated by subsequent intransigence of one or more of the belligerents, poor command and control of one or more of the forces, or conditions of outlawry, banditry or anarchy. In such conditions, peacekeeping forces are normally authorised to use force in self defence, *and in defence of the missions they are assigned*, which may include monitoring and facilitating implementation of an existing truce agreement in support of diplomatic efforts to reach a political settlement, *or support or safeguarding humanitarian relief efforts*.[10]

It is significant that this definition was promulgated in the US military establishment just at the time that the Chairman of the Joint Chiefs of Staff was publicly avowing that the Implementation Force in Bosnia-Herzegovina would do no such things (see Chapter 11).

It should be noted that it was in this context and at this time that the relationship between military and civilian agencies began to alter very rapidly, as the increasing complexity of the various operations (and in the 1990s the sheer volume of peace operations multiplied ten-fold) required a much greater degree of cooperation between the military and the civilians, until finally the Head of Mission was more usually a civilian, with a Force Commander but one of his several subordinate functionaries. UNPROFOR in 1992 was the last UN peace operation with a military Head of Mission; by 1993 UNPROFOR in Bosnia-Herzegovina was *supporting* a humanitarian operation, where the UNHCR was the lead agency and a Special Representative of the Secretary-General of the UN was the Head of Mission. Posing more difficulties for the military than has been generally recognized, mission organizations thus became more horizontal than the vertical organizations which had been typical of the era of military dominance of 'traditional' peace operations. Thus the Chief Administrative Officer (CAO), the Commissioner of Civilian Police and the Senior Political Advisor, who at the beginning of the 1990s were subordinate to the Force Commander, were by the end of that decade sitting around the table with him as his equals, and the Force Commander was no longer at the head of that table.

It is also significant, if little appreciated, that this horizontalism in operational organizations has continued to obtain, despite the fact that the majority of 'modern' peace operations have been enforcement operations, mandated under Chapter VII of the Charter of the UN. Such operations, connoting a greater reliance on armed force because of anticipating a less permissive security environment, cause the military even greater unease with the concept of civilian management, accompanied by horizontal structures, of a field operation. (It is for just this reason that the NATO-led KFOR is *not* an organizational component of UNMIK. NATO has no equivalent of a representative of the UN Secretary-General present in the field, and pretty clearly does not intend to have one – see Chapter 25: 'NATO'.)

But there has developed another strain even of that 'Second Generation': as Pugh says:

> There has been a shift into coercive engineering by dominant states armed with a moral design to safeguard human rights, in which human-itarian missions and humanitarian intervention have been increasingly integrated. Governments have adapted their representations of (peace support operations) to the discourses of ethics, humanitarianism, justice and the 'will of the international community'.[11]

We might call it Generation 2.5. But there is more, as Pugh continues:

> However, where inhabitants are deemed unable to determine their futures without paternalistic guidance, external actors are so intrusive...that the imposition is tantamount to a protectorate. International financial institu-tions, UN administrators, NGOs, intergovernmental aid agencies, private companies, external 'peace support' forces, teams of monitors, outside civilian police and judges attempt to control territory, economic resources and public policy.[12]

Pugh has thus (albeit somewhat caustically) described a form of external administration, actually external governance, which represents those 'ideals of global liberal governance' that bring (or seek to install) a 'liberal peace', and the 'imposition is tantamount to a protectorate'. We might call this 'Third Generation Peacekeeping – External Governance/Administration'.

Of course, these 'generations' are by no means a linear progression: 'First Generation' operations, such as those in the Middle East and especially in the case of Cyprus (United Nations Force in Cyprus UNFICYP), continue into the present; and the UN operation in the Congo became (briefly) an enforcement operation in 1962.

The Agenda for Peace

As was said earlier, this book will concentrate on humanitarian operations just because these are the most critical and complex, but it is not intended that discussion of these problems of inter-agency, civil-military cooperation would be limited, as the problems themselves are not limited, to just these types of missions. In fact, the entire spectrum of peace operations of all types may be and frequently is a continuum: preventive diplomacy when it succeeds may entail a traditional peacekeeping operation. If prevention fails, the conflict may degenerate into a man-made humanitarian emergency which will aggravate or which may cause an accompanying natural disaster.

What may then typically follow will be some form of civil war. In the intra-state conflicts which have been the most common threats to and breaches of the peace since the end of the Cold War, 90% of the casualties have been civilians (in the First World War the civilian casualties were 10% of the total; in the Second World War the civilian casualty rate rose to 50%). Of the predominant civilian casualties in modern conflicts, nearly 90% have been children, women and the elderly: nearly bereft of men (who are fighting or dead); in agrarian societies tied to their land for their sustenance and therefore unable to displace or seek refuge; and with little or no medical support when they fall ill or are injured. And we must not forget how enormously destructive these 'operations other than war' can be: in just three short years (1992–95) Bosnia-Herzegovina was destroyed – nearly 60% of her infrastructure was at least severely damaged – and about two-thirds of her pre-war population were either internally displaced or made into refugees. All this was done with weapons seldom larger than medium artillery howitzers, giving perhaps new meaning to that tired and tiring term 'weapons of mass destruction'.

And it is *these* images which will flood the media, stinging people and governments[13] to do – what? Then it may seem that the only thing we cannot do is nothing, *but this complex humanitarian emergency will often feature a security environment so risky that a peace enforcement operation may be essential to enable and to support the relief effort.*

It was somewhat in that spirit of a holistic approach to the maintenance of international peace and security, and in an environment of optimism soon to be sadly disabused, that UN Secretary-General Boutros Boutros-Ghali prepared his *Agenda for Peace* in 1992.[14] The *Agenda* was originally intended (as its full title describes) to define and to describe preventive diplomacy, peacemaking and peacekeeping. It was thought to do this principally but not solely by setting out basic doctrine and offering some working definitions.

In effect, the *Agenda* went beyond that by providing, as Ernst Schmidl has described it, a 'model chronology of the development of a conflict'.[15] However, the concept of a linear chronology, while a useful analytical tool, was in practice a significant flaw in the concept, as the various sources and natures of threats to the peace do not arise sequentially. The course of a conflict will show unexpected escalations and de-escalations, indeed phases may overlap and even run concur-rently. Sometimes it really does seem like a tale told by an idiot, or perhaps more like a radio being tuned by one, the cursor scraping up and down the dial, pro-ducing few recognizable signals and no patterns. Naturally, then, the repertoire of responses to a situation where the only certainty is uncertainty, the only constant is change, must be similarly flexible. As this was soon apparent, BBG abandoned the concept of a linear chronology, and in his *Supplement to the Agenda for Peace* (published in 1995) he included 'enforcement' and 'sanctions' as additional categories of responses. Further, the *Supplement* noted significant qualitative changes in the nature of UN peace missions; most significantly:

A second qualitative change is the use of United Nations forces to protect humanitarian operations. Humanitarian agencies endeavour to provide succour to civilian victims of war wherever they may be. Too often the warring parties make it difficult or impossible for them to do so. This is sometimes because of the exigencies of wars but more often because the relief of a particular population is contrary to the war aims of one or other of the parties. There is also a growing tendency for the combatants to divert relief supplies for their own purposes. Because the wars are intra-state conflicts, the humanitarian agencies often have to undertake their tasks in ... chaotic and lawless conditions.

This has led ... to a new kind of United Nations operation. Even though the use of force is authorized under Chapter VII of the Charter, the United Nations remains neutral and impartial between the parties, without a mandate to stop the aggressor (if one can be identified) or impose a cessation of hostilities. Nor is this peace-keeping as practiced hitherto, because the hostilities continue and there is often no agreement between the warring parties on which a peace-keeping mandate can be based.[16]

Mary Kaldor, in her theory of 'new wars', shows how this is part of 'a new political economy of war, in which a range of new militaries – the decaying remnants of state armies, paramilitary groups (often financed by governments), self-defence units, mercenaries and international troops – engage in new forms of violence'.[17] Of particular significance to this study, Kaldor writes that 'Since the new wars are, in a sense, a mixture of war, crime and human rights violations, so the agents of cosmopolitan law-enforcement have to be a mixture of soldiers and policemen.'[18] Sir Michael Rose, in a slightly different context (but referring, as does Kaldor, to Bosnia-Herzegovina), has called this 'a new form of warfare – humanitarian war'.[19]

This, then is one scenario in which modern peace operations, especially humanitarian relief operations may occur: an internal conflict, no agreement between conflicted parties, widespread violence which may be directed against relief agencies, theft of relief supplies by the combatants who may themselves be the *disjectra membra* of a failed or faltering state, and relief operations nevertheless to be mounted, in great haste and in the face of what the *Supplement* described as 'a breakdown of law and order, and general banditry and chaos'. Under these circumstances there clearly is little question of any agency being able to cope alone with such a complex humanitarian emergency – how we will put this act together is the subject of this book.

Peacekeeping and world order: a critical theory

There is a view of what may generally be called peace-support operations which suggests that 'they sustain a particular order of world politics that privileges the rich and powerful states in their efforts to control or isolate unruly parts of the world'. This 'deconstruction' of peace operations may support the argument, as Michael Pugh does argue, that such operations 'serve a narrow, problem solving purpose – to doctor the dysfunctions of the global political economy within a framework of liberal imperialism'. This leads Pugh to judge that 'modern versions of peacekeeping can be considered as forms of riot control directed against the unruly parts of the world to uphold the liberal peace'.[20] Pugh quotes Mark Duffield's description of the liberal peace as establishing 'the values of market economics, statism and political plurality, and thus comes to represent the ideals of liberal governance'.[21] Duffield himself says that 'The aim of liberal peace is to transform the dysfunctional and war-affected societies ... into cooperative, representative and, especially, stable entities.'[22] Pugh 'presents an alternative consideration of (peace support operations), by examining the framework of world order politics within which (they) occur'. Thus critical theory 'contemplates alternative world orders deriving from an understanding of social struggles created by adverse impacts of economic globalization'.

Notwithstanding the possibility, indeed the probability of 'alternative world orders', which may or may not be superior to the present reality, it is that present reality which is the subject of this work. (I also do not accept the blanket implication that those who seek to manage modern conflicts are entirely disconnected from the social origins of conflict.) This reality, as unsatisfactory as it is, will obtain unless and until another reality becomes as widely operative as that which has shaped the recent past, the present and the foreseeable future. Practitioners must deal here with perceived current conditions defining operations which have been intended, in the words of the Charter of the United Nations, Article 1.1: 'To maintain international peace and security ... for the prevention and removal of threats to the peace ... for the suppression of acts of aggression of other breaches of the peace ... and ... adjustment or settlement of international peace or situations which might lead to a breach of the peace.'

While one need not 'take the prevailing international framework as incontestable', that contest, if there is one, is well outside the scope of this book, which will indeed be expressly concerned with 'problem-solving to smooth the functioning of the system'.[23] Furthermore, if to Duffield's description of liberal peace was added, 'and a civil society under the rule of law', most would find the prospect of a such a 'peace' not an entirely bad objective for a world order – if there indeed is, or is ever to be, any such thing. And, as it happens, there is at least one writer who tends to support just that view.

The liberal peace of Paris

Roland Paris[24] has described peace-building missions in the 1990s as 'guided by a generally unstated but widely accepted theory of conflict management: the notion that promoting "liberalization" in countries that had recently experienced civil wars would help to create the conditions for a stable and lasting peace'. He has termed the belief 'that democratization and marketization will foster peace in war-shattered states Wilsonianism'. Specifically, this means that:

> In the political realm, liberalization means democratization, or the promotion of periodic and genuine elections, constitutional limitations on the exercise of governmental power, and respect for basic civil liberties, including freedom of speech, assembly, and conscience. In the economic realm, liberalization means marketization, or movement toward a market-oriented economic model, including measures aimed at minimizing government intrusion in the economy, and maximizing the freedom for private investors, producers, and consumers to pursue their respective economic interests.

Paris accepts these broad objectives: 'The purpose of this book...is not to reject the Wilsonian peace-building strategy in its entirety, but to expose the weaknesses of the naïve version of Wilsonianism that informed the missions of the 1990s.' He argues that:

> Peacebuilders should preserve the broad goal of converting war-shattered states into liberal market democracies, because well-established liberal market democracies tend to be peaceful both in their domestic affairs and their relations with other states. The challenge, however, is to devise methods of achieving this Wilsonian goal without endangering the very peace that the liberalization process is supposed to consolidate.

'To this end,' Paris proposes 'a new peace-building strategy called "Institutionalization Before Liberalization," which recognizes that liberalization constitutes "inherently tumultuous transformations that have the potential to undermine a fragile peace" '.

Paris' thesis then is concerned not with the substance of the liberal peace, the origins of which he traces to Enlightenment philosophers such as Locke and Adam Smith, and which gained modern prominence with the presidency of Woodrow Wilson, who was himself 'a scholar of liberal political theory'. Paris is more concerned with the process of liberalization, especially where its proponents assume, often incorrectly, the presence of 'effective state institutions' and tend to 'ignore the question of whether functioning governments exist'.[25]

The Liberal Peace according to Paris, then, has its weakness not in substance but in process – not in liberalism, but in liberalization: in taking for granted the existence of an effective state, the dangers of creating one are ignored.

An example of this right goal–wrong way syndrome was the resurgence of violence in Kosovo/Mitrovica: in rioting over three days of 16–19 March 2004,

19 people were killed, 9,000 were injured, 4,000 lost their homes and nearly 800 houses and about 30 Orthodox religious sites were destroyed. The OSCE report on this quoted observers who said that the incidents 'had been directly provoked by excited and uncritical broadcasting on the night of 16 March'.

> The OSCE's Representative on the Freedom of the Media has said that if it had not been for the reckless and sensational reporting, the events could have taken a different turn and might not have become so vicious and brutal. Others have remarked that if the media had taken more measured actions and weighed their possible consequences, the riots might not have taken place at all.

The report asked, 'Why did the capacity to do this not exist, after several years of media development programmes sponsored by the OSCE and others?'[26] Paris would no doubt agree that the peacebuilders' intentions were good, but that they had overestimated the local governing capacity, and underestimated the dangers of letting them have their heads too soon. Liberalization, not liberalism, was where the danger lay.

In defence of human rights – 'The best lack all conviction'

Nearly paralleling complaints about liberal peace, are charges that the West (and/or the North) is imposing western (or northern) cultural values in a form of cross-cultural aggression, or cultural imperialism as it is also often called. Notwithstanding that this is a favourite response of despots to critics of their despotism, a sort of a sham cultural 'domestic jurisdiction', it is an argument to which libertarians must respond.

It is a principle learned in the hard school of the twentieth century that nothing generates violence so surely as continued violations of human rights and community aspirations, which are frequently linked. Apprehension of systemic violations of rights is thus one of the clearest signs of impending conflict, and early warning is one of the major components of successful prevention, so we need to be clear on this issue – or at least, more clear than some of the arguments against human rights have been.

From the outset of her work as Chair of the Drafting Committee for the Universal Declaration of Human Rights (UDHR), Eleanor Roosevelt had been concerned about this issue. She decided very early that the Declaration should be based on the 'four freedoms' her husband had enunciated: freedom of speech and belief, freedom from fear and want.[27] As Mary Ann Glendon has written:

> One of the most common and unfortunate misunderstandings today involves the notion that the Declaration was meant to impose a single model of right conduct rather than to provide a common standard

that can be brought to life in different cultures in a legitimate variety of ways. This confusion has fostered suspicion of the Universal Declaration in many quarters, and lends credibility to the charge of Western cultural imperialism so often leveled against the entire human rights movement.

In fact, Mrs Roosevelt's drafting committee included (in addition to herself) members from the United States, the Phillipines, Canada, India, the USSR, Chile, China, France and the Lebanon. Of the actual framers, one was Chinese, one was a French Jew who had lost 29 relatives in death camps, one was a Greek Orthodox Arab from the Lebanon, and one was Russian.

Nevertheless, as Glendon writes of the struggle for approval of the Declaration, 'the proposition that human rights are *universal*, belonging to "all members of the human family," challenged the traditional view that the relation between a sovereign state and is own citizens was that nation's own exclusive business'. Rene Cassin, the French Jew with such bitter memories of Hitler's camps, retorted to Soviet criticism in just this vein that in 1933 Hitler had replied to the League of Nations in just that way, to deflect criticism and to justify actions by the German government against its own citizens.[28] In the event, 23 of 30 articles of the Declaration 'were approved without nays or abstentions',[29] and the Universal Declaration of Human Rights was ratified by the General Assembly of the United Nations on 10 December 1948. Although the USSR delegation abstained from the final voting, their signature on the 1975 Helsinki Final Act, which founded the Conference on Security and Cooperation in Europe, was tacit acceptance of the UDHR. Glendon sums up:

> All in all, it has been estimated that the Declaration has inspired or served as the model for the rights provisions of some ninety constitutions. The great majority of nations have also signed the two 1966 Covenants based on the Declaration: 144 for the Covenant on Civil and Political Rights and 142 for the Covenant in Economic, Social and Cultural Rights as of May 15, 2000. And in 1993 . . . 171 countries at the Vienna Conference on Human Rights affirmed . . . their 'commitment to the purposes and principles contained in the Charter of the United Nations and in the Universal Declaration of Human Rights'.[30]

But the controversy over universality has not gone away. Fortunately, Michael Ingatieff has addressed the contemporary manifestation of this issue with exemplary clarity.[31]

Ignatieff notes that 'the cultural challenge to the universality of human rights arises from three distinct sources – from resurgent Islam, from within the West itself, and from East Asia. Each of these challenges is independent of the others, but taken together, they have raised substantial questions about the cross-cultural validity – and hence the legitimacy – of human rights norms'. He surveys each of these sources of dissent, but then goes to the heart of the matter:

> The language of human rights is the only universally available moral vernacular that validates the claims of women and children against the oppression they experience in patriarchal and tribal societies; it is the only vernacular that enables independent persons to perceive themselves as moral agents and to act against practices – arranged marriages, purdah, civic disenfranchisement, genital mutilation, domestic slavery, and so on – that are ratified by the weight and authority of their cultures. These agents seek out human rights protection precisely because it legitimizes their protests against oppression.

Ignatieff observes most usefully for the benefit of practitioners who must face these criticisms that 'what makes human rights demands legitimate is that they emanate from the bottom, from the powerless', and that 'Rights are universal because they define the universal interests of the powerless – namely, that power be exercised over them in ways that respect their autonomy as agents.' He concludes that 'The doctrine of human rights is morally universal because it says that all human beings need certain specific freedoms "from"; it does not go on to define what their freedom "to" should comprise.'

In judging these criticisms and arguments, then, it will be useful to ask if we are hearing from the oppressed or the oppressors, from the top or the bottom – and we must be aware that modern scoundrels have more refuges than Dr Johnson could ever have dreamt. Or, as William Butler Yeats might have described the contemporary confusion on rights issues:

> The best lack all conviction,
> While the worst are filled with passionate intensity.

Peacekeeping reconstructed

The deconstructions of peace operations, and their deconstructors, need to be recognized and confronted, if we are to act at all. These will include the self-doubting of those charged to act as well as of those who study the actions of others who do act. This is true especially of those in the West who either believe, for example, that human rights are 'a twentieth-century fiction dependant on the rights traditions of the United States, the United Kingdom, and France and therefore inapplicable in cultures that do not share this historical matrix of liberal individualism,' or those for whom 'postmodernist relativism began as an intellectual fad on western university campuses'.[32] It will include as well those who maintain that all peace operations are in fact Western ideals, constructs and practices, serving Western goals or at least promulgating Western values.

Notwithstanding those reservations, and whatever our self-doubts, whatever the state of Western self-ennui, whatever our distractions, we will continue to live and function in a highly volatile world, one which is constantly bursting into flames around us. When it does, we put aside the distraction and the temptation of imagined alternate worlds and world orders, and we react to unmistakeable dangers as we must and as we can.

Peacekeeping in the post-Cold War era is evolving much more rapidly than any body of doctrine which might support and inform the theory and the practice of these operations. The virtual disappearance of inter-state war, the almost continuous eruptions of intra-state conflicts, states which must be seen through the prism of the three-centuries old Peace of Westphalia yet who instead of protecting their people are too often the greatest threats those people will ever face, the abrupt demise of one of the only two true superpowers in the twentieth century, the almost as sudden end to the age of colonies, the rise and proliferation of regional organizations, the same with NGOs – clearly, academics and practitioners alike have much to ponder in a world all too real and all too dangerous.

The challenge is clear and the need is urgent. We must resolve the internal problems of building inter-agency partnerships before we can effectively engage jointly in the external problems of the emergency we have been sent to address. Ignoring those internal challenges, of coordination and cooperation, just does not work, nor does trying to resolve the inter-agency and the domestic problems simultaneously. The latter is the most commonly attempted – our experience being less in aid of the distressed population than coming to us at their expense. And what have we made of that experience so far?

Academics and practitioners are not engaged in hermetic pursuits, but need to study together a world at least as dangerous as it has always been. For those who live in a faltering or a failed state, as for those who might seek by their intervention to ameliorate those conditions, the world is possibly more dangerous than ever before.

Nearly a decade and a half after the Cold War, it is high time for us to have caught up to a changed world order, such as it is. Whatever our agencies and organizations, we ought to know our roles and our tasks, and what authorities and resources we may expect in the execution of those roles, and we ought to know the statutory and practical limitations imposed on our mandates. Equally important, we must be able to find out quickly who else is working this problem, and learn all of the above about them, and then enter into constructive and empathetic partnering relationships with them. We cannot do this now without great difficulty, without unacceptable misunderstandings and at an unreasonable cost in scarce time.

The Charter of the United Nations was written in 1945, the UDHR in 1948 and the Geneva Conventions in 1949. Yet today we cannot really determine the effect on peace operations of state sovereignty, we debate endlessly and seriously whether the title of the Universal Declaration on Human Rights might contain an oxymoron, and the superpower seems (or pretends to seem) not to understand the Geneva Conventions at all.

We are left, inevitably, with a set of problems of civil-military, interagency cooperation in response to a complex humanitarian emergency which are now long overdue for resolution. Lines of authority, allocation of responsibilities and the design of coordinating mechanisms are still far too often subject to conflicting claims and to historic prejudice, as well as to the immaturity of the organizations and of the practitioners.

Part II

PRIDE AND PREJUDICE
Military culture and popular perceptions

Harriet thought, 'The trouble with prejudice is, there's usually a
reason for it'.

(Olivia Manning, *The Balkan Trilogy:
The Great Fortune*, 1960)

4

INTRODUCTION

On 6 October 1998, in commemoration of 50 years of peacekeeping, the first Dag Hammarskjold medals were presented to commemorate three distinguished peacekeepers who had lost their lives 'in the service of peace'. Medals were presented to the family of the first peacekeeper to have been killed in operations, Commandant Rene'de Labarrière, as well as to the families of Count Folke Bernadotte and Dag Hammarskjold. In the past 50 years, almost 1,600 peacekeepers, military and civilian, have died on nearly 50 UN peacekeeping operations. Thirty-six of those operations, three-fourths of the total, have been deployed since 1990, and just over half the total casualties have occurred in that decade. Over 750,000 soldiers and policemen and women, from 119 of the 186 UN member states, have participated in peacekeeping operations.

But the military have not been alone in modern peace operations, and civilians have borne their share of the dangers; as *The Economist* has reported:

> In the past decade (i.e. since 1994), more than 200 of the United Nations' civilian staff have been killed by 'malicious acts' in 45 countries. Nearly 300 more, civilians and peacekeepers, have been taken hostage. The International Committee of the Red Cross (ICRC) has lost 40 of its staff on mission over the same period. Hundreds of other unarmed aid workers have been killed, maimed, abducted and assaulted as they have tried to help people in some of the world's most benighted places.[1]

Despite their acknowledged contributions to the maintenance of international peace and security, the military remains a traditional target of prejudice. Paradoxically, that body of prejudice seems more robust and ubiquitous, the further we get from 'classical' military operations and roles, and reaches its apogee just as military forces are applied to the more diverse challenges of pre- and post-conflict tasks. Such phrases as 'brutal and licentious soldiery'[2] have been so commonly accepted and repeated that they have become a virtual shorthand for anti-militarism. Indeed, these stereotypes have penetrated the military culture, such that soldiers often take a perverse pride in their poor image, revelling in their cultural ghetto: 'Never explain, never complain', was the advice given

John Masters on joining his regiment in India in 1935. Rudyard Kipling's 'Tommy' expresses both a traditional anti-military prejudice, and the soldier's wounded pride in his apartness:

> O it's Tommy this, an' Tommy that, an' 'Tommy go away';
> But it's 'Thank you, Mister Atkins', when the band begins to play –
> For it's Tommy this, an' Tommy that, an' 'Chuck him out, the brute!'
> But it's 'Saviour of 'is country' when the guns begin to shoot

More modern and more sophisticated expressions of anti-military culture have in fact been one of the less obvious by-products of the very closeness of civil-military relations in recent peace operations. A journalist, invited to attend a US Army exercise held in Fort Polk, Louisiana[3], which was intended to foster closer relations with civil agencies, afterwards wrote of his experience saying that, 'The military counts on firepower and intimidation to get its point across.' The writer continued, while 'NGOs (Non Governmental Organizations) provide assistance to all . . . (to the) military this looks . . . like providing aid to the enemy'. He warned that 'the military tends to draw fire'.[4] The ICRC, in their 'Report on the Use of Armed Protection for Humanitarian Assistance', advised that 'the concerned components of the Movement should not avail themselves of armed protection for their operations when this is offered by UN troops during an enforcement action under Chapter VII or when it is possible that the UNO will sooner or later be considered as a party to the conflict by the local population or by the belligerents'.[5] At York University in the United Kingdom, in 1998 the Post-War Reconstruction and Development Unit (PRDU) hosted a joint Ministry of Defence/Academic symposium to discuss civil-military issues. The symposium concluded that, 'with training', soldiers could learn to stop destroying and be taught to build. A writer for *The Atlantic Monthly*, describing the US military in Bosnia-Herzegovina, spoke of the soldiers' 'radical, disfiguring haircuts'.[6]

Laura Miller has summarized the syndrome:

> in the 1990's . . . relief workers have become pro-military intervention, but remained essentially anti-military. These workers have experienced the need for armed intervention . . . Nevertheless, aid workers have not developed a favourable view of soldiers. . . . relief workers view armed tasks as necessary . . . but they would not carry out these tasks themselves and they still disdain the use of weapons.[7]

'Meanwhile', as Dandeker and Gow note, 'military personnel can be frustrated by NGO's reluctance to recognize the importance of military command and control . . ., and irritated by the disdain for their armed but "dirty" work . . .'[8] Indeed, in nations which have conscription, such as Germany, the Netherlands, the Scandinavians and (until recently) France, NGO service has often been an acceptable alternate to military service; thus NGOs may include those who have self-selected on the basis of pacifism, adding another layer to anti-military prejudice.

The cultural antipathies underlying this are too important for the passivity of 'never explain, never complain'. It is the responsibility of the military to represent itself better, to counter anachronistic stereotypes, to tell its own story, to explain its own culture, mission and capabilities. To do this, it must know itself better, for the military are too often not their own best advertisement. As I have said, the military language and behaviour might be deliberately intended to alienate outsiders – the prejudice is mutual.

I will not enter into discussions of what constitutes success or failure in peace operations. I do not believe that 'success' is in fact a function, nor an achievable goal, of such an intervention. An external intervention may contribute to the management of conflict, to the prevention of and to the recovery from violent conflict. As Mary Kaldor has written of missions such as Operation Artemis, the EU intervention in the Democratic Republic of the Congo in 2003, 'The goal is not victory but cessation of violence, in order to provide space for political solutions.'[9] The avoidance of conflict recidivism, the restoration of genuine and enduring peace and the shape of long-term political solutions, are largely functions of the parties to the conflict. It is their responsibility to live peacefully, to manage their conflicts non-violently, which is at issue. It is the parties to the conflict who will determine whether they will succeed or fail in their desire, if that is their desire, to live in peace. Where that is not their desire or their intentions, there is little that any third party (or parties) can do to enforce peace. If the parties prefer violent conflict to peaceful resolutions, if they prefer to traduce and to scapegoat the outsiders, then they will live on in a pre-modern, asocietal state, waging their wars by whatever means they can produce or glean.

Under such conditions of non-cooperation, there will be very little that can be done against their will to resolve their conflicts, or to manage them peacefully. All that can be expected of an intervention in such cases is that it will conduct its affairs as efficiently as possible, that it will not introduce conflicts of its own making, that it will contribute to solutions and not worsen the problems it came to help alleviate. Indeed, in these interventions, as often in war, success or failure is not the best measure of the efficacy of an organization. As Gabriel and Savage have written, 'Victory or defeat is *not* a condition of measurement, since, clearly, even defeated armies can maintain high rates of cohesion, as a multiplicity of examples... attest.'[10]

Another reason I will not consider mission success or failure further in this book is simply that civil-military relationships have in no instance of which I am aware been central to the success or failure of a mission. Haiti 'failed' because too much was expected and too little, especially time, was provided; Somalia because inordinate and uncoordinated force was used to address an economic and cultural conflict; the UN did not achieve its objectives in Bosnia because too little was done too late; various Middle East peace plans have failed because no implementing mechanisms acceptable to the parties could be found. In none of these cases was civil-military cooperation a central issue because in none of these cases was there a workable plan on which there *might* have been such cooperation.

However, cooperation does have much to do with *efficiency*, which almost certainly has somewhere its equivalency in lives saved and lost, and efficiency will surely be a major factor in mission costs, which has much to do with the sustainability of the mission.

So this is the 'success' we should seek, and should seek to measure: cohesiveness among the elements of the intervention (in whatever form it may take), effectiveness in achieving an achievable mandate, avoidance of unrealistic expectations, avoidance of waste, minimizing of costs and dangers, doing no further harm. These will not ensure, although they may foster and help to maintain, peace. As is often said of the Principles of War, their observance will not ensure success, but their contravention usually, eventually, will result in failure.

5

THE ROLE AND INFLUENCE OF CULTURES

An approach to more mature and empathetic relationships among the various agencies – civilian, military, international, regional, national and NGOs – will develop naturally when the diverse agencies are understood as cultures: having histories and doctrines, comprising social mechanisms and consisting, above all, of people.

Organizations are or they come to be cultures. Charles Handy has written that:

> organizations are as different as the nations of the world. They have differing cultures – sets of values and norms and beliefs – reflected in different structures and systems.... Strong pervasive cultures turn organizations into cohesive tribes with distinctive clannish feelings. The values and traditions of the tribe are reinforced by its private language, its catch-phrases and its tales of past heroes and dramas. The way of life is enshrined in rituals so that rule books and manuals are almost unnecessary; custom and tradition provide the answers.[1]

Dandeker and Gow have said that 'culture comprises a set of ideas, beliefs and symbols that provide a definition of the world for a group or organisation and guides for action'.[2] They also differentiate between informal and formal culture as, for example, the corporate culture which consists of policies and doctrines, and the informal which consists of legends, history and shared beliefs, the latter possibly being apocryphal – but not the less important for that. In fact, I suggest that it is the informal culture which is the most enduring, and, subjectively, the most revealing of the organization as a culture. For example, the largely negative initial reactions of soldiers to recent attempts at social engineering in the militaries of the world, in respect of minorities, homosexuals and women in their ranks, says more about the hearts and minds of soldiers than does the prevailing legislation. Moreover, it is this informal culture which provides the inertia which will be the true measure of the pace of change; it is in this milieu that effective change will occur – or not.

Possibly the most complex of these organizations-as-cultures is the one agency seemingly best known but least understood: the military. I will argue that the military, as a highly structured culture with a long and (surprisingly) cohesive history, is actually the more accessible, just because of its history and the complexity of its culture – the more code we have, the easier that code is to break. I will further argue that the reason civilians seldom even attempt to break the military code, is principally because the military is traditionally and frequently the object of prejudice. As Albert Einstein has said, 'That a man can take pleasure in marching in formation to the strains of a band is enough to make me despise him. He has only been given his big brain by mistake.'[3] And in 1916 Aldous Huxley thought that the spreading military culture would militarize culture, and feared therefore the 'collapse of English civilisation'.[4] Later Huxley, in *Brave New World Revisited*, echoed Einstein (in quoting Hermann Rauschning):

> Marching diverts men's thoughts. Marching kills thought. Marching makes an end of individuality. Marching is the indispensable magic stroke performed to accustom the people to a mechanical, quasi-ritualistic activity until it becomes second nature.[5]

This systemic generalization, this denial of diversity, this stereotyping, *is prejudice*. Of course such prejudice is entirely unworthy of those who, among others like them, have nevertheless produced and reinforced this behaviour until it has become itself almost a part of our culture. It remains an inescapable fact that democratic societies tend to look down their collective noses at their own armies. Such prejudice may have diverse roots, and many triggers. These are nearly impossible to analyse in any operative, collective sense – indeed, a description of prejudice involves generalizations, which themselves verge on prejudice. When confronted with organizations with histories, doctrines and cultures, however, there will be clearly apparent a cohesiveness of group responses to any challenge, and these can be described generally.

The causes of those responses may include a sense of compulsion to group behaviour, which may be fostered and maintained by the group, and which can be made to override individual persuasion. In addition to this enforced group behaviour, there will often be quite spontaneous individual responses which, in a cohesive group of persons with similar motivations, training and experience, will be at once collectively uniform and quite genuinely representative of personal belief. It is this latter set of personal, but collectively similar responses, in which I believe prejudice resides, and these may be triggered by such emotions as fear, anger, envy and resentment. I might call these triggers collectively by an acronym – *Fear, Envy, Anger, Resentment: FEAR.*

These FEAR-reactions may be irrational, and they may be deeply buried in the individual's consciousness. Indeed, individuals acting from FEAR will commonly deny, even to themselves, that they are prejudiced, or that they experience fear or envy or resentment, even when their behaviour, individually and in their groups, may clearly indicate an irrational, possibly misguided, dislike of another group.

When their dislike of a group is simultaneous with their dislike of nearly all the individuals in that group, there I suggest is pre-judgement – prejudice.

Beyond its FEAR-driven sources, prejudice is sustained by three mechanisms. The first is a simplistic impression: that soldiers are associated with war and violence. That has been until the twentieth century a fair description of military forces, but modern military forces are capable of far more than combat functions. Nevertheless this generalized, anachronistic view will seldom lend itself to much consideration of what modern soldiers *can* do. The second prejudicial mechanism is to generalize, to stereotype, on a lowest common denominator model: *all* soldiers do (insert your own verb), what perhaps *one* soldier or *one* unit did (what you may have said they all do). On this view, diversity is not likely, it is indeed virtually impossible. As Kofi Annan has said, intolerance is, essentially, 'a rejection of diversity'.[6] In the third mechanism of prejudice, change is ignored or denied, and the anachronism is taken as the constant. The loop completes itself; unchecked, it perpetuates itself.

Culture, then, is like a rule-book, and the rules may be written or unwritten, but they will powerfully influence the lives and the conduct of individuals, of groups – and of organizations. The influence may be overt and acknowledged, or it may be subliminal to the point that it is barely if at all acknowledged – but it is always there. We will next look at how the military culture affects soldiers and civilians, often without their conscious knowledge of that influence.

6

COHESION AND CONTINUITY

'The clangour of their shields'

The cohesiveness of the long history of the military has been a traditional brake on progress, but change and the pace of change have caught up with and imposed modern dynamism on a culture not always so receptive to new ideas, new technologies nor necessarily quick to react to altered circumstances. To the extent that today's military organizations have been formed by the richness of their past, their modern challenge is to be served by their history, not limited by it. We should look at some examples of that history-as-culture, and how they contribute to the sense of belonging to, how they impart a duty to preserve, a heritage. We can then see how a cultural heritage, rather than imposing stasis, can instead provide a framework for managing change.

I will describe my own experience, in which I thought I was beginning my career, when in fact I was entering a culture.

Forty years ago I descended from a train in a remote part of northern Ontario, gathered my few bags and walked over the planked station platform to an open jeep, a smart salute and a jolting ride to an already-then old and somewhat primitive army camp. I was reporting to my first station as a new Second Lieutenant, and walking straight into the pages of a book I had read as a teenager:

Nearly thirty years before that, another new Second Lieutenant, John Masters, reported in to his first station: writing of the experience later in his life, he said simply, 'I had come to my home'. He immediately felt the very long history of the place and the occasion:

> The local hillmen said that these palms marked the line of Alexander the Great's outposts. The clumps were descended from the dates Alexander's soldiers had brought from the banks of the Tigris. Certainly the trees rose in the places any officer would have chosen for an outpost line, and history confirms that this was indeed the farthest limit of Alexander's penetration to the east. I thought perhaps a young Macedonian officer climbed this path to inspect his posts. They were strangers here too, and the clangour of their shields on the rock echoed over twenty-two hundred years into my ears.[1]

Masters was reporting on the eve of the Second World War; I was, I was sure, reporting on the eve of the Third. The Berlin Wall was a year old, and Soviet missiles had just been discovered in Cuba.

On the next day I was able to survey my surroundings in a little more detail. The activities in this small and isolated camp were as if they were final rehearsals for a military tattoo. From beyond a copse came the rattle of small arms fire and the drumming of heavy machine guns – the firing ranges were only a mile from the Officers' Mess. A rifle company was drilling on the parade square, with a section of the regimental band, in preparation for a Ceremonial Guard of Honour – I didn't know it yet, but I had already been named the Ensign of the Regimental Colour for that parade. Nearly 40 feet overhead, soldiers from another battalion, parachute infantry, were 'jabbing' out of a mock-up aircraft – the 'mock tower' – practicing their exit drills. I suddenly recalled almost verbatim a similar occasion in the life of the hero of another book, *Northwest Passage*, by Kenneth Roberts, which had in fact started me on this road. It is 1759, and Langdon Towne has arrived at Crown Point, the encampment of Roger's Rangers:

> The place was alive with men. There must have been 2000 of them at work...Behind the fort scarlet-clad companies drilled against a background of acres of tents. I could hear the rattle of wheezy drums, thumping out orders to the drilling men.
>
> The ceaseless and all-pervading activity filled me with anxiety, for I longed to be a part of that activity, and I was afraid there might not be room for me.

Towne was there in no small part because of one moment of self-illumination:

> Suddenly...I began to have an unexpected powerful yearning; I wanted one of those green caps to wear. In my mind's eye I saw myself returning to Portsmouth and Kittery, swaggering in green buckskins and with a Scotch cap tilted becomingly on the side of my head...I looked at Hunk, and saw that he, too, was staring, fascinated, at the green cap so securely perched above Sergeant McNott's ear.[2]

For me, it had been the maroon beret, with the eight-pointed star above the left eye, of the barrack sentry when I had first entered another camp to enlist, three years before. And I think I had always known exactly how a young man much like me might have felt about that Ranger uniform, 200 years before. And forty years later, I feel it still.

Three years a soldier before I became an officer, I had already stood in those drilling ranks long enough to know that those soldiers were not unwillingly subject to what could easily seem, to an outsider, dehumanizing. Some years later

I would encounter, reading in John Keegan, the cultural antecedents to this ceremonial drill, he recalls

> [an] archaeological pang in catching a glimpse of a Guards sergeant marching backwards before his squad who were learning the slow-march on the Sandhurst drill-square; the angle of his outstretched arms and upraised stick, his perfectly practiced disregard for any obstacle in his backward path, the exhortatory rictus of his expression exactly mirrored the image, sketched from life... of a Guards sergeant drilling his recruits on the Horse Guards parade 170 years before; and through that reflection I suddenly understood the function – choreographic, ritualistic, perhaps even aesthetic, certainly much more than tactical – which drill plays in the life of long-service armies.[3]

That evening I had another lesson in the power and the cohesiveness of the culture which was to be entrusted to me.

The battalion to which I had been posted had a tradition of placing officers and NCOs on the US Army's Ranger Course, a gruelling six-week course conducted in the swamps of Georgia. The Ranger 'Tab' was one of the most prized badges any soldier could wear, and the Canadian pre-Ranger training was reputed to be tougher than the course itself. Canadians had a reputation for performing very well on the course, which even its proudest graduates admitted was characterized more by physical than by tactical challenges. Our Commanding Officer had distinguished himself on the course when over 40 years of age, which had made him a legend in our Army. Several of our officers and NCOs had also been 'tabbed',[4] that is, they had completed the US Ranger course, and one of them was my escort for my first days. In the course of our conversations, he had shown me his copy of the Rangers' Code, which I instantly recognized from its source to be apocryphal. In Roberts' novel, Sergeant McNott is giving a briefing to Langdon Towne and Hunk Marriner at Crown Point in 1759, on the eve of their departure with Roger's Rangers for the raid on St Francis; he concludes, in just the words of that modern US Ranger 'Code':

> You got to tell the truth about what you see and what you do. You can lie all you please when you tell other folks about the Rangers, but don't never lie to a Ranger or an officer.

Was life imitating art, or had Roberts actually found such a Code in his researches?[5] It seemed not to matter, and I kept my revelation to myself. It was good apocrypha, and legends (which are always a mix of fact and fiction) are important to culture. Culture, we are reminded, need not rest solely on objective facts; what Omer Bartov has termed 'the invention of memory'[6] will also serve, *if it fits the facts* – such as they may be known.

In real life, Rogers remained 'loyal' during the American Revolution. After the Battle of White Plains he and his Rangers made their way to Toronto (then known as Yorktown), and they have their existence there yet today as a reserve infantry regiment: The Queen's York Rangers ('1st Americans'). In 1996, I attended a re-enactment of the Battle of White Plains, held on the original site. Present there was a 'replica group' of the Queen's American Rangers (as Roger's Rangers were styled during the Revolution); the enactors were quite knowledgeable of the Roberts novel and the real incidents Roberts describes, and many had visited their real-life modern models in Toronto. Several members of that Canadian 'militia' Regiment have served on recent peacekeeping and peace enforcement missions with the Canadian Army. I might have met some of them in Croatia or in Bosnia – two centuries after Crown Point and White Plains, a book written in the year of my birth might have brought soldiers younger than my own children, and me, to meet in the midst of a very model of a modern major conflict.

I have dwelt on this literary aspect of the military culture, even though I am aware that a high standard of literary awareness is not, in the popular perception, a prominent characteristic of the military rank and file. As Paul Fussell, in his book, *The Great War and Modern Memory*,[7] observed of Sir Douglas Haig, the commander of the British forces in the First World War, 'one powerful legacy of Haig's performance is the conviction among the imaginative and intelligent of today of the irredeemable defectiveness of all civil and military leaders'. I very well recall, at the time of the My Lai atrocity, the dismissal of the entire US Army officer corps, by a popular 'opinion maker' of the day, as beer swilling, ex-fraternity, political illiterates. There was, sadly, something to be said at that time, even for such an obvious oversimplification.

But an awareness of their culture, and a surprisingly high standard of literacy even among a group who may often have little formal education, is just one of those things about the military, which is often NOT quite as it might seem.

By the beginning of the twentieth century, it was common that the soldiers' literacy was a significant aspect of the development, influence and preservation of the military culture. Theodore Ropp has said that 'The (American) Civil War was the first great war in which really large numbers of literate men fought as common soldiers.'[8] Fussell has written eloquently of the influence of English literature on English soldiers of nearly a century ago. He cites the example of a British soldier of First World War, 'hardly educated at all', recalling 'the mood of Clarence's dream when he was pacing on the hatches of the ship at night with the Duke of Gloucester, talking of the Wars of the Roses'. Fussell goes on to say that:

> By 1914, it was possible for soldiers to be not merely literate but rigorously literary.... There were few of any rank who had not been assured that the greatest of modern literatures was the English and who did not feel an appropriate pleasure in that assurance.

Fussell then describes a British Private, one John Ball, who has spent a pre-Somme afternoon discussing literature with his friends, as having 'no feeling that literature is not very near the centre of normal experience, no sense that it belongs to intellectuals or teachers or critics'. 'Indeed', says Fussell, 'the *Oxford Book of English Verse* presides over the Great War in a way that has never been sufficiently appreciated'.[9]

Something very like this, this consciousness of a larger culture and of a soldier's rightful place in it, undoubtedly operated as well on the other side of the lines: Modris Eksteins has cited 'the nineteenth century German accomplishment in education...(as) the most important single human component...of Germany's rise to industrial and military pre-eminence in Europe by 1914'.[10] Paul Bauemer, the anti-hero of Remarque's *All Quiet on the Western Front*, goes directly from school, with his schoolmates, through the useful brutalities of Corporal Himmelstoss and into the trenches. A principal factor in their motivation to enlist had been Kantorek, their schoolmaster. Bauemer soldiers on more or less stoically in his diminishing company of ex-school boys until that very quiet day in October 1918 when, like Wilfred Owen, he falls mere weeks before the Armistice[11] – they might almost have gone down together.

And so the events, the culture and the history of soldiers and soldiering are preserved and promulgated by art, especially by literature, and in a way that raw memories, even directly received – and that direct experience bearing on only one generation – could never have done. Those Great War authors have and will continue to affect profoundly the succeeding generations of soldiers, as their successors will in their turn continue literally to immortalize the collective experience of the military culture for, as Ford Maddox Ford said:

> it is not unusual in human beings who have witnessed the sack of a city or the falling to pieces of a people to desire to set down what they have witnessed for the benefit of unknown heirs or of generations infinitely remote; or, if you please, just to get the sight out of their heads.[12]

This, then, is the military culture: colourful, ubiquitous, unexpectedly but continuously recurring, just as my youthful literary encounter with Rogers' Rangers had popped up in real life years later on my first day in my new regiment. The culture is often binding in ways quite subliminal – but nonetheless powerful and compelling, as that 'Code' had been to me, and to those who followed it, *including some who might never have heard of the Ranger Code*. It is like Proust's tisane-dipped *madeleine*, or 'that little phrase' in the Vinteuil Sonata; as Malroux described them, those instinctive memories worked to preserve what time would otherwise have destroyed,[13] and it is in just this manner that the 'customs of the service' push the buttons of memory, keeping alive a legendary past for those who will themselves, even if all unwittingly, pass eventually into their own legends.

I shall return later to consider in more detail the relationship of culture to change – a barrier or a window, and sometimes both. But first we need to look more closely at the military organization as a culture, which I will present in the next chapter.

7

A CLOSER LOOK AT MILITARY ORGANIZATIONAL CULTURE

There are, as Olivia Manning's Harriet observed, all too often some reasons for prejudices or, more charitably, misunderstandings. It is particularly unfortunate that the military do so much to foster and to sustain the prejudices they endure. Clearly the misunderstandings which underlie those prejudices must be appreciated if they are to be avoided.

Military leadership is deliberately and overtly paternalistic. This alone is frequently enough to alienate civilians who witness or who have experienced this; 'paternalism' may have for many an immediately negative connotation. Nevertheless the regimental system which is almost unique to British Commonwealth armies, and which has several times been unsuccessfully imitated by the US Army, is organized as an extended family. In that 'regimental family' there are both formal and informal structures. An example of the latter are the 'associations', consisting of the former members of a regiment, who continue to advise the current generation of formal leaders and soldiers, preserving legends and traditions, and performing many of the functions of tribal elders. And always there is that paternalistic style, for, as Ewart Alan Macintosh wrote in his First World War poem, *In Memoriam*:

> they were only your fathers
> But I was your officer.

It will follow naturally then that a paternalistic military culture will foster hierarchical, vertical organization. While authority is centralized, usually at a fairly senior level, there is a high degree of accountability at all levels. The chain of command is normally inviolate. Although authority is limited by orders, procedures and doctrine, responsibility is absolute and may not be set aside under any circumstances. This last is very important to an understanding of the military culture: under no circumstances of confusion, ambiguity, fatigue or danger, may an officer be excused one fragment of his responsibility, not only for his own actions, but for any actions which may be performed by any person under his command. Naturally, therefore, this includes acts of omission, and most armies regard 'an act, or neglect of an act' as equally serious. Indeed, 'neglect' is considered to indicate shortcomings fundamentally more serious than circumstances might seem to indicate: the officer or NCO who fails to take action is considered to be guilty of a far greater transgression than one who acts in error.

Just as civilians who would work effectively with a military force must appreciate these characteristics of military command and responsibility, so the military must learn to appreciate the civilian, especially the NGO, culture. There the organization is much flatter, not to say nearly horizontal. Authority is decentralized to the maximum practicable extent, and accountability is based on results. This of course implies flexibility and rapidity of response, which can be very valuable characteristics of an emergency relief operation. However, the seemingly *ad hoc* nature of the immediate response has its disadvantages: other or future operations may be compromised by isolated actions with unintended consequences; a desire to get supplies through may compromise an overall mandate; unnecessary dangers may be encountered.

It is commonly apprehended that the military is an authoritarian organization, and it is further commonly believed that officers and NCOs are persons of great authority. This belief inspires in many persons, variously, a whole range of negative responses, and these may include any or all of fear, resentment, envy. This commonly arises from confusing authority with responsibility.

To the extent that a military organization is authoritative, the authority of individual members is severely limited. This is in no small part designed to prevent abuses, but is also an important legal mechanism. Officers and NCOs have life and death responsibilities, and these must be circumscribed by the fact that they are the legal authorities of a social organization, and are at the service of the society which created them. Laws, regulations, custom, tradition, mandates and procedures impose complex restrictions on the authority of leaders who may be required to use deadly force, and who may expose their followers to deadly peril.[1] Their responsibilities, on the other hand are, as I have said, virtually unlimited.

The case of Romeo Dallaire, the United Nations Assistance Mission for Rwanda (UNAMIR), illustrates the juxtaposition of severely limited authority with unlimited responsibilities.[2] He was unable to generate any effective preventive action by warning in good time, on 11 January 1994, of impending genocide, he was prevented by DPKO (Department of United Nations Peacekeeping Operations) from seizing an arms cache, which was to be used to initiate the genocide, and the Security Council (on 21 April) reduced his Force by 90% to a strength of 270.[3] He has since been sued for negligence by a group of Kigali survivors (their advocate was a Canadian lawyer with a reputation for defending human rights), and has been censored by the Belgian Senate for 'imprudence'. And yet – who even remembers who was the head of the DPKO at the time, or the name of his deputy, or who were the Special Representative of, and the Military Advisor to, the Secretary-General? Or knows where they are now?[4] Who knows what nations were asked for additional troops, and refused to contribute? Who remembers President Clinton's apology to the Rwandan Government (in 1998) for his Government's refusal to allow the use of the term genocide in

1994?[5] Of all those 'authority figures', only Dallaire continues to be hounded, and haunted, by his responsibilities then. Stephen Lewis, a member of the Panel of Eminent Persons who investigated the events of 1994 for the OAU (Organization for African Unity), has said, 'Personally speaking, I don't know how Madeleine Albright lives with it'[6]; Romeo Dallaire, it seemed, just about couldn't. Yet Lewis, a former Canadian ambassador to the UN, also said, 'If there is one exemplary human being in all of this, it's General Dallaire.'[7]

The distinction between authority and responsibility is vital, yet misunderstandings arising from failure to appreciate this are common. Those who see the military leaders as possessing great authority will be frustrated, often disbelieving, when they encounter manifestations of the limitations of the authority of officers. Unable to realize how circumscribed the officer's authority may be, they may be quick to detect non-cooperation or unwillingness to help. The officer who tries to explain that he cannot do something because he may not, rarely has a sympathetic reception. On the other hand, an officer who may seem anxious to consider, to avoid, unforeseen consequences, is being mindful of his all-encompassing responsibilities – and may expect as little sympathy for his concerns.

One example of a negative image which arises from the exercise of authority which is remote from the responsibilities of those on the ground, concerns the issue of force protection.

The IFOR, intended to enforce the General Framework Agreement for Peace in Bosnia-Herzegovina (the Dayton Agreement), deployed in late 1995 in the shadow of the US Presidential Elections. The issue of US ground troops' involvement in this operation had itself been overshadowed by the experience in Somalia in 1993. That mission was and is still poorly understood, and many 'lessons' seem to have been drawn deliberately to support partisan views of other issues. Nevertheless, as a result the American *vox populi* was then inferred (at least by the politicians and by the media) to be almost entirely negative towards peace operations in general, and towards the United Nations in particular (the incumbent Secretary-General was then in the process of being forced from office as deliberate US policy).

A major issue in the United States thus became, and remains, casualties, any incidence, or even the risk, of which (it was thought) would have fatally undermined not only the second Clinton presidency, but US involvement in any peace operation. Bosnia-Herzegovina was not worth the bones of a single Ohio paratrooper.[8] Although politically motivated, this was supported enthusiastically by at least the higher ranks of the US military. Meanwhile, the US allies had convinced themselves that, without the participation of US ground troops, the operation in Bosnia could not be mounted at all. Thus security, just one of (traditionally) ten principles of war (see Chapter 23), became the overriding concern, and a new function was born – Force Protection.

Force Protection – the concept was born with capitals – became a major function of, indeed a major limitation on the operation of the US forces. By extension this came to be true of the entire force, and eventually of all NATO.

A Force Protection staff section was created, with tentacles at all levels of staff and command, in NATO and in IFOR. IFOR troops wore complete body protection at all times, were cantoned, and were closely regulated in their movements 'beyond the wire'. Contact with locals was strictly limited, and was nearly entirely reactive – as William Langewiesche has written of US soldiers in Bosnia, 'contact was limited by orders that required GIs to remain armed, helmeted and clothed in their camouflaged combat gear'.[9] A guide had become the law; doctrine had become dogma. The Allies might chafe under these restrictions, and they did. Even though Langewiesche observed that, 'None of the other coalition troops went around like this – not even in the notoriously tough territory around Mostar,'[10] most of the allies largely conformed to US leadership in this as in other issues.[11] There was and remains only sporadic military action to apprehend suspected war criminals,[12] resettlement has been equally patchy and largely unavailing, and peace has so far been considered to be the simple absence of war. The largest and most powerful single military formation then in the field in the entire world, hunkered down in their camps and hoped for quiet – a setting the troops themselves derided in terms such as 'Fort Apache' and 'turtle gear' operations. As William Pfaff wrote, 'The U.S. forces' problem (in Kosovo) is due in part to their crippling doctrine that subordinates military mission to force protection.'[13]

At the same time, senior US officers often described their involvement in peace operations as prejudicial to their profession and to their responsibilities to the nation. The decay of combat skills was widely anticipated, and seniors reminded their juniors, and the press, that their responsibility was to fight their nation's wars – whatever that might mean. That it might have been easier to prevent 'the nation's wars' was not considered, nor was it considered, at least from the outset, how many of their combat skills were in fact being exercised to their fullest extent, every day, in Bosnia.

Bill Nash, a former Major General who commanded the first US division to deploy with IFOR in Bosnia, has recently written that, 'Overall, we found that the improvements gained in difficult battle staff and command skills while in Bosnian far outweighed any losses in specific war-fighting tasks while deployed for peacekeeping.' Nash concludes that 'what is gained in an operational environment more than compensates for the specific skill levels that may be degraded, and those skills are generally more easily and quickly recovered'.[14] Naturally, however given the narrow 'warrior' attitudes which prevailed then, there was little interest in, indeed bare tolerance for, those civilian agencies that were not going to be around to fight 'America's wars'.

Of course, other nations and armies, whose experience was quite different from the Americans', would vacillate on these issues, and would at the tactical level display more flexibility in their operations. However, the damage was being done: prejudices were being sustained and reinforced, diversity was denied. Soldiers were seen, by the media and by their civilian 'partners', as being passive, remote, inflexible, ineffective on the real issues of peace and security. Perhaps more importantly, the locals perceived them this way – the soldiers might have been alien invaders.[15]

The disgraceful lengths to which professional soldiers could be led by their Governments' and hence their officers' preoccupation with Force Protection were never more clearly nor better illustrated than by the 'at-our-peril' speech given by the IFOR Ground FC, a British general:

> At our peril does IFOR get involved in police work. At our peril do we join in the search for war criminals or the evidence of war crimes. At our peril do we deploy our soldiers to guard the sites of mass graves, probable or suspected.[16]

Just how unarmed and unprotected civilians, exposed to those 'perils', and many others as well, might react to the military's preoccupation with their own security, seems beyond the ability of the military (at least the United States, plus at least one British general) to imagine. It was for just this reason that Lieutenant-General Sir Michael Rose generally did not wear protective gear in Sarajevo: 'I had long taken the decision not to wear a flak jacket or helmet when travelling in Bosnia, because it created a barrier when talking to people who did not have such protection.'[17] And Martin Bell of the BBC said:

> The flak jacket was like a badge of indemnity, a status that I did not wish to claim. And there came a time when I discarded it to walk the streets of Sarajevo ... It may have been a lapse of security, but it was also plain good manners.[18]

Although I have said that the military culture is cohesive and ubiquitous, this does not mean that the military culture is monolithic. UNPROFOR initially had contingents from 19 nations, and they were Protestant, Catholic and Orthodox Christians, Muslims (in Bosnia, deliberately mirroring the Bosnians themselves) and Buddhists; the soldiers were from every continent and nearly every region of the globe. Could their diversity have been any less than in any other so variously founded organization? To deny them their natural diversity could only be a manifestation of that second mechanism of prejudice. Socially and professionally cohesive the world's militaries may be, but they find it no easier to speak with a common voice, nor are they any more or any less susceptible to groupthink or thought control, than might be any comparable grouping of diplomats, of NGOs, or of international organizations. Sir Michael Rose encountered the cultural diversity of NATO and the UN peacekeepers:

> [NATO] was a war-fighting alliance designed to deter an attack by the Warsaw Pact against Europe; whereas the UN had been formed to bring about, by peaceful means, the settlement of international disputes. *The respective cultures of the two organizations were poles apart.*[19]

Woodward noticed this as well:

> The use of airpower (in Bosnia in 1994) also introduced into the field a second military organization – NATO – whose criteria, *culture*, doctrine and political guidance were vastly different from the UN and from peacekeeping operations.[20]

It should be borne in mind that there were present in UNPOFOR at that time several contingents contributed by NATO members – British, Canadians, Dutch, French, plus staff officers from Norway and Denmark; thus an unusual number of the peacekeepers would have had extensive NATO experience – and vice-versa, of course. What made the difference here however was the effect of an organization creating a micro-culture, introducing striking differences within the over-arching framework of a shared military culture.

The problem of *military* cross-cultural disconnects is recurring as the EU prepares to assume its largest and most important regional security role to date: relieving the NATO-led SFOR in Bosnia-Herzegovina. Critical to this handover is a seamless sharing of intelligence, but the EU has in fact expanded more rapidly than has NATO, and secrets-sharing has come to a near halt as NATO has refused to accept all of the 'new Europeans' into its complete confidence. Bulgaria's designated ambassador and military representative to NATO, and the commander-in-chief of her air force, have been refused access to NATO classified documents. Turkey, for reasons which obviously have little or nothing to do with security, has nevertheless blocked the access of the delegations of Malta and Cyprus. As a result, it has been said that NATO-EU cooperation 'is simply not developing' and that cooperation 'has almost come to a standstill'.[21]

The military is not a monoculture, but with all its similarities continues to be comprised of national elements and contingents which will display the varieties of their parent nations, regions, histories, religions and services, just as do their civilian partners. It is because of their differences – in roles and in capabilities – that they need each other, and have value for each other at all. The challenge for inter-agency cooperation is to manage these differences so that each element contributes its best, and so that an emergency reaction is not crippled by the very diversity which should be its major strength.

8

CULTURE AND CHANGE

A barrier or a window?

The third component of prejudice towards the military is the denial of change: the stereotype, if it ever was authentic, has become an anachronism.

Change has been the only constant of the past decade, especially in the shape and nature of peace operations.

With the apparent, even if temporary, lessening of the veto threat,[1] mandates have been more proactive, and have been more interventionist as well. 'Regional arrangements and agencies' as prescribed in Chapter VIII of the Charter of the United Nations (only one of the present regional or sub-regional organizations existed when the Charter was written), are more prominent and more capable than in the previously bi-polar environment. Conflicts are more commonly within states, which may invoke the protection of their sovereignty to forestall intervention, even as the breakdown of governance that often accompanies intra-state conflicts may render that sovereignty of less positive significance. The resource and humanitarian crises that have caused, and/or have resulted from, intra-state conflict have been more complex, and these complex emergencies demand a broadly based inter-agency response by military and civilian agencies working in concert.

Responding to the increased complexity of the emergencies encountered in the 1990s, the array of NGOs has proliferated in number and scope, and their influence has increased greatly. Enforcement mandates, given faltering or failing governance and resultant widespread violations of human rights, have been much more common. These have entailed earlier and more extensive use of force in an intervention – as the crises have increased in severity and complexity, force has escalated just as the importance of host consent has tended to decline. Force, or the threat of force, has in fact been used deliberately to induce and to maintain consent.

Finally, the issue, indeed the very concept of state sovereignty is being re-appreciated, and the perceived legitimacy of governments is being shaped by a new awareness of such issues as fundamental rights and freedoms of peoples.

These post-Cold War conflicts thus typically involve state collapse, man-made humanitarian emergencies and violent struggles among a variety of non-state forces. These 'manifest conflicts' are often a resurgence of long-standing latent conflicts, and often seem virtually intractable. The response to such conflicts usually requires unarmed civilian agencies to deploy in situations of extreme danger, where the state (if there was one) has been reduced to impotence and there are no responsible negotiating partners. Such a situation will require that security must be imposed if relief is to be effective. And thus is born what the Canadian International Peacekeeping Training Centre calls 'The New Peacekeeping Partnership'. This then is the scenario in which civilian and military need each other as never before – whether or not either is prepared to recognize this mutual interdependence.

The military cannot be, and has not been, immune to these changes, and changes in the military there certainly have been. Attitudes and practices have been altered by experience, and things are not as they were. A very brief look at an earlier UN operation, now concluded, will illustrate this.

Little reported at the time, and little examined since, the United Nations Transition Administration in Eastern Slavonia (UNTAES) deployed at the same time as IFOR, and with the same mandate – and there most similarities ended. Despite having an American Head of Mission (HOM), UNTAES was, as the title indicates, a UN enforcement mission, mandated under Chapter VII of The UN Charter. The HOM was a civilian, and the Force Commander (FC) was subordinate to him (NATO troops in the field have no comparable diplomatic or political leadership at the operational level). Although much smaller than IFOR, the UNTAES force structure was adequate for its role (it was more than four times the strength of the former Sector East of UNPROFOR, which it replaced), and had firepower, mobility and protection appropriate to its enforcement mandate. In contrast to IFOR, UNTAES was actively patrolling in very small, often dismounted groups, employing the security measures deemed appropriate by tactical commanders, maintaining contact with locals at all levels. That Force was a powerful and positive presence everywhere in its area of operations. It was also, in terms of its mandate, reasonably successful in demilitarization, resettlement and confidence building. For so long as UNTAES was deployed – which was very probably not long enough – as Dr Ingrid Lehmann has said, 'peace was given its chance' in Eastern Slavonia.[2]

It has been said that UNTAES, and not I/SFOR, was the past which was the prologue for the current international effort in Kosovo, and it is true that the Kosovo Force (KFOR) differs sharply in many important aspects, especially in its behaviour and its attitudes, from I/SFOR.

Among the first images of the KFOR deployment were pictures of American soldiers, who had stacked their arms and turtle gear to play pick-up basketball with local youths. British soldiers patrol the streets of Pristina with small arms and wearing only berets on their heads. When French soldiers in Mitrovica and Americans in Gnjilane wear full protective gear, they do so in response to a situation, which specifically demands that level of protection.[3] The Civil-Military Operations Coordination Centre (CMOCC) in Pristina was provided, and nearly entirely manned, by KFOR. In that CMOCC could be heard, quite openly by any who care to attend, frank and complete discussions of the intimate details of civil-military coordination, mostly among military officers from a force which is not even one of the four 'pillars' of the United Nations Interim Administration Mission in Kosovo (UNMIK). Yet on one morning an officer (an American) ended his presentation with the motto, 'Support your Pillar!'[4] Can the T-shirts be far behind? The spots are changing, but are the perceptions changing? One civilian, remarking on this, said to me he thought the military were changing and adapting their attitudes and practices more, and more rapidly, than were their civilian 'counterparts'.

But how does the military culture meet the need for change – is the culture a part of the problem, or is it a part of the solution?

For many years the military culture has indeed acted as a check on change, often with catastrophic results. Military preparedness has been popularly characterized as 'preparing for the last war but one'; the French, especially, are said to have been ready in 1914 for 1870, and in 1939 for 1914. The glacis of Ulm, the inner defences of the city, were renovated and improved in 1924, although the last land battle there was Napoleon's defeat of Mack in 1805. However, that actual battle took place 20 kilometres to the east of the city, so the glacis was not used even then. When, in the 1860s, the Emperor Franz-Joseph announced his intention to demolish Vienna's glacis and return it to the people, the city had not been directly threatened since the occupation by Napoleon, also in 1805. *However*, in 1805 Vienna was surrendered without a fight, so *that* glacis was not used even then, either. Nevertheless, fifty-five years later, the Emperor's proposal was met by the collective outrage of the Imperial and Royal General Staff. Despite their protests, the project nevertheless went ahead, an early example of a peace dividend; the ground thus vacated became the famous Ring. That, you might infer, is the trouble with military installations and plans: the enemy always does something else, or comes from somewhere else, and the whole thing has been a waste of time. The Maginot Line stands as the definitive metaphor for this sort of 'preparedness'.

Military preparedness might thus seem to have been an oxymoron and, on the record, such a perception is far from groundless.

Two examples of lessons not learnt were the American Civil War (1861–65), and the Crimean War (1854); failure of the military to learn from these led directly to the disastrous, and clearly foreshadowed, land battles of the First World War.

The US Civil War had many of the components of a modern war: Rifles, machine guns, railways, the telegraph, wire. The only things lacking from the Civil War battlefield, compared to that of 1914, were indirect fire artillery and aviation – although balloons were used for reconnaissance and artillery spotting. Nevertheless, the Civil War was little studied in the nineteenth century, largely just because it had been fought mostly by amateurs, and by Americans, against whom there was a thus a double cultural bias. Despite that, as John Keegan has written, the Civil War attracted many foreign observers,[5] their contributions seem to have been largely disregarded. This disregard was most succinctly expressed by the Chief of the Prussian General Staff, Moltke, who, invited to send observers to the Confederate Army, replied that he was disinclined to study 'the movements of armed mobs'.[6] The results of many of the battles seemed to justify that dismissive judgement.

The British Army, for their part, was in the latter half of the nineteenth century bumbling out of one of their 'signal disasters', although just what was signalled by the Crimean War was unclear at the time. As Winston Churchill put it, the British Army suffered horrendous casualties, a sickness rate which exceeded the rate of battle casualties, and near defeat, partly 'because it did not occur to the Government of the greatest engineering country in the world to ease the movement of supplies ... by laying down five miles of light railway'.[7] The public outcry over the bungling – public opinion was already having a great influence on British policy – led grudgingly and despite much official footdragging to a series of reforms which began only in 1868, and were not completed until 1906.[8] Flogging was abolished, short service was introduced, the infantry was equipped with breech-loading (but still single shot) rifles and, after an especially hard struggle with the entire establishment, commission and promotion by purchase were abolished in 1871.[9] Nevertheless, for long after, wrote James Morris, 'Some of the army's anachronisms survived because of its Imperial role: the hollow square, volley firing, the frontal cavalry charge – *all these would be disastrous in a European war.*'[10]

And that is essentially why the First World War was fought as it was: as Bruce Patton said, 'defensive firepower had made obsolete all of the established practices for getting an offensive underway. As in 1914, the (Civil War) enlisted man paid with his life for the High Command's education in this matter.'[11] And so in the First World War, men 'went over the top' in densely packed waves, and died in them, too – at the rate of 20,000 per day, for 51 months. Except in the cavalry, who largely stood idle for four years,[12] following which they were dismissed from most armies. Thus, the only proper lesson to have been drawn from the Charge of the Light Brigade had – after more than half a century – finally been learnt.

It seems that, in the nineteenth century, military culture was an effective barrier to change.

Things were a little different in the twentieth century, and armies tried to do better than to 'prepare for the last war but one'. The results were a bit mixed: the German experience of the First World War led them to *Blitzkrieg*; the French built the Maginot Line; the Anglo-Americans launched strategic air campaigns. It took the last half of the twentieth century to prove that air campaigns will be effective only when they are joint campaigns, coordinated with the other services. It has also seemingly taken our unsatisfactory experiences with bombing campaigns in the Second World War, in Korea, in Vietnam and in Serbia, to prove repeatedly that aerial weapons were and are still as characterized by H.G. Wells in 1908 (before anybody had an air force of any description): 'at once enormously destructive and entirely indecisive'.[13] As Michael Ingatieff described the NATO air campaign in Kosovo-Serbia nearly a century later: 'Brave American pilots were upstairs at 15,000 feet watching people going from house to house with machine guns and knives and couldn't stop the ethnic cleansing'.[14]

As comfortable as these derogatory views of the military culture may be, they have become truly anachronisms. There is ample evidence, as my colleague observed that day in the CMOCC in Pristina, that the military are collectively catching up to change and the pace of change, and are far from the tightly bound reactionaries they are sometimes type-cast to be. It is today a very good question who are the reactionaries: civilians who disdain the military, or soldiers trying to come to grips with a bewildering menu of new mandates, roles and tasks?

A visit to the modern German officer factory in Dresden might serve as an example of change as an essential component of a military education. Although the school was established in its modern form only in 1998, it was until 1945 the traditional 'old school' of the Reichswehr and, later, the Wehrmacht, and was probably the prototype of 'The Officer Factory' so savagely parodied by H.H. Kirst (in his novel of that name). Rommel, Stauffenberg, de Maizere were trained there.

About 1,200 cadets now train here each year, and most go on to the University of the German Armed Forces – it generally takes almost seven years of intensive training to produce an officer in the Bundeswehr, about what it takes for a physician or a lawyer. For nearly fifty years the Bundeswehr has had only one role: the defence of the Federal Republic. Cadets interviewed in Dresden recently expressed their goals as 'neutralizing problems to buy time for political solutions'. Their ambitions are decidedly shaped by today's conflicts, not yesterday's: they have 'moral ambitions: to permit the rule of law in places where lawlessness prevails'. 'Even press relations are a part of a German officer's schooling these days... For this reason, the ten character traits of the officer's profile include "self-assuredness and self-control when liasing with the media." '

As regards the controversial modernization of the Bundeswehr, where many may operate vehicles and machines older than they, the Cadets cite a directive of the General Inspector, dated 1993, in which it is reiterated that the officers of the Bundeswehr must 'endure hardships over and above the generally accepted measure'. Some things never change.[15] It should be noted, however, that these changes were not worked by 20-year old Cadets: the changes were effected by officers of the two older generations, themselves products of the 'single role' Bundeswehr. For those elders, today's military structures and roles were, less than a decade ago, utterly unthinkable.[16]

Thus the bearers of the tradition have simultaneously worked the necessary changes, not just to training but also to attitudes, while preserving the more austere traditions of service and of hardihood. These former Cold Warriors seem to have decisively broken the last-war-but-one syndrome. Nevertheless, these young Germans' attitudes must be contrasted to those of the West Pointers cited by David Lipsky (see Chapter 11): '(West Point) cadets exhibit negative attitudes towards peacekeeping and global missions.'

9

CIVIL-MILITARY CULTURES IN COLLISION

Festina Lente

Do nothing in haste; look well to each step; and from the beginning
think what may be the end.
(Edward Whymper, *Scrambles Amongst the Alps*, 1871)

We will discuss a situation in which the 'partner agencies' have found themselves, with all their reservations about each other, nevertheless and however uneasily working together to resolve a serious and urgent relief operation, one which must be mounted in the face of continuing violent conflict. The dangers faced by the outsiders will be no less than those being faced by their putative beneficiaries.

Their responses to this situation will illustrate their cultures in collision. So we will consider their joint plans, and their own conflicts, and then ask what might or should have been done to avoid or mitigate the circumstances. In what follows, I have synthesized several different occasions, some of which I have experienced and some of which have been related to me by those who have experienced the sort of organizational culture shock I describe here. As Michael C. Williams has written of the difficulties UNPROFOR and UNHCR faced in coordinating humanitarian relief in Bosnia-Herzegovina, despite everyone's best efforts, 'convoy operations remained a contentious part of civil-military cooperation in Bosnia, largely because of the near-constant threat of local blockages and harassment'.[1]

And so a humanitarian NGO might request, late of an evening, a military escort for an urgent relief convoy, which is to be dispatched at first light the next day. The officer who receives the request demurs, saying her troops cannot be readied in such a short time. The NGO bridles, and asks just how much time is required to get ready to drive 50 miles. The officer explains that the troops must be fully and carefully briefed for the operation, that the route must be proven (for mines, road conditions, checkpoints, bridge classifications). Radio frequencies must be allocated and sets checked, and coordination with other military units along the route must be established. The vehicles must be thoroughly inspected before and after each convoy. The convoy must include a vehicle repair team and medical personnel. This will all take several hours to arrange, and the troops must be rested. The officer suggests a 24-hour delay. Fatally for her credibility, she says she needs time to complete her battle procedure.

The NGO does not blow up over this, but asks acidly 'What battle, what operation?', and says the route has been in constant use and there have been no mines nor checkpoints there for months. To make a long story just somewhat shorter, there are always pressure points in military organizations, and several now get pushed, and the mission is on – for first light tomorrow.

In the event, not too much goes wrong – no drivers fall asleep at the wheel, there is no fighting at the crossing point, nobody gets lost, nobody breaks down. There is however a checkpoint no one knew anything about, and there is a necklace of anti-tank and anti-personnel mines across the road. The road warriors at the checkpoint are heavily armed, and high on something more than slivovitz. There is another peacekeeping unit in the area, but our Convoy Escort Commander did not get their frequency and cannot call them. This is rapidly becoming something for another day, as E.M. Forster might have said. It now develops, however, that the checkpoint 'commander' wants to negotiate. If some of the supplies might be left for his men, the mines could be cleared and the barrier raised, and the convoy could roll. The NGO is all for it – there's more where this came from, and the people really need these supplies. The officer now puts her foot down: freedom of movement is non-negotiable; still less is it to be purchased at gunpoint. Moreover, this checkpoint is in violation of the Zone of Separation Agreement, and it is going to be removed, not bargained over. She, the officer, is accountable for observing the mandate, not selling it. Finally, if we did this, we would have to do it everywhere in the province – probably even when we return this way later today.

Not *too* much went wrong.

This region did not really need any more conflicts, but there we are: misunderstanding *among the peacekeepers* is now complete. It is probably too late to resolve this today, but what might have been done to prevent this? And what must be done to prevent the recurrence of such incidents?

Of course all this, and all these possibilities, should have been discussed before – it is called coordination, and that's what the CMOCC is there for. Even more to the point, we see some gaps in the training of both parties. Opportunities for this type of training are far from lacking: the website of the International Association of Peacekeeping Training Centres lists centres, academies, ministries and offices conducting training on all the points encountered here.[2]

But let us assume what is in fact usually the case: both the NGO and the officer are of good will, and neither wants to repeat this experience, so they agree to meet and try to resolve their problems. They are, whether they realize it or not, in a classic negotiation situation, and they probably have not been trained for that either, but they at least recognize the need to create some common ground.

The officer might first try to explain what she means by 'battle procedure' which, she now recognizes, is a fairly formidable term and she devoutly wishes somebody would think of a better. However, she explains it as:

> That whole process by which a commander receives orders, warns the troops, conducts a reconnaissance, develops a plan, issues orders and deploys the forces to execute the mission. The essence of battle procedure is concurrent activity.

She goes on to explain that her troops had been fairly busy recently, and their vehicles as well. Both were overdue for rest, and exceeding those limits is one of the most dangerous things you can do here. She guesses (she still does not know for sure) that that neighbouring unit may have known, or at least suspected, that the Zone of Separation might have been violated, and could have given warning – if asked, but she (the officer) did not have any contact with them. She reiterated, politely but forcefully, that the mandate was not up for bargaining, especially in respect of freedom of movement. She advised the NGO of what he should have been aware: she had over 50 soldiers out there, and probably not more than a handful of her NCOs really understood the mission – most had only hastily prepared route cards. If anyone had broken down or gotten separated from the convoy for any reason, we might now be dealing with a hostage situation. Except for her: she would be on the way home, and to no heroine's welcome, either (*but I was your officer*). The bottom lines for her were two: the maintenance of the mandate, and the safety of her troops. Warming somewhat to her theme, she said these were sacred charges to her, and she was enjoined by her superiors, and trusted by her subordinates, not to take unnecessary risks.

The NGO probably replied that he was grateful for her frankness, but he had a few points to make as well:

The people left in those mountains were mostly elderly, women and children; their men dead or fled – or both. They were always a poor people, and now facing a very harsh winter. They had had no autumn harvest, nor would there be any in the spring – their fields were extensively mined. Speaking of bottom lines, he said, this is it: this is the complex humanitarian emergency we signed on to deal with, and I intend to deal with it. That is my sacred charge, and I am accountable to *myself* in dealing with it. Despite our best efforts, many of those people will not survive this winter, and risks are acceptable in the face of a crisis like this.

If a mediator were present to assist in these negotiations, it might be observed that the common ground is looming up before the officer and the NGO, if only they can recognize it.

Both are idealistic and dedicated, and both are *there* – they are not back in a headquarters, still less in some foreign capitol. They do want the supplies to get through, and neither now has any grounds to doubt the other's professionalism. Their differences are *cultural and social*, not professional, still less are they personal. Given that mutual recognition, they have quickly learned some valuable lessons about each other, and education is well on the way to replacing the prejudices which each has brought to this partnership. We may now leave them to build a sustainable relationship.

We wish them well in persuading their respective superiors that they are each on the right track.

Perhaps, if we had been mediating that negotiating session, we might have observed on some tendencies that should be better appreciated. Some of these might be:

- The military is mission-oriented: the officer spoke passionately of her troops and her mandate.
- The NGO is victim-oriented: he spoke with equal passion of the people he hopes to save.

As Rear Admiral Claes Tornberg puts it:

> There are professions which are victim-oriented, such as the humanitarian organizations and the NGOs. Other professions, like the military..., tend to be more mission-oriented. The two approaches are not always compatible and cause counter-productive agendas and inefficiencies of operations.[3]

- The officer is to a certain extent captive of a system that limits her authority, but recognizes virtually no limits on her responsibilities – and she would not have it any other way.
- The officer has been preparing for war, and much of her training is certainly useful in trying to end, or to prevent, war. But her vocabulary necessarily represents the harsher realities of her profession: the term 'battle procedure' does not fall easily on the civilian ear. Had she explained it in the first place, instead of resorting to jargon, it would be hard to resist the logic and the prudence of preparing thoroughly to do something complicated and possibly dangerous.
- The NGO must be cognizant of hidden complexities that, if properly managed, may be transparent; if poorly managed, they may be tragic.
- The military must do a much better job of explaining how they see those complexities, and just what the unintended consequences of precipitate action might be. Then a real appreciation of the factors affecting the operation, and a joint consideration of the courses open, can be undertaken in a rational manner.
- In other words, the military decision loop is fairly broad: thorough, deliberate, painstaking; the NGO decision loop is relatively tight: agile, quick. The military may miss some opportunities, but the NGO may miss some things important to realizing opportunities. It should not be difficult to synthesize the two approaches, combining more flexible reactions with more thorough preparations. It is principally a matter of better communications, and some common training might be a good start in that direction.

- The NGO is perfectly aware of the military attitudes towards civilians, especially NGOs, and if he has not read Lipsky's book about West Point, he has had plenty of opportunities to observe that attitude in action. The key to overcoming this will be respect and courtesy – it is no coincidence that these are key attributes of successful negotiators.

Clearly, it is the military's responsibility to present themselves, as individuals and as members of an honoured profession, clearly and precisely. Only in this way can civilian prejudice be overcome, and solid relationships built. But the military must work harder to overcome their *own prejudices*, and courtesy is a good place to start. The civilians have shown little propensity to study the military profession, and are still less likely to even attempt to penetrate military jargon. It has so far fallen to the military to study their civilian counterparts – the military profession is after all a social product, and ignorance of the society from which the army has sprung, for the protection of which it was created, in whose employ it serves, is not acceptable.

10

UNIT ROTATIONS

Les Absents se Trompent

The customary rotation of military units into and out of a mission, usually at six-month intervals, has given rise to serious misunderstandings with the civilian components of the mission, has resulted in a perceived lack of depth in the military commitment and has become yet another cause for trust to be withheld.

Civilian agencies, and individuals, are often in the crisis area long before the military arrive, and may remain long after the military have left. The reasons for the seeming slow reaction of military units, which are not unavoidable, are discussed separately in Chapter 22. The relatively early termination of a military force often results from a combination of factors; among these may be success in creating a positive security environment and confidence that stability can be maintained without external security forces, coupled with the enormous cost, mostly borne by the troop contributor nations, of maintaining a military force in the field.

There remains, however, the fact that individual civilians do remain at their posts much longer than the military units – members of the OSCE (Organisation for Security and Cooperation in Europe) average 18 months en poste. A distinction must be made here between the military field units and the headquarters staff members. The latter customarily remain at their positions at least one year, and often longer. Nevertheless, the perception that the military presence is collectively transient and superficial, which is undoubtedly derived from the bi-annual rotations, remains and is seriously divisive. There are, however, inherent in the nature of the military mission good reasons for the relatively frequent rotations of units.

The first factor to be considered is that few nations are comfortable that they have enough military forces, and most nations' militaries are multiply tasked in their own countries. Towards the end of the Cold War, the Canadian Forces officially had 55 separate roles and tasks, of which peacekeeping operations was only one. Since the end of the Cold War, the strength of the Canadian Forces has approximately halved. However, the list of tasks and the resources they demand has, with the exception of forces stationed in the Federal Republic of Germany, remained essentially the same. Most NATO nations, and many others, are in a similar situation.

Second, and connected to the first, the various roles of a military unit usually call for varying degrees of exclusively military training, both of individuals and the collective training of units. While it is true that individual training benefits in the short term from almost any deployment, there will remain skills that can only be instilled and maintained under specific and rigorous training. These are principally, but not exclusively, combat skills. These individual combat skills, which will unavoidably deteriorate over time, must be complimented by collective skills. Units are teams, and working together effectively, both within a given unit such as an infantry battalion, and with detachments from other types of units, such as engineers, artillery and armour, requires a concentration in time and space of these units. This training of various arms in effective teams of all arms, entails dedicated time and training facilities which are difficult and expensive to provide.

The alternative to providing individual and collective combat training for military forces is to convert them to gendarmeries, paramilitary organizations without combat roles or capabilities. This has been rejected by nearly all governments as an irreversible deterioration of forces, which are, after all, created and intended for the defence of their country. So countries limit the period of a peacekeeping deployment to that in which they consider their units can continue to have a useful general military capability, without comprehensive post-deployment individual and collective re-training – upon the completion of which the next emergency cannot be expected to wait.

Third, military field deployments entail an environment usually unremittingly harsh. Inadequate shelter, prolonged exposure, physical hardship, poor sanitation and lack of fresh food typify the life of soldiers living in very small detachments on observation posts and checkpoints, conducting patrols in all weathers and climates. As units are normally kept as small as possible on peacekeeping operations, time off is limited and often almost non-existent. In professional armies, which most peacekeeping contingents are, soldiers are very often married, and nearly all of the NCOs and officers are. Young soldiers separated from young families have their tolerable limits for such deprivation. The backbone of a military unit is its junior ranks, and in no army are these any more than badly paid. The civilian members of UNMIK are today paid more in subsistence allowances than the annual salary of a soldier or junior NCO in KFOR.[1] Only a very high degree of physical and mental fitness permits the soldiers to sustain such a harsh life, and this has its limits in the most professional and dedicated units.

There is of course an alternative to unit rotation, which would be individual replacements. This would preserve a core of experience and expertise that, it might be thought, would sustain unit effectiveness at a more even level. This also has been rejected by most contributors, and for reasons directly derived from the nature of the military culture. It is these cultural reasons that are central to maintaining the practice of unit rotations.

The military culture is one of cohesion – of maintaining group identities and loyalties despite all the forces that threaten, and may destroy, the identity of the group. Military leaders know how little impact external factors may have on the motivation of soldiers. As Gabriel and Savage put it, 'It appears that a continued sense of "cause", at whatever level of saliency, is not very important to military cohesion.'[2] S.L.A. Marshall adds that the things that will induce one to risk life bravely are 'the same things which induce one to face life bravely – friendship, loyalty to responsibility, and knowledge that he is a repository of the faith and the confidence of others'. He quotes a general who commanded a division in Sicily in the Second World War as saying that 'men do not fight for a cause but because they do not want to let their comrades down'.[3] Gabriel and Savage state that, in the Second World War, 'the main factor in combat cohesion was found in the primary group'. That group was minimally viable and sustainable when it was founded on squads of ten, or platoons of thirty.

The extraordinary cohesiveness of the Wehrmacht despite seriatim disasters was in no small part based on the preservation of relatively large primary groups, typically at the company (100+) level[4] – and this in a force suffering repeated, catastrophic losses – in July 1944, for example, in the Central Army Group, 28 of 38 committed divisions were destroyed with the loss of nearly half a million soldiers. Yet they continued to rotate whole divisions, or the *disjecta membra* of divisions, to reconstitute primary groups.[5] Later, in the Korean conflict, under a system of individual replacements, the group 'collapsed' to a buddy system, which was not sustainable, and cohesion, under far less pressure than in the Second World War, similarly collapsed.[6]

The continuity of this aspect of the military culture was reiterated recently when a US Marine Lieutenant-Colonel told Chris Hedges, just before crossing into Kuwait at the start of the Gulf War in 1991, 'Just remember that none of these boys is fighting for home, for the flag, for all that crap the politicians feed the public. They are fighting for each other, just for each other.'[7]

This lesson, then, has been learned at great cost in lives and fortunes, and is not to be discarded: soldiers work for each other, not for causes. There are literally no limits to their devotion to their primary groups, yet to be sustainable these must be fairly large. The armies of the British Commonwealth are normally formed around a regimental system, although in practice this usually means battalions of around 6–800 men. Even there, the social unit is usually the company, just as the Wehrmacht had it in Second World War. These will train together, work together, play together – and all very hard, and for quite a long time, as long as they are together. The relationships thus formed endure for lifetimes: the website of my Regiment is filled every day with emails from old soldiers looking for comrades from 20 and 30 years ago.

So, today, the battalions which have trained together for the mission will deploy together, they will stay together, and eventually, when it is their time, they will leave together. In much the same terms, Nash has described this as a major component of the performance of his division: 'almost the entire division deployed together to Bosnia. We were therefore able to maintain unit integrity far more than any unit since the 1995 and 1996 period. The benefits of unit cohesion to long-term readiness are most significant, maybe critical'.[8]

But is the perception, that these unit rotations decrease the overall peacekeeping mission effectiveness, accurate? It is my view that it is not. The cohesiveness of the unit enhances and sustains its members' preparations, and the similarity of their training and their organization with those of their predecessors equally enhances the effectiveness of the handover between units. The replacement of one unit by another is in fact a collective combat skill in which both the outgoing and the incoming unit will have been identically trained, and each will know what is expected of it, and what to expect from the other. In a combat situation, such a relief would commonly be executed in less than 24 hours; in peacekeeping operations a relief usually takes at least two weeks. Nor does a unit always rotate 100% of its strength: the Austrians replace one-half of the unit each six months, and the newcomer will be paired with a comrade who has been in the mission for at least three months. While it is true that a new unit can be wrong-footed by unexpected situations – and the parties will commonly deliberately attempt to contrive this – the learning is quick, and mistakes are seldom repeated. Indeed, it is to be thought the process could be accelerated if those civilian agencies longer in that particular field were to be more congenially alert to the learning curve of a new unit, and if civil-military cooperation were to begin in that handover/working in period. But even without the early contributions of the partner agencies, the military are not fools, and can only rarely be repeatedly fooled.

Unit rotations are important to the culture and the nature of the military contingents, and the extent to which they adversely affect operational effectiveness should not be exaggerated.

11

THE US FORCES

The military antipodeans

The Pentagon is not the right locus for the generation of U.S. foreign policy.

(Wesley Clark, former Supreme
Allied Commander Europe[1])

The emergence of US forces in peace operations since the Cold War has introduced a new note into already familiar problems of civil-military coopera-tion in these types of operations. The inexperience of the American forces has been exacerbated by high-level scepticism about the appropriateness of such missions for the American military. At the same time, the very large numbers of Americans deployed on recent peace operations, together with the commanding role they have assumed, indeed as they have insisted upon as a condition of their participation (as in Haiti, Somalia, Bosnia and Kosovo), has made it increasingly common that the civilians' experience with the military has been with the American military. This has been unfortunate, as a judgement of the American military has been widely inferred to be typical of military forces in general. This is far from being the case, therefore it is appropriate now to consider in more detail the *sui generis* nature of the armed forces of the United States.

The nineteenth-century Europeans who scorned the 'armed mobs' of the American Civil War have been mirrored, especially since the Second World War, by the US military class, who have in some isolation from the main developed their own strains of military doctrine, structures and procedures. This is not the context in which to discuss in detail the development of the current diplomatic practices of the United States, nor to describe other than very briefly the uniquely American military doctrines which have arisen from those practices. However, there has at least since the end of the Cold War era been a reversal of the traditional relationship between, and thus of the functions appropriate to, diplomats and the military in the United States. This has led to some rather odd developments in the US military establishment, and these developments have in their turn contributed to a transatlantic schism between the American and the European military communities. This has had its consequences for the conduct of modern multi-agency peace operations, especially those led or dominated by US forces, and these effects have been generally insalubrious.

That this military intra-communal conflict indeed mirrors (or has pre-figured) a growing rift among the traditional Cold War allies is of course a part of a much larger problem. US–European cultural and historic myopia are scarcely of recent origin. However, the recent weakening of formal alliances and the simultaneous proliferation of *ad hoc* coalitions, have severely complicated international and regional responses to complex humanitarian emergencies. These recent coalitions have included regional organizations and NGOs, especially in Europe, where for example the UNMIK leads efforts by two specialized agencies of the UN, the EU, the OSCE and NATO, plus about 500 NGOs. Beyond Europe, European regional organizations, such as the EU in the Middle East and the OSCE across Eurasia, as well as European-based NGOs, such as CARE International and MSF, are important actors. Transatlantic differences among agencies – international and regional, governmental and non-governmental, civilian and military – thus are readily manifested in the structures and practices of peace operations, and not only in Europe. The relations among the various and varied military and civilian agencies, and their potential for peace operations partnerships, are particularly vulnerable to the resultant bickering.

American foreign and security policies and structures today reflect a curious ambivalence towards Europe, if not the entire non-American world. This is partly a result of America's perception of its historic uniqueness, what Henry Kissinger has described as the assumption 'that America is possessed of an exceptional nature expressed in unrivalled virtue and unrivalled power'.[2] This fabula rasa of American exceptionalism is also partly a result of feeling themselves thrust into a quasi-imperial role they have not sought and do not want. These factors in part arise from, in part contribute to, a resurgence of neo-conservative isolationism. It is almost a reversion – and by no means entirely an unconscious one – to the spirit of George Washington's Farewell Address: 'The great rule of conduct for us in regard to foreign nations, is, in extending our commercial relations to have with them as little *political* connection as possible.'[3]

The experiences of the United States in Vietnam and in Somalia, poles apart in respect of the relative intensity of those conflicts, and in their degrees of international involvement, have nevertheless reinforced American scepticism, in the people and in the polity, about limited wars and about military coalitions. This attitude has come to include as well a quite narrow interpretation as to where the nation's interests lie, and where their military might therefore properly be hazarded. At its most extreme, this narrowness of application of American effort was demonstrated in the United States' reaction to the events of 1994 in Rwanda which, it has been widely surmised, resulted from the Vietnam as much as from the Somalia experiences. As Dana Priest has written, in her excellent book, *The Mission*, 'Somalia left a mark on the American military psyche that has dominated military planning' – and not just military planning, as she elsewhere makes clear.[4]

Thus the deeper historic background has joined with perceptions of recent experiences to produce in US foreign and military policies something like the duck-billed platypus: an almost hermetic environment has first produced and then preserved a unique system, which may now be seen to be anachronistic. The US military seems to be not just preparing for that last war but one, but seems as well to be preparing for a type of symmetrical, inter-state warfare which finds no threat or model in the modern world at all. It is in accordance with this view that war is seen not as a continuation of diplomacy, rather that military force is threatened or used *in place of diplomacy* at the first sign of any threat. Indeed, the US government now speaks of *coercive diplomacy*, and avers that the lesson of Munich, as of Bosnia (see Woodward), is that diplomacy *not* accompanied by the use of force would be unavailing (this used to be called gunboat diplomacy, as though that were not an oxymoron).

This is, then, that complete inversion of the relationship between foreign and military policies. It is in direct contrast to norms obtaining in almost every other democratic government in the world (one of the major criterion for the admission of new members to NATO has been civilian control of the military, euphemized by the NATO staff as 'democratic-style civil-military relations'[5]).

Priest describes how this process has recently gained impetus:

> (William Perry, who became Secretary of Defence in January 1994) was the first to see that the military could be used to 'shape' the world in peacetime, by using military-to-military relations to seduce countries into the U.S. sphere of ideas and geo-political interests. This vision became part of the Clinton administration's National Security Strategy, which guides the military's overall operations. The strategy directed the CinCs (Commanders-in-Chiefs) to 'shape, prepare, respond' all over the globe.[6]

And Joseph S. Nye corroborates almost exactly:

> While Congress has been willing to spend 16 per cent of the national budget on defense, the percentage devoted to international affairs has shrunk from 4 per cent in the 1960s to just 1 per cent today. . . . Over a thousand people work on the staff of the smallest regional military command headquarters, far more than the total assigned to the Americas at the Departments of State, Commerce, Treasury and Agriculture.[7]

The inversion of the US government's military and diplomatic roles and precedence has provided a *sui generis* model of gunboat diplomats, a model not commonly associated with democracy nor democracies. This militarization of US foreign policy has combined in one functional branch of the US government that which had normally been a collegial function of at least the entire Executive branch of the government, with regular oversight by the Legislative branch.

Placing policy development in the same hands as those traditionally concerned only with certain aspects of its implementation, has distorted the entire function of the US government. This has had significant impact on the development and practice of peace operations, as manifest in the traditional US disdain for limited warfare which, as Priest observes, is 'a concept with which the military, and particularly the Army, remained uncomfortable'.[8] David Lipsky, in his excellent study of the United States Military Academy, has made it abundantly clear just how uncomfortable the US Army is with this concept:

> A Pentagon administrator asks me, 'What do you think we are socializing (West Point cadets) for up there? War-fighting. Everything is geared to war fighting. When they leave, what do they do? Peacekeeping. When was the last time anyone did war-fighting? But they spend four years...in their mind, that's what the Army is'. The official shows me studies: cadets exhibit negative attitudes toward peacekeeping and global missions.[9]

James Traub describes the internal dichotomy of the US officer corps in more detail:

> Despite the increasingly widespread acceptance of peacekeeping in the ranks of the military, the conservative thinkers who staffed the upper reaches of the Bush foreign-policy apparatus adhered to the 'fight and win wars' philosophy. They came in, as James Dobbins puts it, with 'an ideological blinker': nation-building didn't work; nation-building represented the triumph of the nanny state on an international scale. Defense Department officials initially planned to abolish the Pentagon's Office of Peacekeeping and Humanitarian Affairs; in the end, however, they contented themselves with changing its name to the far more manly Office of Stability Operations, and then ignoring it as much as possible. Even after 9/11, President Bush said, 'We're not into nation-building; we're focused on justice'.
>
> The administration made its aversion unmistakable when the Army announced in May 2002 that the Peacekeeping Institute would be closed. The Army explained the closing as a budgetary decision, but very few of the current or retired soldiers and civilian experts who constitute Washington's peacekeeping community were convinced. 'I think the decision was made at the highest level', said Beth C. DeGrasse, who conducted the 2002 survey of leading military commanders. 'People in the O.S.D'. – the Office of the Secretary of Defense – 'will tell you that peacekeeping was a dirty word there'.[10]

So it would be no surprise when a third-year West Point cadet would tell Lipsky he was not interested in Kosovo: 'We want to deal with something legitimate.

We don't feel like baby-sitting'. James Dobbins *et al.* summarize American professional attitudes towards peace-support operations:

> The United States...tends to staff each new operation as though it were its first and destined to be its last. Service in such missions has never been regarded as career enhancing for American military or Foreign Service officers. Recruitment is often a problem, terms tend to be short, and few individuals volunteer for more than one mission.[11]

It is not just generals and cadets who do not like peace operations, as demonstrated by Anthony Cordesman, Arleigh A. Burke Professor of Strategy at the Washington Center for Strategy and International Relations, in an interview which he gave to the German current affairs magazine, *Der Spiegel*:

> You know, Canada and many European nations undertake peace operations, only so long as there are no risks, minor costs and absolutely no casualties. In such cases they are quite unnecessary, little more than ushers in a theatre. The preservation of peace is an act of violence. Naturally, we would like to have allies with us.[12]

This institutional discomfort with 'operations other than war' has also had its entirely intended consequences for such issues as apprehension of those accused of war crimes (Shalikashvili, when Chairman of the Joint Chiefs of Staff: 'I made it clear that I would not support using the military to hunt down war criminals... We weren't going to take them unless we stumbled on them.')[13]

The pronounced aversion of the modern US military to the risks of peace operations has also become virtual policy in any US-led coalitions – at least for the American contingents. Priest calls this 'a kind of agoraphobia: only if the troops were kept isolated behind barbed wire would the military agree to a peacekeeping mission'.[14] And finally, the US military attitude towards their putative civilian partners in peace operations – those whom militaries more experienced at these 'operations other than war' have come to consider indispensable players – seems concerned more with limiting their nuisance impact. Priest notes that, in planning for the IFOR in Bosnia-Herzegovina, the American military 'didn't want to be saddled with rescuing civilian aid workers either – even U.S. citizens who might get into trouble in Bosnia'.[15] Thus it is precisely those 'aggravated peace operations' which the American leadership of IFOR had absolutely no intention of pursuing.

It was not ever thus with the US military. In fact, the post-WWII occupation of Germany, so often and so carelessly cited in recent optimistic pronunciamentios by US officials in respect of Afghanistan and Iraq, provides an historic model which today's generals, admirals and professors might well re-visit:

> A wave of military civil-affairs units swept into Europe immediately following WWII to set the stage for the Marshall Plan...The Army, under a U.S. military governor, quickly turned its few remaining infantry

and cavalry units in Germany into a gendarmerie.... Soldiers helped rebuild water systems and electrical plants; repaired sewage pipes, roads, and bridges; and dealt with massive numbers of concentration camp survivors and former slave laborers. They guarded monuments and fine arts collections, and carried seed to farmers and coal to stoves.... '*not a job for soldiers*,' scoffed General Lucius Clay, who later became military governor of Germany.[16]

And it was especially fortunate, indeed it was especially fortunate for the Germans themselves, that the attitude of the victorious allies towards the apprehension and trial of Nazi war criminals was very different from the attitude of NATO in the former Yugoslavia fifty years later. In Germany, the trial of accused individuals and their acquittal or conviction by due process was an essential step in relieving the larger population from perceptions of collective guilt; in the former Yugoslavia such rehabilitation has scarcely even begun, and the notorious Karadzic and the equally odious Mladic are regarded as Serbian heroes.

US officers who today disdain the duties their Second World War predecessors continued for *eight years*, and who have neglected to develop a genuine cooperation with the wide range of civilian agencies which are indispensable to these functions, do a disservice to one of the finest traditions of their own services. Nevertheless, as Priest observes:

> Twelve years of reluctant nation-building and the United States still hadn't spawned an effective civilian corps of aid workers, agronomists, teachers, engineers – a real peace corps – to take charge of reconstruction in Afghanistan or anywhere else. Relations between the military and civilian sectors remained ad hoc. So was coordination between U. S. and international aid agencies.[17]

Clearly, the essential concomitant of regime change must be nation building, a lesson clearly learnt by the victors of the Second World War from the mistakes of the victors of the First World War, as in the Pottery Barn principle of which Secretary of State Powell failed to convince President George Bush before the invasion of Iraq in 2004.[18]

This unusual dichotomy – the false lessons of Somalia, and the role reversal in US foreign and defence policies – has again been played out in Liberia. There can be no more telling irony, nor one more starkly illustrative, of that interdepartmental role reversal than the changing of the spots of Colin Powell, late General, US Army, and former Chairman, Joint Chiefs of Staff; Secretary of State in the first administration of George W. Bush.

As Chairman, General Powell was, with Caspar Weinberger, then Secretary of Defence, one of the authors of what was variously referred to as the Weinberger (or the Powell, or the Weinberger-Powell) Doctrine. This doctrine consisted of an ultraconservative body of checks on the use of the US military, which was eventually formalized as Presidential Decision Directive (PDD) 25. Very briefly, PDD 25 demanded that a military deployment advance US interests, and be a response to a valid threat to international security. In the case of a peacekeeping operation, there should be a cease-fire and the consent of the parties in conflict; in the case of a peace enforcement operation, there must be a significant threat. Adequate means to support the operation must be available from the outset, the consequences of inaction must be clearly unacceptable and – the *conditio sine qua non* – there must be a realistic criteria for concluding the operation (the exit strategy).

The problem with this neat formulation is that a complex humanitarian emergency is so complex just in that there are seldom any clear answers to most of the above points. One analyst called it 'a checklist for doing nothing'. However, as Powell himself put it, 'many of my generation...vowed that when our turn came to call the shots, we would not quietly acquiesce in half-hearted warfare for half-baked reasons that the American people could not understand or support'.[19] Richard Holbrooke reports that Powell was especially opposed to American involvement in pre-Dayton Bosnia. Holbrooke observed specifically that these were the scars left by Vietnam and Somalia, which he called the Vietmalia Syndrome.[20] Madeleine Albright, then US Ambassador to the United Nations, challenged Powell directly: 'What's the point of having this superb military that you're always talking about if we can't use it?'[21]

And then it came to Colin Powell to become the Secretary of State in the George W. Bush government. Analysts of Powell's first press conference as the designated Secretary, on 18 December 2000, speculated that this government would be far less interventionist than had been the Clinton administration, that there would be 'clearer thresholds for the use of military forces, and that these would have more to do with traditional national-security interests than with "humanitarian intervention" as in Somalia and Kosovo'. It was also observed that, 'Given General Powell's famous doctrine – essentially that Washington should use force only if there is a clear strategic and political goal, popular support, an exit strategy, and overwhelming numbers – many wonder whether he would have supported a Kosovo war'. However, as Karl Kaiser, an advisor to the German government and long time analyst of American–German relations, put it: 'The world does not consist of situations where you can apply the Powell doctrine, where you gather the force, know what to do, apply that force and get out. In politics, you need allies, institutions and multilateral approaches, not merely American power.'[22] Writing of perceived misadventures in Iraq, Mark Danner called it 'A Doctrine Left Behind'.[23]

But then came Liberia – again.

Unless Mr Powell is to favour us with a second volume to his memoirs, we may never know just where his epiphany lay. Perhaps he had become aware of Nye's seminal classification of hard and soft power:

> Military...and economic power are both examples of hard command power that can be used to induce others to change their position. Hard power can rest on inducements (carrots) or threats (sticks). But there is

also an indirect way to exercise power. A country may obtain the outcomes it wants in world politics because other countries want to follow it, admiring its values, emulating its example, aspiring to its level of prosperity and openness. In this sense, it is just as important to set the agenda in world politics and attract others as it is to force them to change through the threat or the use of military or economic weapons. This aspect of power – getting others to want what you want – I call soft power. It co-opts people rather than coerces them.

Soft power rests on the ability to set the political agenda in a way that shapes the preferences of others.... Soft power is also more than persuasion or the ability to move people by argument. It is the ability to entice and attract. And attraction often leads to acquiescence of imitation.

Soft power arises in large part from our values. These values are expressed in our culture, in the policies we follow inside our country, and in the way we handle ourselves internationally.[24]

Values; example; entice and attract; culture; co-opt rather than coerce; attraction leading to acquiescence: soft power. And then on 24 July 2003, Mr Powell, in an interview with *The Washington Times*,

showed himself to be a strong advocate of interceding in Liberia... The Secretary acknowledged that American involvement would be primarily on a humanitarian basis, but he said action was necessary to avoid a catastrophe comparable to the carnage in Rwanda. In Liberia, if you ask the question, 'What is our strategic, vital interest?,' it would be hard to define it in that way... But we do have an interest in making sure West Africa doesn't simply come apart. We do have an interest in showing the people of Africa that we can support efforts to stabilize a tragic situation as we work with others to bring relief to people – people who are desperately in need.[25]

However, 'two days after Secretary of State Colin L. Powell called for the speedy deployment of troops to Liberia, the top two American military officers warned... of significant dangers facing United States military involvement there and called for a clear mission strategy for its successful end before any troops are sent'. ' "It is potentially a very dangerous situation," said General Peter Pace (USMC, Vice Chairman of the Joint Chiefs of Staff)', who 'cited an ominous precedent, the failed relief mission to Somalia'. 'General Meyers (USAF, Chairman of the Joint Chiefs of Staff) laid out the military's broad requirements for potential deployment to Liberia, using a formulation paralleling the so-called Powell doctrine, which Mr Powell had laid out when he was chairman of the Joint Chiefs from October 1989 to September 1993'. 'It's not a pretty situation,' said General Meyers.[26]

To the Secretary of State, it must have seemed that the State-Defence competition was all tied up, with Defence leading. The Defence budget is sixteen times that of State; Vietnam and Somalia trump Rwanda; General Powell's doctrine has become Secretary Powell's albatross.

In 1971 the military philosopher and historian Morris Janowitz re-issued his classic *The Professional Soldier*. Presciently he foresaw a challenge to the American military to adapt to a post-Cold War era with an entirely new set of challenges, where threats to security might be other than military, and might require other than narrowly militaristic responses. He said that 'Military leaders must be prepared to assist in accurately estimating the consequences of the threat or the use of force *against the potentials for persuasion and conflict resolution.*' He suggested that one option was for the military establishment to transform itself into a constabulary force, and he described a constabulary as being 'continuously prepared to act, *committed to the minimum use of force, and seeks viable international relations, rather than victory.*'[27]

Writing thirty years later, Susan Woodward describes how the problem Janowitz had posed was ignored, and how his solution, had it even been remembered, would have been rejected:

> Between late 1997 and spring, 1999, (U.S.) policy debate over Kosovo focused almost entirely on what were called the lessons of Bosnia. These were said to be: force should not be the last resort but should be used early in a conflict, and diplomacy must be backed by the threat of force.[28]

These, then, are some important aspects of the US military culture. But it most emphatically is not the European military culture, nor is it the Canadian military culture. *Sui generis* though it may be, the US forces nevertheless manifest a pervasive cultural model, and one which if not entirely predominant, as in the case of Force Protection, is powerfully influential, as in the case of treatment of war criminals. Olivia Manning was right again – there is indeed too often a reason for prejudice.

But then, if there *is* good reason, perhaps that is *not* prejudice, but rather a matter of facing the facts of American influence on international affairs, especially on peace operations – without FEAR. As Leon Gordenker has so precisely understated it: 'The quality and depth of the broad public debate in the United States before Washington loosed its military might on Iraq suggests that the internalization of international norms in American political life is remarkably thin.'[29] If we are to understand the tactical doctrines, structures and procedures of the armed forces of the United States in the field, we must have an appreciation of the perceived strategic context. This will require as well an understanding of the domestic political environment, which has so far shaped the very limited American experience of peace operations.

Nevertheless, it must be admitted that the Americans – military and diplomats – seem to be learning: the US Commanding General in Afghanistan (quoted in my preface) who at the start of his mission wanted nothing to do with nation building, and who shortly after leaving Afghanistan was able to observe that peace in Afghanistan was being jeopardized by lack of *development* efforts *by the international community* – had learned much. And in an interview in January 2004, the US Commanding General, and leader of the 38-nation alliance of occupying forces in Iraq, described his mission as 'about gaining and retaining the consent of the Iraqi people. That's what we're here for, fighting a war, *and building a nation*'.[30] The education of these two American generals was however relatively belated, and had certainly been very expensive, but seems to have comprised lessons that most *other* twenty-first century General Officers would not have needed to learn.

But we should not necessarily read too much into the self-second guessing of two officers' reflections on how they *might* or *should* have conducted their operations – but did not. The US Army Peace Institute which was ordered closed by Secretary of Defence Rumsfeld (see Chapter 25) hangs on to life and mission by a thread, and even the name has changed, as the term 'peace operations' is formally out of favour – the current term 'stability operations' carries no connotation of the broad civil-military basing understood as essential to peace operations. Meanwhile, the US Joint Readiness Centre and the National Training Centre are (notwithstanding the several quasi-academic civil-military centres for a few US officers) the only pre-theatre collective training centres for overseas-destined formations, and these are principally combat training centres. They are intended to prepare forces for 'war fighting'.

Indeed, the very term 'war' is being used in ways to connote operations which a short time ago would, for very good reasons, have been called something else.

Andrew J. Bacevich, in his book, *The New American Militarism*,[31] elaborates on the current American use of the term 'war'.

Bacevich says the Cold War was really the Third World War, and it lasted from 1947 to 1989. The Fourth World War, he says, 'after a brief interval of peace, corresponding roughly to the 1990s', 'commenced on September 11, 2001'.[32] Elsewhere, however, he places the real origins of that Fourth World War with the enunciation by President Carter in 1980 of what came to be known as 'The Carter Doctrine': the Persian Gulf was to be off-limits to any outside force, which would 'be repelled by any means necessary, including military force'. The Carter Doctrine placed the Gulf at the centre of the 'vital interests' of the country. The gloves were off: three decades of covert involvement in the Gulf gave way to an overt military involvement which Carter's successors have continuously expanded and reinforced. President Reagan used armed force unilaterally in the region on four occasions: Beirut in 1983; against Libya in 1986; the Tanker War of 1984–88; and in assisting Afghan 'freedom fighters' throughout the 1980s. In the period leading up to the 1991 Gulf War, a series of structural and doctrinal changes in the US military institutionalized the Carter Doctrine-based policies of four Administrations, from Carter to Clinton. In the 1990s, American officers who spoke of 'Operations other than War (OOTWA)', 'Situations Short of War' and 'Low-intensity Operations', did so tongue in cheek, clearly hoping never to get sent to one of those. Peacekeeping was, as Cordesman said, something for somebody else, and was no concern to the legions of a superpower. And anyway, 'the preservation of peace is an act of violence'.

'A superpower doesn't do windows', runs the sarcastic aphorism; it seems they do not do peace, either.

And so when, in February 2004, Vice-Chairman of the Joint Chiefs of Staff General Peter Pace (USMC) said, to a dozen or so journalists in a 'conversation' hosted by the Council on Foreign Relations, 'We are a nation at war. We have been at war since *before* September 11th 2001', his statement was allowed to stand unchallenged.[33] They all knew – or thought they knew – or didn't want to admit they didn't know – exactly what he meant.[34]

The American peoples' confusion over issues and definitions surrounding war and peace are not surprising: on 29 May 2005 the *New York Times* reported a surge in violence 'across Iraq', raising the total Iraqis killed in that month to 'about 650', while 'at least 63 American troops...have been killed'.[35] On that day, the Times also reported breathlessly that 'This is an America of $130,000 Hummers and $12,000 mother-baby diamond tennis bracelet sets, of $600 jeans, $800 haircuts and slick new magazines advertising $400 bottles of wine.'[36]

As this is being written (2005), a US Civil Affairs Command unit that was preparing to deploy to Iraq, was reportedly at only 30% of its authorized strength. That shortfall was to be made up by individual backfills from other commands, who were to be deployed with little or no training in civil affairs. And finally, the US Army Civil Affairs and Psychological Operations Command, which has traditionally relied heavily on reservists from various civilian fields, has recently determined that, insofar as possible, they will deploy overseas only regular forces personnel, thus further distancing the military from civilian influence on military affairs.

* * *

From the International Herald Tribune, 25 August 2003:

> Monrovia, Liberia: A U.S. Marine rapid-reaction force of 150 troops headed back to warships off Liberia on Sunday, ending significant American military deployment on the ground after 11 days.... Asked whether the 11-day U.S. deployment seemed adequate in length, (Colonel Theophilus) Tawiah (chief of staff for the African force) laughed, 'You'd have to ask the Americans about that,' he said.

12

PRIDE AND PREJUDICE

You never get a second chance to make a
first impression

Jane Austen's original title for her first novel was *First Impressions*; these seem to be about the only ones commonly exchanged between the military and their partners-to-be. In his 1972 introduction to the Penguin Classic Edition of *Pride and Prejudice*, Toby Tanner suggested that the principals might themselves have entitled a fiction about them *Dignity and Perception*. He goes on to suggest that:

> the book is, most importantly, about pre-judging and re-judging. It is a drama of recognition – re-cognition, that act by which the mind can look again at a thing and if necessary make revisions and amendments until it sees the thing as it really is.[1]

In closing this part of the book, we will review just how the military lends itself to pre-judgement, and to see how we might set the stage for the necessary re-cognition, 'to see the thing as it really is'.

What then might be some of the signals the military sends, and how might those signals be received? Try this list, and see if you do not spot yourself, or your reactions, in this mirror (Table 12.1).

This list can of course be lengthened, and it's a game any number can play. We recall that CMOCC in Pristina, entirely provided by the military, for all who wished to use it – and how few NGOs, for just that reason, used it at all. Nevertheless, the military are not chameleons, they are *armed* forces, and they are

Table 12.1 Pride and prejudice

When the military is	They may be seen as
Self-assured	Arrogant
Systematic	Inflexible
Coordinating	Controlling
Resourceful	Resource-rich
Doing things for people	Doing things to people

armed for very good reasons, and they are *there* for equally good reasons. Clearly, no one should wish them to be other than peerlessly good at what they are to do. As Christopher Bellamy of Cranfield University has written:

> To ensure the success of existing peace-support operations, armed forces with the ethos and physique of war-fighting soldiers have to be recruited and trained. No-one else can be relied on if peacekeeping suddenly regresses into civil war, and studies have shown that no-one else gets the necessary respect from local people in the immediate aftermath of a bloody conflict. But such soldiers, well-disciplined – and that is the key – can be the best peacekeepers and take to the task enthusiastically. A partially trained *gendarmerie*, or an army trained only for peacekeeping duties, is unlikely to be effective. The warrior ethos must remain, but it must be imbued with flexibility and humanity, and a willingness to mix with the locals. . . . It is possible to mix combat readiness with compassion, and that is the challenge for many armed forces in the first quarter of the 21st century.[2]

And, Bellamy added, this is no place for amateurs, or newcomers to the profession: 'local populations have most respect for peacekeepers who are also unmistakably professional soldiers, robust in their manner and well-equipped'.

There are other things about the military, which the military should perhaps explain better, but which civilians who will work with the military need to understand. For just one example:

A German journalist of my acquaintance spoke mockingly of the numbers of KFOR soldiers she had seen in and around Pristina engaged in sports and in fitness centres – boys will be boys, she implied. I told her that physical fitness for soldiers is neither merely sport nor is it a fetish, but is definitely linked to ability to resist stress, which produces fatigue; fear is an extreme form of stress. As S.L.A. Marshall wrote:

> Will power, determination, mental poise, and muscle control all march hand-in-hand with the general health and well being of the man. Fatigue will beat men down as quickly as any other condition, for fatigue brings fear with it.[3]

And, as Lord Chalfont said of Field Marshall Montgomery,

> The first aim of his relationship with the troops . . . was to give them confidence in his capacity to look after their physical needs; the second was to give them confidence in their own ability. This was the root of his obsession with physical training. The men must *feel* that they were well prepared for action, even if the actual process of physical jerks did little to prepare them for combat.[4]

Montgomery himself, summarizing a series of exercises conducted early in 1941, cited the fitness of the soldiers:

> It is interesting to note how the daily sick rate drops as the troops become fit and hard. The average daily admission to hospital in . . . 5 Corps during the past winter has been 10 per day per division of 16,000 men. On this exercise which lasted five days the sick rate dropped to 5 per day per division. It was wet and cold, and the troops had no billets.[5]

Exercise is also the best non-medical treatment for stress, and it's a lot cheaper than medicine. But fitness is often very difficult to maintain in a mission. Those who were in Sarajevo with UNPROFOR in the summer of 1992 were estimated to have lost over 10% of body weight, and many had difficulty sleeping and eating for weeks after they left. Almost none were completely healthy, and likely none were physically fit. And what gym would I visit in Pristina today? It would almost certainly be a military facility, if any – and if they would let me in.

Physical fitness is deeply rooted in the military culture, but it is not a fetish. Physical fitness fulfils best the requirement to withstand the stressors of physical hardship and danger, to remain alert in spite of fatigue and to persevere in the most discouraging circumstances. To the very considerable extent that civilians share this exposure, they would do well to consider and perhaps to emulate that concern for physical conditioning.

It would be naïve to ignore that much of the resentment of the military stems from envy. As Dr Johnson said, over 200 years ago, 'Every man thinks meanly of himself for not having been a soldier, or not having been at sea.' That envy, however deep it may lie in the consciousness, is rudely awakened in the most pacific souls by suspicion of poaching – on resources, roles – just because the flexibility of the military, and their multiple capabilities are so widely and self-evidently known, even when so unwillingly acknowledged. The story of the Canadian naval supply ship's repair crew who flew ashore, in helicopters never intended to fly over land,[6] to dismantle generators and air conditioners in a hospital in Belet Huen, and repaired them on board their ship, then re-installed them in the hospital so blood could be stored so surgery could be carried out – is not a story you will hear from NGOs who could never have managed that. In similar circumstances, in East Timor:

> The UN CIMIC Team had to intervene a couple of times to explain to INTERFET (Intervention Force in East Timor) the fundamental principle that military resources should complement, not replace civilian resources. In one particular incident, a national military contingent performed an excellent job in cleaning up and restoring a hospital. However, before the riots that hospital had been run by MSF (Medicins Sans Frontieres), and the MSF team were now ready to return, *but were barred by their charter from working alongside armed military personnel.*

MSF therefore requested the UN CIMIC (Civil-Military Cooperation) Team politely to persuade the military to relinquish the hospital and start working at a nearby military hospital instead. Fortunately, the military contingent agreed and the matter was resolved amicably.[7]

It was reported that, notwithstanding the above, 'The humanitarian agencies fully shared the opinion of the FC that the primary need was for combat forces, so that security and humanitarian access could be restored without delay.' It would seem, however, that in this case the military had gone a bit too far – but 'the matter was resolved amicably'. The report does not record how the MSF expressed their gratitude to the military who first saved and then restored 'their' hospital. (One might be permitted to wonder what the world's peacekeepers and MSF today think of each others' Nobel Prizes.) This case does raise the interesting possibility, however, that the NGOs are making distinctions their 'beneficiaries' would not: the locals likely do not care, may not even know, of these differences among the foreign community – it may be, it probably is, of very small matter to them who helps them, still less who gets the credit. This raises a further intriguing possibility: the *international* civilians seem content to have the military support *them*. But when the military comes into contact with and begins directly to serve the needy, *then* we have a relationship which is no longer *complimentary*, but is *competitive*, and something must be done.

That situation which arose between MSF and the military in East Timor occurred in 2000. Lest we might think that those Nobel Laureates are today working better together, MSF has warned us in 2005, in an *Emergency Alert*, that:

Pierre Salignon, General Director of the international medical humanitarian organization Doctors Without Borders/Médecins Sans Frontières (MSF) in France, recently returned from a visit to Haiti. He describes the extreme violence reigning in Port au Prince's poorest neighborhoods and how the United Nations Stabilization Mission in Haiti (Minustah) – far from restoring calm – has been drawn into a war against supporters of former President Aristide. As the security situation continues to deteriorate in Haiti's capital, MSF has called on all armed groups in the city to respect the safety of civilians and allow immediate access to emergency medical care for those wounded in clashes.

Minustah cannot 'reestablish peace' in Port au Prince. Because of its mandate from the UN Security Council allowing it to use force in order to accomplish its 'mission,' it has become an armed player in the conflict, a source of violence against civilians during police operations in the slums. No longer taken aback by 'collateral damage' caused by UN soldiers, one of its representatives even sees it as the price that has to be paid in order to 'stabilize' Port au Prince. No matter if Minustah is now seen by a significant segment of the population as an occupation force, buttressing a transitional government with limited powers.[8]

Karns and Minsk have written of 'the threat to the legitimacy of the UN's own humanitarian agencies posed by governments and military organizations bypassing them in crisis situations'. They cite the (then) High Commissioner for Refugees, Mrs Sadako Ogata:

> The military can support but should not substitute for agencies with humanitarian mandates. The experience and expertise to deal with the human dimension of crises – the suffering of civilians, their traumas, the terror of flight, the pain and uncertainty of exile – are with us, the civilian humanitarian agencies.[9]

And thus does the redoubtable Mrs Ogata dismiss the experience of those three-quarters of a million uniformed peacekeepers, who have encountered all of those things in their missions over the past nearly six decades.

There is another very large red herring across the path to better understanding of the military, and this is the legend of military apartness from their founding society. Dandeker and Gow state that 'The functional imperatives of war and military operations ensure that the Services stand apart from civilian society.'[10] If this were true in the past, it is only exceptionally true today, even though this perception may be powerful and ubiquitous enough to have nearly displaced objective reality. It has however been a long-standing principle that, at least in a democracy, 'the army is the mirror of the society'. As Andrew Lambert has described the nineteenth century Royal Navy:

> The Navy took on the particular character the State required. *It was distinctive, but not different.* Armed forces that do not reflect the wishes of the society from which they take their funding and human resources are doomed to decay, or to overthrow their masters. That the Royal Navy did not go down either path is testimony to its central place in the national identity.[11]

Even an entirely voluntary professional military like Canada's indeed mirrors its society, even if by inversion. As Martin Bell put it, 'It (the military) does not exactly reflect the society that it comes from, but it does reflect the *best* of that society.'[12] The Canadian military, it is true, stands somewhat apart from a nation traditionally disinterested in its military but passionate about its defence, just as people little interested in fitness may be passionate about sport. This indeed can lead to a gladiator syndrome, but not one of the design or choosing of the military – it is the Canadian civil society whose involvement with the Canadian military is much like that of the average American's involvement with the National Football League. It is not commonly the desire of Canadian soldiers to be Praetorian Guardsmen, but it is common for Canadian society tacitly, even if unintentionally, to assign that role to Canadian soldiers. If the peoples' interest in the military is largely vicarious, that is scarcely a military shortcoming.

And so to a certain extent this apartness, even if exaggerated in the public perception, may arise naturally from the fact of a completely voluntary military. But the military are far from the only profession to adopt over time – or to be assigned by the larger society – an almost tribal culture. The apartheid of the military is indeed much less in nations with conscription, and British and American officers have noted a difference since their politicians and diplomats have come from a generation that has never done military service. As David Lipsky described the process:

> When the (U.S.) draft ended in 1975, civilian and military culture shook hands, exchanged phone numbers and started to lose track of each other; military theorists worry that most Americans have no firsthand knowledge of how their Army lives or what their Army does.[13]

A fear of alienation of the military from the larger society is a part of the determination of successive German governments to maintain conscription, even if downsizing, and access to the population of the former German Democratic Republic, have made it unnecessary. (The Cold War Bundeswehr had a peacetime strength of just under 600,000, drawn from a population of 60 million; the current Bundeswehr strength of 273,000 is drawn from a population of nearly 80 million.) Nevertheless, the Bundeswehr is to consist of 'citizens in uniform', even if the presence of a relatively small number of conscripted recruits actually shackles the entire force to their level.[14]

Another form of prejudice, the origin of which is quite obscure and the analysis of which yields only the gaping disappointment of another encounter with the irrational, is undoubtedly a FEAR response. This is the widespread belief that alliance with the military will compromise the partner agencies, the minute the military uses – or even threatens – force. Possibly the heart of this matter lies in confusing the terms 'neutrality' and 'impartiality'. The distinction is not mere semantics.

Satish Nambiar, who in 1992 was the first Commander of the UNPROFOR in the former Yugoslavia, has written that 'Enforcement actions, by their very nature, are subjective and biased towards one side or the other'.[15] And we recall the ICRC's solemn injunction (see Chapter 3) against involvement in an enforcement operation: 'the concerned components of the Movement should not avail themselves of armed protection for their operations when this is offered by UN troops during an enforcement action under Chapter VII or when it is possible that the UNO will sooner or later be considered as a party to the conflict by the local population or by the belligerents'.

Why is the capacity, and the will, to answer force with force, seen as compromising impartiality? Why is the prevention of conflict recurrence, the protection of life and property, using all authorized means, seen as 'subjective and biased'? It would seem that police, in responding to a civil disturbance, might use all means necessary, including deadly force, to restore law and order, without automatically forfeiting their impartiality. They may have been, they hopefully will have been, completely impartial in the measures they have employed to restore law and order. The police should have been utterly unconcerned with who was involved in violence, in looting, in refusing to keep the peace, and they should have been entirely even-handed in their response to violations. They will have been objective in maintaining law and order, and that objectivity will not have been objectively compromised by their use of appropriate force as a last resort. Why then is it so commonly postulated that the use of military force to restore peace must irretrievably compromise the military's impartiality? And why does the military – indeed a former UN FC – seem so commonly to accept that judgement, especially as a limitation, *ab initio*, on an enforcement operation: that it cannot be impartial?

Thakur and Schnabel initially maintain that peacekeepers 'cannot join the fray without taking sides...But to take sides is to become aligned to one and therefore the enemy of the other'. However, their own good sense soon leads them to recognize that 'the need for impartial peacekeepers should not automatically translate into moral equivalence among the conflict parties on the ground'. They conclude:

> Timidity masquerading as political neutrality has also led to the operational failure to confront openly those who challenge peacekeeping missions in the field. The United Nations, while striving to remain impartial, should suspend its long-standing attachment to neutrality between belligerents if one or several pursue morally reprehensible goals in repugnant ways. That is, the United Nations should no longer extend, directly or indirectly, a seal of moral equivalency in its relationships with combatants. Impartiality should not translate into complicity with evil. The UN Charter sets out the principles that the organization must defend and the values that it must uphold. The reluctance to distinguish victim from aggressor implies a degree of moral equivalency between the two and damages the institution of UN peacekeeping.[16]

Of course, these are often precisely the conditions which will have summoned up a peace enforcement operation in the first place.

No one who intervenes in any situation in any form remains neutral: involvement is not neutrality. Neutrality is inactivity, and peacekeepers are neither, or they would stay home and be something else, like academics – perhaps even political scientists. In the deliberately strong words of the recently released *Report of the Panel on United Nations Peace Operations*:

> where one party to a peace agreement clearly and incontrovertibly is violating its terms, continued equal treatment of all parties by the United Nations can in the best-case result in ineffectiveness and in the worst may amount to complicity with evil.[17]

Peacekeepers are involved in the causes, solutions and the resolution of conflicts. They are, usually, impartial – that is to say, they are usually *fair* – and they always attempt to be so. This is no less true of military than it is of civilian peacekeepers. That does not mean never condemning infractions of the peace, nor the violations that may continue, by one or the other of the 'parties'. The mandate will be enforced impartially, that is to say fairly, and all transgressions reacted to equally – regardless of who has transgressed, no matter for what ostensible reason.

We need as well to recognize that even peace has its enemies. Not all those 'hosts' in an intervention operations area will welcome, support or even accept peace – which, it has been well said, is more than just the absence of war. As Robert Kaplan has said, 'a large number of people on this planet, to whom the comfort and stability of middle-class life is utterly unknown, find war and a barracks existence a step up rather than a step down'.[18] In the spring of 2000, as armed militias from Kosovo and probably Albania were conducting a brutal guerrilla campaign to de-stabilize Macedonia, one of the guerrilla leaders was interviewed on Austrian TV, and was asked what he would do if the conflict were peacefully resolved. 'Panther', as he styled himself, pondered this novel idea at some length, then, and speaking excellent German, mused that perhaps he would just go back to the Ford assembly line in Cologne. It took but scant imagination to realize how little Panther wished to return to putting windshield wipers on Escorts – nor what it might take to send him back to Cologne.

Seymour Hersh describes how this tactic – waging war on peace itself – functions today in Afghanistan. He quotes 'a Pentagon expert on Afghanistan' who tells him that 'the resurgence of the Taliban did not begin until early (2003)'. They had begun to realize that encouraging instability was the key to undermining Karzai's regime – and that the way to do it was 'not to fight (U.S.) soldiers, but U.N. officials and aid workers'[19] – which is why the civilian casualty rate in modern peace operations has been so high (see Chapter 4).

Occasionally, the only effective and appropriate reaction will be to use force, which the military will have been mandated to do. Why then is this perceived as compromising their impartiality? Why cannot armed force be used impartially *for* the mandate; why must it be perceived as having been *against* a 'party', and thus having compromised forever the credibility of not only the military, but of any agencies which may be associated with them? Why should civilian agencies 'fear that their organization's neutrality will be compromised by sharing data with the military?'[20]

The moral high ground seems to be getting a little crowded here, and there is no room left on it for the use of armed force – nor, it seems, for armed forces. Do the civilian agencies and workers really believe that the military can have been involved – with some notable successes – in peacekeeping for over 50 years without having also developed a sense of the value of impartiality, or that they need today to be reproved, shunned, for doing what their mandate said they should do, and which everyone expected they would do? And when, as it has been judged of the peacekeepers in Rwanda and in Srebrenica, they have not done enough, who then casts the first stone, of those still flying so thickly? Yet the police who use force to stop a riot are asked only if the level of force was appropriate – and fire fighters fight fires, and physicians fight illness and disease, with all the resources available and appropriate, nor would any sensible citizen expect less of them.

The issue of contamination of humanitarian operations by the military continues, and is now so strong that Evans and Sahnoun report that 'this terminology... carries a great deal of baggage, so much so that it is now effectively unusable... *Humanitarian relief organisations like the International Committee of the Red Cross (ICRC) and Medicins Sans Frontiers (MSF) object to the word* humanitarian *in a context that so often involves military action*'.[21] And Call and Stanley solemnly inform us that, 'Most military forces are not appropriate for public security tasks, since their training, equipment and doctrine emphasize the use of overwhelming force *rather than the controlled application of force*'.[22] Just as though, on the one hand, Article 51 of the Charter had never been written; on the other hand, as though side arms will always be enough. And have Call and Stanley truly never heard of Rules of Engagement, which authorize and control force as, inter alia, minimal and a last resort? And this, it would seem, is a fair indication of the state of informed discussion after a half-century of military peacekeeping.

Bell similarly concluded:

> The case for intervention is not to help one side against another, but the weak against the strong, the unarmed against the armed; to take the side of the everyday victims of the war who, until now, have had no protection. It is really a question, finally, *of whether we care*.[23]

And that is the only kind of impartiality we can afford: we are all against violence, against all violations of human rights, against all the scourges of war, and we must oppose, taking all necessary measures, whomsoever may engage in these evils. As Bell also said, 'it isn't involvement but indifference that makes for bad practice'. If police forces can enforce the law, impartially – and they do, then military forces can enforce the peace, impartially – and they do.

Part III

SENSE AND SENSIBILITY
The military as a partner agency

C'est manifique, mais ce n'est pas la guerre.
(Marshall Bosquet, 1854)

13

INTRODUCTION

In Jane Austen's novel *Sense and Sensibility*, she makes use of a distinction between *sense* and *sensibility* which had been available to the English language for nearly one hundred years: the latter half of the eighteenth century was known as the 'Age of Sensibility'. The juxtaposition of the two terms was intended to convey a distinction between the objective knowledge of an event or fact: the sense; sensibility referred to a more subjective interpretation of knowledge which we might today call empathy. As Austen makes clear, the sense of Elinor and the sensibility of Marianne are not necessarily in conflict, but might be – ought to be – complimentary. It might even be said that Elinor *knew*; Marianne *understood*. This in fact is just what we are seeking: not simply to know more, but to understand better. And so it is now time to turn to a more principled description of the military, and their relationships with 'the humans'.

14

WAR AND PEACE
Matters of principle

It will be apparent from what has been said so far that the militaries of all nations have in common that they are a highly structured community – or communities, for the world's militaries are as diverse as the societies which have produced them, which they are intended to serve and which, intentionally or not, they mirror. It will come as no surprise, then, that the soldiers' art is a highly principled one. One can only begin to understand, to appreciate, such a community through an understanding of the principles on which it is based.

All soldiers, or at least all officers, are systematically educated in the principles of war. They have been in every epoch, in every culture, throughout the history of the world's second oldest profession. That these principles have varied through the ages and across cultures is natural, but as a body of teaching they have been remarkably consistent, nor have accepted principles in one age or place been invalidated by changes in tactics, or technology; on the contrary, the principles still in use today are those which have stood the tests of universality, and have been confirmed and reconfirmed throughout the long history of the military culture. Count Alfred von Schlieffen, Chief of the German Staff from 1892 to 1906 was the author of the German plan for total victory in the west. The Schlieffen Plan was based on the Battle of Cannae, which took place in 216 BC. Nevertheless, as Schlieffen said, 'In two thousand years weapons and tactics have completely changed…but the principles of war remain unchanged'.[1] An oft-quoted work on the principles of war is Sun Tzu's *The Art of War*, written in about 500 BC. Thus, when Sun Tzu said, 'There is no instance of a country having benefited from prolonged warfare,' we know instinctively that what he said then is just as true today – which is why our politicians always promise short operations.

The principles of war are not laws of war – despite some academics' approach to teaching military 'science', the military profession is not fundamentally a scientific one – Sun Tzu did not loosely title his work *The Art of War*. So the principles we will now discuss are 'guidance unto the wise; laws only for fools'. A textbook which I was issued almost 40 years ago, and which I have still in my possession, puts it like this:

> the principles that guide action in war…are not laws…nor rules…they
> simply indicate a course of action that has been successful in the past

and serve as a warning that disregard of them involves risk and has often brought failure.[2]

The observance of these principles, let us be clear, is no guarantee of success, but their frequent contravention may well ensure failure.

These principles, moreover, are not just principles of war, they are indeed the principles of all military operations and actions, and have indeed often been imitated in other spheres as well: industry is continually rediscovering them. Flexibly and properly applied, and adapted, they might be the principles of almost any collective actions, civil or military, in war – as well as in peace. In what follows, then, I will describe the principles of war, as they were presented in my book of forty years ago, and I will briefly re-interpret them as they might more specifically apply to modern peace operations. Let me add only, before we begin, that this is no mere conventional, or received wisdom, but the collective guidance of history – and nothing more than guidance. Doctrine is not dogma, and these certainly are not short-cuts for thinking. As G.F.R. Henderson said in his *Life of Stonewall Jackson*, 'Providence is more inclined to side with the big brains than with the big battalions'.

The selection and maintenance of the aim

'The selection and maintenance of the aim must be regarded as the "Master" Principle. It has therefore been placed first', says my text, and so we shall also consider this Master Principle as a *primes inter pares*.

This principle has two parts: *selection* and *maintenance*. The aim must be a brief statement, usually just one sentence, of just what is to be achieved. The statement must be capable of being adapted for each level at which it is to be applied, thus representing a descending continuum from the strategic, through the operational to the tactical levels of operations. Thus, in peace operations mandated by the United Nations, the Security Council Resolution, the mission of a peacekeeping force, and the orders given to an outpost must be mutually contributory to the achievement of a common goal, and these must be clearly communicated and instantly understandable at all levels. That NCO or junior officer commanding the outpost ought to be able to read the UNSCR and see therein with perfect clarity his own mission. There is no place in this process for mission creep – as my text has it, 'Once the aim is decided, all efforts must be directed to its attainment *until a changed situation calls for a re-appreciation and consequently a new aim*.'[3] We will discuss mission creep in Bosnia in more detail (see Chapter 17) and will review the invidious process by which previous directions were simply re-enforced by seemingly tireless reiterations of aims and measures which had already failed, and always with no re-appreciation of the resources and measures for which a changed situation so clearly called.

It may seem self-evident that *the aim must be a continuum*, a cohesive statement applicable, with adaptation, yet recognizable at the strategic, operational and tactical levels of application, but this can by no means be taken for granted. The tragic events surrounding the deaths in Mogadishu in October 1993 of 18 US soldiers – and probably more than 500 Somalis – were not just a failed operation, they were also a *mistaken* operation, not least because the operational and tactical aims were not contributory to the strategic aim.

The strategic aims of the United Nations Operation in Somalia, or UNOSOM II, as the operation had by then become, were clearly stated in UNSCR 814 of 26 March 1993 *inter alia* as:

> 4. to provide humanitarian and other assistance to the people of Somalia in rehabilitating their political institutions and economy and promoting political settlement and national reconciliation[4]

How the subsequent plan to remove General Mohammed Farah Aidid as the leader of the Habr Gidr clan and its political and military arm, the Somalia National Alliance (SMA), gained legitimacy is not entirely clear. The apparently proximate cause was a reaction to the killing on 5 June 1993 of 24 Pakistani UN soldiers, and UNSCR 837 of 5 June authorized the 'arrest and detention for prosecution, trial and punishment' of 'those responsible for the armed attacks' and 'those responsible for publicly inciting such attacks'.[5] There was however a vendetta aimed at Aideed of some longer standing: the (then) Secretary-General of the UN, Bhoutros Bhoutros-Ghali was known as 'a longtime enemy' of the clan and its leader, dating from his service as the Foreign Minister of Egypt. And Jonathon Howe, the retired US Navy Admiral and former Deputy National Security Advisor to President Bush, who had become the Secretary-General's Special Representative in Somalia (and thus head of UNOSOM II), was of the same view: he 'was convinced that getting rid of the warlord... would cut through the tangle of tribal hatred that sustained war, anarchy and famine' and, after the killing of the Pakistanis, Howe 'authorised a $25,000 bounty for the warlord.... More than anyone, Howe had been responsible for bringing the Rangers to Mogadishu'.[6]

It only deepens the tragedy of the deaths and injuries, to soldiers and civilians, that a 'successful' outcome of the Ranger and Delta Force operation would have been as damaging to the mission as was its failure. As one local citizen, who described himself as 'disappointed in the Americans', explained it:

> Didn't the Americans realize that for every leader they arrested there were dozens of brothers, cousins, sons, and nephews to take his place? Setbacks just strengthened the clan's resolve. Even if the Hadr Gidr were somehow crippled or destroyed, wouldn't that just elevate the next most powerful clan? Or did the Americans expect Somalia to suddenly sprout full-fledged Jeffersonian democracy?[7]

And that was just the point that seems to have entirely escaped both the Secretary-General and his Special Representative: an operational aim had been selected which not only did not serve the strategic aim, but would have defeated that aim in order to gain a tactical advantage which was itself highly questionable (and it *was* vigorously questioned, especially in the US Joint Chiefs of Staff). An earlier raid on Aidid's residence on 12 June, which was said by the ICRC to have resulted in 54 Somalis dead and 250 wounded, 'bolstered Aidid's status, and badly undercut the UN's humanitarian image. Moderates opposed to Aidid now rallied behind him'.[8]

Four days after the Ranger deaths, President Clinton announced on 7 October the withdrawal of all US combat forces by the end of March 1994; several countries announced they would follow suit. An emerging US doctrine for the use of US combat troops in 'operations other than war' was almost mortally wounded as well. This resulted in the promulgation of that extremely limiting 'Weinberger-Powell Doctrine', formally embodied in PDD 25, with effects on US involvement in subsequent peace operations which are still to be reckoned with in the international community (see Chapter 11). It can only be imagined what further unintended *strategic* consequences might have been unleashed by *tactical* success on 3 October; it is hard to imagine how the peace operation could have survived the success, any more than it did the failure, of an operation so at odds with its own goals. Thus, Susan Woodward in a slightly different context noted that 'Unity of policy is even more important than unity of command'.[9]

But that does not mean that the aim, once selected, is to become as a set of shackles on the organization or on the operation. Derek Boothby, who was the Deputy Transitional Administrator for the United Nations Transitional Authority in Eastern Slavonia (UNTAES) put it this way:

> there are basically two ways the SRSG (Special Representative of the Secretary-General) can regard his or her mandate: either it is a ceiling, under which the operation may be developed up to its legislated roof, or it is a floor on which the operation may be imaginatively constructed without any limit as to the height that may be attained.[10]

The aim must be clearly communicated to those who are to carry it out. The Headquarters of UNPROFOR was initially placed in Sarajevo, so we were told, because Bosnia was neutral and peaceful. What those in that Headquarters were never told was that it had been hoped that a UN presence there would act as a brake on, might in fact deter, Bosnia's slide into civil war. Had the soldiers been told this, their reaction is impossible to estimate, but the troop contributing governments might have had much to say about such an extension of an already difficult and complex mission – in any event, nothing was said of this hidden aim. That is not to say that such a deterrent operation might not have been undertaken – as we know, a year later, in Macedonia, the mission which would eventually become UNPREDEP (United Nations Preventive Deployment) was launched on very short notice, and with a seemingly positive effect on nearly those same dangers. However, had that initial aim, or purpose, of HQ UNPROFOR been clearly stated, that statement should have driven a sober appreciation of the real challenges and opportunities, and likely as well an appropriate resource base for a very hazardous undertaking. That, it may be hoped, would have resulted in a force of something more than what was sent – about 350 staff officers and NCOs with pistols, plus some UN Military Observers and Civilian Police *without* pistols – *or nothing*, which would have been about as effective.[11]

The selected aim must be maintained, and it must be safeguarded from deterioration or abridgement, for so long as it remains appropriate and achievable. As it is surpassed or achieved, or as circumstances change fundamentally, the process by which the initial aim was selected must be repeated. We have seen in Bosnia how the aim of safeguarding the UN Protected Areas in Croatia was jeopardized, then fell victim to, the distractions of events in Bosnia, with no re-appreciation of how developments there were affecting operations in Croatia. The main aim of UNPROFOR was the 'Vance Plan', in Croatia. Although this was the raison d'etre for the entire force, it was, within less than six months of the deployment of UNPROFOR, very much a secondary operation.

Post-conflict peace-building operations nearly always entail a long-term transformation of the conflict and the comprehensive reformation of the society. Short-term commitments, as may often be stated by the contributors to the mission, are often merely cynical ploys to a domestic audience. Such talk of short-term goals, however, jeopardizes the long-term commitment which is really required, while offering reassurance to non-compliers that they need only wait out the international community. As Dennis McNamara, the (then) UN High Commissioner for Refugees has written:

> There is a lot of talk about 'exit strategy' in peacekeeping operations. This can be a dangerous preoccupation. What is needed is a clear strategy, not for exit but for careful transformation of the mission through its different phases. The initial peacekeeping emphasis should phase into a peace-building one linked to establishing the basis for sustainable development. The short-sighted elections-and-out strategy in Cambodia will not, hopefully, be repeated.[12]

Long-term goals must not be compromised by short-term strategies, however comforting these latter may be to the strategoi and to their domestic audiences.[13] The careful selection of the aim, and the equally careful management of that aim, at the strategic level, should produce a top-down continuum of do-able goals, and should as well produce a realistic bottom-up estimate of the requirements for the mission. Those who must consent to and support the mission must also be clearly informed from the outset just what is realistically entailed in this undertaking. If they have been misled, it will be no surprise that the sustainment of the mission will be uncertain. There can be no greater danger to success than a mis-statement of the aim.

Maintenance of morale

'Success in war depends more on moral than on physical qualities. Numbers, armament and resources cannot compensate for lack of courage, energy, skill and the bold offensive spirit which springs from a ... determination to conquer,' reads our text. Liddell-Hart notes 'the general truth of Napoleon's oft-quoted dictum that in war "the moral is to the physical as three to one"'. While this may not offer a precise measure of performance in any given situation, 'it does not impair the judgement that they will offer less (resistance) if they are taken by surprise than if they are on the alert; less if they are weary and hungry than if they are fresh and well fed'.[14]

We have already seen how physical fitness affects morale, and thus performance, and it is obvious that this is as true in peace, and in peace operations, as it is in war or indeed in any undertakings. As John Adams put it, 'Exercise invigorates, and enlivens all the faculties of body and mind ... It spreads a gladness and satisfaction over our minds and qualifies us for every sort of business, and every sort of pleasure.'[15]

A major component of morale which must be considered further is information: the extent to which those who are to do something understand intimately what they are to do, how they are to do it, and especially why – we are well beyond the age of not asking 'why'. Ingrid Lehmann has written of the importance of information campaigns in peace operations, and has posited three audiences for information: international, national and mission internal.[16] In 1992 the Croatian Government launched a vigorous disinformation campaign, designed to shift the blame for their own non-compliance with solemn agreements, and the deleterious affects this was having on the Croatian people, onto the United Nations, and onto the peacekeepers they were in fact so actively thwarting. Scapegoating, Lehmann has termed it. The United Nations' response to this was termed 'passive P.R'. – the modern form of 'never explain, never complain'. So almost the only voice the peacekeepers ever heard in Croatia was the one that blamed them for everything, charged them with outrageously inappropriate responsibilities, and credited them with absolutely nothing of positive value.

Eventually, hearing nothing to the contrary, the soldiers began to believe the only voices they heard, and eventually so did those who should have known better; the latter including the international media, as well as those whose responsibility to answer such disinformation, was entirely abrogated. Morale plummeted, and so did performance, as the soldiers either came to believe the lies, or believed that the lies would prevail no matter what they did. Finally, in early 1995, the renewal of the UN mandate in Croatia could only be secured by changing the name of the Force (ironically, to United Nations Confidence Restoration Operation (UNCRO)); there were few tears shed when the discredited force was swept aside by the Croatian Army in its cleansing of the United Nations Protected Areas later in that year. Much worse was ahead for the United Nations, and for the Blue Helmets, on the 'level killing fields' of the former Yugoslavia, where questions of morale, understandably, were seldom raised.

Offensive action

'Offensive action is the necessary forerunner of victory; it may be delayed, but until the initiative is seized and the offensive taken victory is impossible.' Here we will have to interpolate fairly freely to apply this principle to peace operations. Perhaps the key word for our purposes is 'initiative', and nearly all soldiers will sense the lack of this principle in their experience of peacekeeping.

Too much of peacekeeping is concerned with the passive aspects of these operations, especially as expressed and experienced in the pursuit and maintenance of consent and impartiality. No successful undertaking can be entirely characterized by the pursuit of entirely passive measures. Not peace, nor justice, nor democracy, to name just a few of the things we hope to foster and maintain in peace operations – just happen, nor are they logical nor even expected outcomes of violent conflicts. The 'third parties', the peacekeepers, are there just because the parties to the conflict cannot resolve their conflict, nor deal with its aftermath, on their own. Where consent is lacking, it must be created. Where evil exists, it must be named and confronted. Where the peace cannot or will not be kept, it must be enforced. Democracy especially is a very tender plant – once sown, it must be protected and nurtured. None of these are passive measures, often none can – at least initially – be reliably left to local initiatives. And so we are back to that key word: initiative. If the outsiders are to have any value, if they are to make any lasting contribution, it will be by seizing the initiative to create and to maintain an environment in which peace will be built and sustained, where democracy and the rule of law can flourish where they have never been known before, or where they, like truth, were numbered among the first casualties.

Let us then, for these purposes, replace the word 'offensive' with 'initiative', but let us not forget that word 'action'.

Security

We have already spoken at some length of an overemphasis on the principle of security, in our discussion of Force Protection (see Chapter 14). The intelligent observation of these principles involves balance among them, some being more or less appropriate to a given situation. One, The Selection and Maintenance of the Aim, we have called the Master Principle, the *primes inter pares*. We have observed in this case how the exaggerated treatment of one principle, security, in fact violates several others, especially that Master Principle. As my text put it, those forty years ago, 'Security does not imply undue precaution and avoidance of all risks, for bold action is essential to success'.

Surprise

It is here, in discussing peace operations, that we will make our only fundamental divergence from this text on the principles of war. A particular characteristic of peace operations is transparency. Aims and means must be clear to all of Lehmann's three audiences: international, local and mission internal. No misunderstandings can be permitted, there must be no surprises, disinformation can be given no place to start. ROE especially must be simple, clear, instantly communicable and subject to no distortion or miscalculation (see Chapter 18). It is not clear what was intended, in IFOR in Bosnia, as with UNTAES in Eastern Slavonia, when ROEs were classified – it is likely that bugbear of a habitually restrictive society that desired that there be some deliberate uncertainty about intentions, as about reactions. However, after the planning for the UN mission in Somalia had been completed in the Headquarters of the US Central Command in Florida in December 1992, the Commander, a USMC General, observed that, in peace operations, the principle of transparency should replace the principle of surprise – but that observation was contained in a classified report.

Concentration of force

The concentration of any resource, personnel or material, may occur in time or in space, and our text advises that in modern military operations it is more usually the former than the latter. Concentration need not imply physical massing, as this is dangerous in modern war, and in peace operations it is usually as impracticable as it is unnecessary. What is necessary is to have resources so disposed so that they are quickly available at a critical or a decisive point. It is a corollary of this principle that reserves, of forces and of material, are always and at all levels readily available for the unforeseen – which must always be foreseen. In the cheese-paring process of structuring forces for peace operations, however, no 'redundancy' is permitted, and reserves, where they exist at all, are usually only produced by withdrawing troops from or reducing them at other points. This is extremely short sighted, as it robs the force of the ability to react to the unexpected. This weakness is quickly sensed by those who may be opposed to the operation, and who may seek to thwart or embarrass the force by presenting them with situations to which they cannot effectively, which usually means quickly, react. This is an important function of another principle, flexibility.

Economy of effort

'Economy of Effort implies a balanced employment of forces', runs my text. This is a subject even more complex in modern peace operations than in conventional war. Especially in the modern complex humanitarian emergency, the array of agencies – governmental, intergovernmental, non-governmental, international, local, military, police and civilian – present an awesome challenge for coordination, sharing of responsibilities and resources, avoiding duplications as much as omissions. We have spoken here at some length of the failures of communications, the competition for resources and the simple lack of knowledge of who one's partners might be, where they are, what might be their needs and capacities, how one might help – how simply to stay out of their way, when that is what is required.

Despite over a decade at what, for simple lack of a better term, we call 'modern peace operations', we are not getting better at this. *Ad hoc* solutions at the tactical level have not been supported by, still less are they the subjects of, an emerging and maturing body of doctrine. The *ad hoc* tactical solutions are often not supported even at the local operational level, and seem even to be unknown at the strategic level. Moreover, these tactical level innovations seem not to transport well between theatres and missions, and so each mission starts up much as though we have not done this all before – the book of lessons learnt is apparently dwarfed by the one on lessons *not* learnt.

A sub-set of this principle, regarded in some texts as a separate principle, is Unity of Command. This is in modern peace operations frequently referred to as Unity of Effort for, as we will later discuss in more detail (Chapter 20), absolute command is frequently impracticable. This is a systemic weakness of United Nations structures. We have spoken of the abrupt organizational shift from a military-led, vertical structure to a civilian-led, horizontal structure which more or less accompanied the dawn of modern peace operations. The pre-Iraq war (re)deployment of United Nations weapons inspectors in Iraq provided a rather different example of this common weakness, and of the dangers such divisiveness can pose.

Although public focus was on the United Nations Monitoring, Verification and Inspection Commission (UNMOVIC) in Iraq, that mission was in fact responsible only for chemical and biological weapons systems, while the International Atomic Energy Agency (IAEA) was responsible for nuclear weapons. The doughty Swede Hans Blix was the Head of UNMOVIC; the IAEA was headed by Mohammed ElBaradei of Egypt. Although Baradei had initially gone to Baghdad with his monitors – and Blix – he remained head of his agency, a specialized agency of the United Nations, in Vienna. While Blix was acting as his own spokesman, the IAEA spokesperson remained in the IAEA offices in Vienna. Thus two heads of mission were from the outset in theatre, though one was unlikely, given his responsibilities for an agency in Vienna, to remain for long away from Vienna, and his spokesperson initially and for some weeks remained in Vienna. Difficulties were expected to arise especially in the case of nuclear investigations: the United Nations Special Commission (UNSCOM), the predecessor mission to UNMOVIC, reported in 1998 'no indications that Iraq was successful in its attempt to produce nuclear weapons'.[17] Iraq is not the type of nation to produce a nuclear weapon programme in five years – if they were assessed as having had no weapons in 1998, what might have been the UN credibility if in 2003 evidence were to be found of a nuclear weapons programme? Or, on the other hand, if *no* such evidence were found? This scarcely seemed a good beginning for cooperation, and we recall that phenomenon of the narcissism of small differences, with some foreboding. How would the UN leadership, so divided at the strategic level in the Security Council, and at the operational level in the field mission, have withstood or reacted to what was clearly to be, among other things, an information battle? For example, how would *Blix* have replied to criticism of the monitoring of *nuclear programmes* in Iraq? In the event, thanks to the enormous good sense, patience and probity of Blix and ElBaradei, complications were avoided – but that is despite, not because of, the operational-level structure.

Flexibility

Flexibility 'entails good training, organization, discipline and staff work, and, above all, that flexibility of mind and rapidity of decision on the part of both the Commander and his subordinates which ensures that time is never lost'. This is to describe one of the weakest aspects of today's peace operations. Given the complexity of the emergencies which peace operations have faced, the sheer scope and the size of the responses, the fragility of local consent, as of international consensus, the tendency has been towards horizontal structures which, at the operational level, are really little more than committees.

Agencies formerly under the direct authority of a Peacekeeping FC, such as Civilian Police, Civil Affairs and Administration, are usually today his co-equals, and all (including that FC) under the leadership of a civilian HOM, such as the SRSG. In fact, unpalatable as this may seem to the military, this is probably the optimal response to the complexity and sensitivity of these situations. The fact remains, however, that it will be an extraordinary group which will more or less voluntarily produce from such an organization operations which are precisely timed, structured and supported. As has been said before, it is organizationally possible to separate officers from the authority necessary to the efficient performance of their duties; it is not possible to separate them from their responsibilities.

The military will have to learn to live with horizontal organizations, and force commanders and their staffs will have to learn that critical resources and functions may in peace operations lie outside their direct orbit. This may suggest some changes to the way in which commanders will plan their operations, and of the time such plans may require for development. In turn, this may indicate some re-thinking of the role of a Chief of Staff of a military peacekeeping force – someone is going to have to attend all these meetings, and pursue all these negotiations.

Cooperation

To a large extent, what is lost in flexibility in the labyrinth of such operations as we have here described must be regained in a spirit of cooperation, which is at the centre of this work. I have suggested here an approach to greater empathy in the inter-organizational setting, based on a cross-cultural communications effort.

Nevertheless, many relationships will remain inherently adversarial, particularly at the higher levels, and often despite considerable will to compromise and to co-operate on the ground. Where these adversarial relationships exist, the resulting conflicts will best be managed by principled negotiations.

There are many who recognize the need for and offer training in Interest-based Negotiations. Among these are of course the Harvard Programme on Negotiations (PON), and some of their collegial organizations such as the United States Institute for Peace (USIP), the Canadian International Institute for Applied Negotiations (CIIAN) and the PPC. The PPC has been running its ten-day course, 'Creating Common Ground: Negotiations and Mediation for Peacekeepers' in conjunction with the CIIAN, twice per year since 1995. In 1998 all graduates of the PPC course were polled to see, among other things, how they were applying what they had learned. Almost all replied that their most common application of negotiating techniques was in interacting with co-workers and partner agencies.

Administration

'Every operational Commander must have a degree of control over the administrative plan within his sphere of command corresponding to the scope of his responsibilities for the operational plan.' So says the text, but here is the rub for the modern commander or manager, for the degree of autonomy of the CAO of a UN mission is usually considered, by all but the CAO, to be disproportionate to his responsibilities for the overall mission. As the Swedish Major General Karl von Horn said, a generation ago, 'They have separated authority from responsibility, with disastrous results'. There will be few peacekeepers, military or civilian, Force Commanders or civilian Heads of Missions, who have not their favourite CAO story. Above all, the CAO is a financial watchdog, he will be reporting directly to New York, and he will usually exercise highly centralized control over all resources, including finances. His disposition of resources critical to the goals of other components of the force will be one of the limitations on planning, and may seriously limit flexibility of response.

Conclusions

So runs the text on the principles of war, and so, approximately parallel, runs the reality of modern peace operations. As in every situation we are reminded that these principles are neither rules nor laws, they are guides. As we have noted, their observance is no guarantee of success – these are also not recipes – but their continual contravention bodes no good. Badly chosen or ill-phrased aims will scarcely yield the miracle of success, morale will always outweigh material aspects, security must be balanced against all other considerations, flexibility and cooperation are more important than ever just because they are more difficult than ever, and no force or mission can achieve much without seizing the initiative when the time is ripe for it to do so. Administration, as always, will be a major factor in deciding upon the do-able, and no responsible commander will overlook its importance – nor can he afford to underestimate the difficulties of securing the sustainment of his operations.

This chapter has been intended to construct a bridge for the principles of war, and to transform them very slightly so that, so abridged, they become guiding principles for peace operations. They provide, as it were, a systems approach to military organizations and their underlying culture. So equipped, we can now turn to more detailed considerations of the military roles in these operations.

15

THE MILITARY ROLES IN SUPPORT
OF HUMANITARIAN OPERATIONS

Generally speaking, almost all peace operations are initiated to relieve human suffering, or they are launched to prevent conflicts which will cause such hardships. The term 'humanitarian' then cannot be the exclusive term some 'humanitarians' would like it to be, anymore than the term humanitarian itself can be used exclusively by the self-appointed members of a humanitarian 'community'. All of those who take part in peace operations may be called peacekeepers, and few of them cannot be called humanitarians.

The military role and involvement in support of humanitarian efforts probably has its origins in 1974 in Cyprus. Up to that time, the military had had the peacekeeping field almost entirely to themselves. The mandate of UNFICYP had since 1964 consisted of only three points: to prevent a recurrence of fighting, to promote law and order, and to contribute to a return to normal conditions.

I was in 1973 the Civil-Military Affairs (CMA) officer,[1] and my duties concerned the third point of the mandate, which was called, in the shorthand of the day, 'normalization'. Just what was meant (or hoped) by 'normal' no one knew, nor asked a second time. I had a deputy and a clerk, and relied on six District CMA officers, all of who were in that capacity serving in secondary duties, devoting what effort could be spared from their more important appointments, such as the Officers' Mess Committee. There was one UN Specialized Agency – UNDP, and one NGO – the World Bank for Reconstruction and Development. I had absolutely nothing to do with either. It was pretty small beer.

All that changed (for my successors) in the week and the aftermath of the Turkish invasion in 1974, and UNFICYP was flooded with internally displaced persons who, as the fighting ended, posed an urgent humanitarian situation. Responsibility for the relief of this emergency was formally assigned to UNFICYP.[2] Naturally, the role and the staff to discharge this were expanded. Eventually the leading role was assumed by UNHCR, with the military function gradually transformed into one of support, rather than leadership.

The actual military role of UNFICYP in respect of displaced persons in Cyprus was quite short-lived – the numbers were never, by the standards of recent cases, great, and many Greek Cypriots were fairly quickly re-settled, either in the remaining Greek Cypriot-held part of the island, or elsewhere. It is in fact rather hard to say what that role might be today, even though the present CMA Staff is still larger than my pre-invasion section, and the military half of the partnership is once again rather singular: one of its erstwhile partners, UNDP, ceased its operations in Cyprus in 1996. The UNHCR programme for Cyprus is managed from Geneva, and asylum seekers are largely handled by the British Government through its Sovereign Base Areas on the island.[3]

So this was not really prologue for what has ensued, and has been continually developing, since UNPROFOR was rather off-handedly directed to take over and re-open the airport in Sarajevo for the delivery of humanitarian relief supplies, in July 1992.[4] This is not the place to review in any detail the short but dense history of modern humanitarian operations, as they have evolved in response to complex emergencies since the end of the Cold War. Suffice it here to reiterate that this process has occurred in a doctrinal vacuum, and that evolution has not meant a controlled developmental process, any more than mission creep is a logical tasking process. We can for the purposes of this chapter only speculate on what are, what might be and what should be the actual tasks of the military in supporting humanitarian agencies and operations.

In the post-Cold War operations as they have evolved, the majority of interventions have been mandated as peace enforcement operations, authorized by the UN Security Council under Chapter VII of the Charter. A principle implication of such a mandate is an increased expectation that force may be used to achieve the mission, accompanied by a decreased expectation of full and uniform consent, by all the parties, to the mission or to its conduct. The issue of consent I will discuss separately; the issue of force is in urgent need of clarification (the matter of control of force I will also discuss separately as under Rules of Engagement).

The role of the military seems to have evolved from the relatively simple military mandate of the era of 'classical', consensual, 'Chapter VI' peacekeeping. There, the mandate was to observe, or to preserve, something that existed, which had physical property – a Cease-fire Line, a Zone of Separation, a Withdrawal Line, a Green Line, a De-Militarized Zone. Consent was assumed, and the use of force was limited to self-defence, an 'inherent right' specified in Article 51 of the Charter. Today, in 'wider peacekeeping', it is more the norm that, in a rather paradoxical pairing of *humanitarian* with *enforcement* operations,[5] the military is asked to create and to maintain precisely what is *not*. This is often euphemistically described as the creation of a 'positive security environment', such as to allow civilian agencies to conduct their operations safely and effectively.[6] Just what specific role armed force is to play, indeed what armed force means – to the military, to the governments of the troop contributors, to those civilian agencies who are to be enabled to work in this environment as well as those who are to be its beneficiaries, and, not least, to international and national public opinion – seems to be the subject principally of *post facto* discussion. That discussion, unfortunately, is not of recent origin. In a peace enforcement operation that was in many ways a prologue to 'modern' operations, the UN Force in the Congo in

1960 (ONUC), posed the questions still unanswered. As Karl von Horn, the Swedish UN FC, wrote:

> The physical difficulties of sticking to the rules of peacekeeping became sharply apparent... Our orders were specific: force was to be used *only* in self-defence, nor were we allowed any latitude however threatening the situation.... orders like these present a commander with a distinct moral problem: whether to risk his men's lives by involving them in a situation where some of them are bound to get shot before having a chance to defend themselves – or whether to risk the failure of a mission (on whose success the lives of many civilians may depend) through a reluctance to expose his soldiers to what he considers an intolerable degree of risk.[7]

Forty years on, and despite our more recent experiences with enforcement operations, especially in Bosnia, Somalia and Rwanda, there are no satisfactory answers to this fundamental question, left over from that first peace enforcement operation.

It is perhaps not too much to say that the military is to be all things to all people – which is of course impossible, and is merely the root of unrealistic expectations and productive of endless dissatisfaction.

What the military can offer, if properly structured and deployed, is protection, communications, logistic support, and robust command and control capacities – all of which will often be critical in a complex emergency response, especially in the earliest stages. The actual tactical role will be defensive in nature: to deter armed aggression by the 'parties', and to protect unarmed humanitarian workers should aggression occur. What the military usually cannot do effectively is to re-settle returning refugees, and the soldiers of democracies are understandably reluctant to undertake law enforcement tasks.[8]

Direct intervention in relief efforts is, however, not the best use of military, nor are military often the best suited to conduct direct assistance tasks. Above all, military force cannot be used offensively in humanitarian operations – they will not 'fight through' the supply convoys.[9] Also, the military should be used to escort convoys, offering deterrence against and protecting from interference, but the military should not normally be employed to deliver the supplies themselves. Nevertheless, the military are very flexible, and can in the short term do almost anything they are asked to do and for which resources are or can be made available.

Ironically, it is just when the military are unable to establish a positive security environment that they may be drawn into assuming tasks more properly belonging to civilian agencies, and there is evidence that this is now happening to coalition forces in Iraq. As a recent report by an officer who has visited Iraq says:

> Iraq remains a semi-hostile environment. Civilian employers have a duty of care for their staff and many of the International Organizations and

NGOs have decided to stay away. Coalition Forces (CF), therefore, have a very significant role at present in Iraq's reconstruction, rather than just in its security.[10]

And all this is no doubt being played out to the intense displeasure of all concerned: the military are resentful of the extension of their roles, and the civilians will be equally resentful of what they consider poaching. What, we may ask, will happen when the climate is right for the civilian agencies to undertake their proper tasks? The situation will not likely be eased at all by the fact that the military, with their traditional flexibility and their very wide repertoire of capabilities, may have done a very good job in these expanded roles. We remember that hospital in East Timor, restored and returned to service by military medics, with whom the MSF could not work alongside and so, unthanked as it seems, the military left the hospital to the NGOs. In Iraq, as then in East Timor, it is likely that neither the civilians *nor* the military will see that the military simply did what needed to be done at a time when only they could do it – *but it was no job for soldiers*, and we can have little expectation that these roles will pass easily to the civilians when the time for that comes.

This does not provide answers to many questions, such as the definition of force and especially the determination of its appropriateness to a given situation, nor is the issue of security of the military force itself a simple one (however much the proponents of Force Protection may wish it were). We cannot draw any lines, on one side of which the military supports the humanitarians, on the other side of which it competes with them. Our recent experience certainly does little if anything to instil mutual trust. The military rightly see themselves subject to an endless round of Monday morning coaching by the very agencies who cannot define a role which has now been the subject of international controversy for a decade. On the other hand, civilians will often only grudgingly admit the necessity for a job to be done which they could not do, and which they consider demeans those who do it for them – *but only a soldier can do it.*

Nevertheless, the military exists to execute policy, not – at least in a democracy – to design policy. Failing the resolution of these issues at the strategic – the political and the diplomatic – level, the workers, civilian and military, must work these out for themselves at the tactical level. This is asking quite a lot – without empathetic, trusting relationships, it is asking the nearly impossible. We can only conclude that it is not surprising that civil-military coordination does not work better, for it is amazing that it works at all.

As in the first part of this book (Chapter 3) we reviewed briefly the changing doctrinal context of the generations of peace operations, it is now time to consider these operations in more detail as their very differing mandates are effected by missions in the field.

16

FIRST-GENERATION
PEACEKEEPING

The Age of Consent

Traditional peacekeeping has been largely undertaken with the consent of the parties to the conflict. This experience has conditioned responses and expectations of goals and tactics profoundly. In these consensual operations the conflict was either ended or it was anticipated that it soon would be at least suspended. The security situation seemed to favour civilian relief agencies, and the risk to them was usually low enough to be acceptable. That relatively permissive security environment did not call for a high degree of cooperation between military forces and civilian agencies, and they tended to operate in relative isolation from one another. That has changed greatly in the past decade or so. To appreciate how this scenario has altered, we need to review the consent issue, to see how it has affected peace operations, then to re-examine how changed circumstances have altered practices – or how they have failed to do so.

The first fifty years of peacekeeping were almost entirely consensual operations: that is to say, they were carried out with the full and explicit consent of the parties to the conflict, of the troop contributor governments and of the Permanent Members of the Security Council. This last was especially important for the approval of a mission, as well as for the design of the mandate. For those fifty years the 'threat' of a Security Council veto was probably the overriding factor in the decision to undertake a peacekeeping mission, and all peacekeeping missions were undertaken in the shadow of that threat. Thus that first half-century was perhaps not fifty years of experience, but one year repeated fifty times: it might be called 'The Age of Consent'.

The circumstances surrounding the launch of the first modern peacekeeping mission, the United Nations Emergency Force (UNEF), in 1956, illustrate several facets of the consent issue, many of them surprising at the time, and some still today not fully appreciated.

The developments in the Middle East, especially with respect to the closing of the Suez Canal by Egypt, the Franco-British military response and the resulting disarray in the international community, are well documented and need not be re-told here.[1] For our purposes, we can begin on 30 October 1956, with the veto in the Security Council, by France and Britain, of a US-sponsored resolution calling upon Israel to withdraw from territories she had occupied in the wake of the Anglo-French invasion. A Soviet amendment designed to dilute the force of the original resolution was also vetoed. The next day, the Yugoslav representative offered a resolution under the 'Uniting for Peace Resolution',[2] to move the issue to an Emergency Special Session of the General Assembly – as this was a procedural matter, it was not subject to veto, and was passed over the objections of France and Britain. The Special Session convened on 1 November.

In discussions with the Secretary-General prior to that Special Session, the Canadian Permanent Representative, Lester B. Pearson, had broached the idea of a peace force, which he eventually proposed to the General Assembly on 4 November, as follows:

> The General Assembly...requests...the Secretary-General to submit...a plan for the setting up, *with the consent of the nations concerned*, of an emergency United Nations Force to secure and supervise the cessation of hostilities.[3]

But there were other things going on (there always are):

'On October 22 the first news of disturbances in Hungary began to reach New York, and the next day it became clear that a full-scale uprising was in progress, and that Soviet forces would be brought in to deal with it.' On October 24, at the 'request' of the Hungarian government, Warsaw Pact forces did enter Hungary.[4] 'Widespread fighting was soon reported between the insurgents, Soviet forces, and Hungarian forces loyal to the Hungarian regime, and on Sunday, October 28, the Security Council voted to consider the question of Soviet action in Hungary.'[5] At 3:00 a.m. on Sunday, 4 November, 45 minutes after Pearson's proposal for a Middle East peace force was approved in the General Assembly, the Soviet Union vetoed an American-proposed Security Council Resolution demanding Soviet withdrawal from Hungary. Five hours later, Radio Budapest played the national anthem, then cried out, 'Help Hungary! Help us! Help us!', and went off the air – essentially for the next forty-five years.[6]

The Secretary-General had been quietly preparing an observer mission to Hungary, to which the USSR had strenuously objected as a violation of sovereignty (whose they did not specify, and they had at any rate the 'consent' of Hungary for *their* intervention).[7] Quite naturally, they perceived the proposed intervention in the Middle East as a highly dangerous precedent that, if they could not prevent, they might effectively derail. Thus on 5 November, in an apparent (but transparent) move to strengthen the action *in the Middle East*, the Soviet Union proposed that the action should be an enforcement mission under Article 42 of the Charter.[8] As this had only been done once before in the history of the United Nations (establishing the UN Command in Korea in 1951), it was highly unlikely in this context that the member states would authorize such a mission (there was indeed to be only one other – in the Congo – in the next thirty-five years). Clearly, the Soviet proposal was not intended to strengthen the prospects for peace, but was based on a canny appreciation of the then-limits on, and the critical importance of, consent.

But, as the Middle East Force was finally deploying, there came one more twist on the consent issue. Canada had agreed to provide an infantry battalion, and the battalion was duly moved from its barracks in British Columbia by rail, 4,400 miles to Halifax, where it was to take ship to the Middle East. On the eve of their sailing, however, Nasser learned from a press release of the name of the regiment from which this battalion was drawn: they were 'The Queen's Own Rifles of Canada'. Nasser was not having anything of the Queen's on his territory, and the battalion returned, sadly disappointed, to their barracks. It was apparently an unpleasant surprise to the United Nations to find that, having secured the consent to the mission, the composition of the Force could be just as contentious – as late as 10 November, Hammarskjold wrote to the Foreign Minister of Egypt to insist that such consent could not reside with one of the 'hosts' without seriously infringing his own authority.

These were not the Secretary-General's final words on the matter, however: 'obviously', Urquhart wrote, 'as a practical matter, the UN must give serious consideration to the views and wishes of Egypt... and give them full weight in deciding on the composition of the Force'.[9] Writing to Burns, the Canadian officer who was to command the Force, Hammarskjold pronounced what may stand as a fundamental principle of consensual operations:

> I frankly fail to see how, as constructed, the UN force could be instrumental in forcing on Egypt a solution of the Canal question other than one freely negotiated.[10]

Much later, in his report to the General Assembly on 24 January 1957, Hammarskjold observed that 'The use of a military force by the UN *other than under Chapter VII*, the enforcement chapter of the Charter, required the consent of the states on whose territory the force was to operate'.[11]

Thus this first modern peacekeeping force encountered nearly all the consent issues which effect such operations today: the fullest consent of the parties in conflict, of the Security Council members and by the governments of the troop contributors, was essential to any intervention. Other issues such as freedom of movement of the force, its composition, its right of entry into the area of operations, the extremely touchy issue of the sovereignty of the 'hosts' – all these issues were played then, and almost none were, nor have they since been, entirely satisfactorily resolved. All have arisen afresh with each new operation, and all have been settled differently (or not at all), and at great cost to the efficiency of the operation of the peacekeeping forces.

Ironically, and tragically, this Force was to founder, nine years later, on just the issue of consent. In finalizing the stationing of the Force, the General Assembly had entered into what came to be known as 'The Good Faith Agreement', which stated, *inter alia*, that the Force could not be 'stationed or operate on the territory of a given country without the consent of the Government of that country'. Egypt undertook to 'be guided, in good faith, by its acceptance' of that resolution. In the course of a period of rising tensions between Syria and Israel, which led in turn to tensions between Egypt and Israel, the Egyptian Government, on 16 May 1967, requested the withdrawal of UNEF. In discussions at the United Nations, the Secretary-General reminded the UNEF Advisory Committee 'that the Force was on Egyptian territory only with the consent of the government and could not remain there without it'.[12] The Force completed its withdrawal by 17 June, but not before 15 UN peacekeepers had been killed in the fighting which had broken out on 5 June, in what came to be known as the Six-Day War.[13]

This was the era of inter-states conflict: 'The Age of Consent'. The questions not answered of those 'consensual' peacekeeping forces – their mandates, their missions, the use of force; above all, the issues of consent, still bedevil the modern peacekeepers of our post-Cold War era.[14] Moreover, these modern, intra-state conflicts have raised new issues, to be layered on those yet outstanding from the first half-century of peacekeeping.

Of course, consent is not solely a military consideration. As Lehmann has written, 'in the new, complex operations, consent implies popular support *or acquiescence*, even in non-democratic or transitional societies'. She adds:

> There are at least three areas in which consent – that is general support for a peacekeeping operation – should exist for it to be carried out successfully:
>
> 1 In the countries in which the UN force is deployed;
> 2 In the troop contributing countries; and
> 3 In the countries that pay the largest share of the bill for peacekeeping.[15]

Nor can it be expected that consent will exist as a natural phenomenon, indeed quite the reverse will often be the case, and the creation of a climate of consent will be a major component of the design of the intervention mission. Lehmann describes the potential value of creating consent, where it might not otherwise have been expected to exist:

> The U.N. mission in Namibia was a high-profile, well-prepared public relations effort in a country that harbored many suspicions against foreign influence in general and against the international peace plan for Namibia in particular. By using 'corporate image-making' and other public relations techniques, the United Nations managed to convince the overwhelming majority of the population in the territory that the international peace plan was in the country's best interest, and that holding free and fair elections leading to independence from South Africa was a desirable goal.[16]

Beyond the public relations aspect of creating a climate of consent, there may arise the need to induce consent more forcefully. As the Secretary-General of the United Nations has described it:

> In any given case, blue helmeted soldiers are likely to encounter many persons who welcome the UN presence and many others who are highly resistant. In such operations, some of which will be mandated to assist societies bordering on anarchy, the old dictum of 'consent of the parties' will be neither right nor wrong; it will be, quite simply, irrelevant.
>
> Much of the literature on peacekeeping treats the consent of the parties as if it were an independent variable. It is not, for the simple reason that the decision of the parties to grant consent is never taken in a vacuum. It is, rather, a function of the alternatives. *If consent carries with it certain rewards, and the failure to grant consent carries with it certain costs, this obviously affects the decision as to whether or not consent will be granted.*[17]

The Secretary-General went on to distinguish between 'coercive' and 'positive' inducement:

The purpose of coercive inducement is 'to intimidate recalcitrants into cooperating'. Operations of this nature will 'take into account that hostile consent was granted only in the face of intimidating force, and that *a credible force is required if consent is to be maintained*'. Despite this, the peace force will assume that much of the host population has freely consented to and supports the operation, thus the aim of an inducement operation is 'to build, not to destroy', controlling with the necessary force the extremists who oppose reconciliation and would continue violent conflict for their own ends. Bluffing is dangerous and must be avoided. There are, however, limits on the use of coercive consent: 'the intimidation factor will erode over time', its usefulness may be constrained by weakness in the consent of the sponsors (see Lehmann) and, most importantly, coercion cannot resolve conflicts.[18]

It is necessary, therefore, to consider a softer, more sustainable approach that will go beyond mere conflict management, and which has the potential for conflict resolution – the Secretary-General has called this 'positive inducement'. By this he means 'the provision of rewards'. These, he says, can be divided into two categories: the first the military refers to as 'civic action', which aims 'to gain the good will and consequent cooperation of the population'. The second group of rewards he terms 'peace incentives', which are aimed specifically at the reconciliation process: these might be assistance and developmental projects, rewarding, indeed requiring, cooperation among antagonists. These may be financial credits, medical care, physical reconstruction. He distinguishes between these positive inducements and humanitarian assistance measures which, while similar, are not the same:

> The primary purpose of humanitarian assistance is to provide succour to those in need. While civic action and peace incentives also help those in

need, their primary purpose is to forward political objectives to gain people's support for a UN operation and to provide leverage in favour of reconciliation. While humanitarian assistance is unconditional, peace incentives are to some extent conditional. Their continuation depends, more or less explicitly, on a certain amount of cooperation towards the objective of political reconciliation.[19]

'It should not be surprising, therefore', Kofi Annan concludes, 'that experience to date has not been promising in regard to effective cooperation between humanitarian providers, on the one hand, and peacemakers and peacekeepers, on the other'.

One example of induced consent, showing both stick and carrot, in that order, was the demilitarization and re-opening of the Djeletovci Oil Fields in Eastern Slavonia by UNTAES in 1996:

By May it was considered by UNTAES that the Serbs were prepared for progress in the negotiations, but were concerned about political correctness.

UNTAES then manifested a show of force. In late June, a mechanized battle group, consisting of an APC battalion with tanks, artillery and attack helicopters, moved up to the oil fields. There was a brief confrontation between the Serbs and a tank squadron, in which the UN tanks fired 10 rounds main armament, and then the Serbs began to withdraw. As a UN officer said, 'We told them it would be a good idea to leave, then we showed them what a good idea it would be to leave, and then they left'.

Agreement was reached on 25 July to return the oil fields to production, and a joint survey mission of Croatian, Serb and UNTAES experts to determine the condition of the fields was initiated. De-mining started on 6 August, and oil exploitation on 15 August. By agreement, UNTAES administers the fields, and revenues are handed to the Croatian government. Mine clearance continues, as do negotiations for re-hiring Serb workers by the Croatian company which will eventually take over full responsibility for the operations. By the end of August, over 150 Serb former employees had been given draft contracts for their re-employment.[20]

And it is at just this point that we see, from a slightly different angle, the conflict, cultural as well as procedural, between the peacekeepers and the humanitarians. We can now begin to re-appreciate the different cultures inherent in the situation in that hospital in East Timor, and we can perhaps now more clearly address the civilians' seeming objection to the soldiers assisting the people directly: did those 'parties' – military and civilian – sense their differing aims? Did the humanitarians (INTERFET soldiers called them 'the Humans') sense an underlining of their own self-admitted weakness, which is that unconditional assistance not only may create dependencies, but may indeed delay resolutions? Perhaps the civilians object instinctively to whatever glove hides an iron fist; was the MSF reaction FEAR-motivated? And all at once, we know we have heard this all before, not just in that hospital in East Timor, but in the minefields of Cambodia.

A DHA report on mine action capacities, published in 1997, observed that 'present arrangements are dysfunctional and have undermined the development of indigenous capabilities when it tried to combine activities geared to meeting the operational requirements of peacekeeping missions and the development of humanitarian mine action programmes'. The reporters further observed that:

> In situations where UN peacekeeping troops are deployed, the UN focal point must ensure that there is a clear delineation of authority and responsibility for all activities related to 'operational' demining and 'humanitarian' mine action. Operational demining should be undertaken in close consultation with the Mine Action Centre or mechanism established to coordinate support for the development of indigenous capabilities.
>
> However, launching a mine action programme within the ambit of a UN Security Council-mandated peace-building mission is problematical. ... In such situations, the development of a humanitarian mine action programme is of secondary concern. The overwhelming focus is on 'operational mine clearance' and inadequate attention is given to building an indigenous capacity and to issues of continuity and sustainability.
>
> The problems encountered in Cambodia, Mozambique and Angola illustrate the importance of an overall plan focused on the development of a humanitarian mine action capability *and not subverting this endeavour to help in the achievement of mission objectives.*[21]

And so we again have elements with similar roles and tasks, indeed very similar people assigned to them, lining up astride adversarial relationships that have little to do with overall programme goals, but seem to have much to do with internal competitions. Is this another dimension to the consent issue, wherein agencies will not consent to the development of partnering relationships, even when there seems every good reason for and advantage to their doing so?

17

SECOND-GENERATION PEACEKEEPING

Crossing the Mogadishu

Since the end of the Cold War, peace operations have taken on a new dimension: the use of force to *enforce* the peace. This is in fact just the use of force which had been envisaged in the Charter of the United Nations. However, as we shall see, this provision and the operations it would have mandated had been extremely rare in the first half-century of the Organization. Thus, although the Charter was written in 1946, we did not at the end of the last century have 50 years' experience with enforcement of peace – we had almost none. We had little idea what peace enforcement might mean, and we are still learning, slowly and painfully, what peace enforcement operations might entail. Since this is just the scenario in which military and civilian agencies are mandated to work in unprecedented combination, we need to look closely at this 'second generation' of peace operations.

The term 'peacekeeping' appears nowhere in the Charter of the United Nations. Chapter VII of the Charter deals with 'Action with Respect to Threats to the Peace, Breaches of the Peace, and Acts of Aggression'. This begins with 'measures not involving the use of armed force' (Article 41) and, should the Security Council consider these inadequate, 'it may take such action by air, sea or land forces as may be necessary to maintain or restore international peace and security' (Article 42). Actions mandated under this Chapter of the Charter are referred to as 'enforcement operations'. During the Cold War – the Age of Consent – there were only two enforcement operations: Korea and the Congo. Since 1990, however, nearly all UN peace operations have been or have become enforcement operations; indeed the Security Council has mandated the invasions of three member states (Iraq, Haiti and Somalia). In the period 1991–94, the Security Council passed eleven resolutions under Chapter VII of the Charter in respect of the former Yugoslavia and Bosnia-Herzegovina. That these resolutions were passed in respect of a mission originally deployed in Croatia as a consensual peacekeeping force, offers an excellent opportunity to contrast the two types of missions, as well as taking us to the birthplace of mission creep.

Enlargements of the UNPROFOR mandate began almost immediately upon its deployment.

On 30 June 1992 the Security Council, by UNSCR 762, authorized UNPROFOR to undertake monitoring of 'the pink zones': Serb-controlled areas of Croatia which were outside the UNPAs. On 7 August the Force was tasked by UNSCR 769 to control entry of civilians into the P.A.s, and to perform immigration and customs functions where the boundaries of the P.A.s were concurrent with international borders. On 6 October the Force was again further tasked to control the demilitarization of the Prevlaka Peninsula, and to take control of the Peruca Dam, both in Croatia (UNSCR 799). Trouble followed promptly: on 22 January 1993, impatient 'with the slow progress in respect of certain economic negotiations', the Croatian Army launched offensives in UNPA South and adjacent 'pink zones'; five days later they attacked the Peruca Dam. The Krajina Serbs responded by breaking into UN weapon storage areas,[1] undoing several months of demilitarization in the area.

It was in Bosnia-Herzegovina, however, that the UN undertook qualitative enlargements of the mandate that were to lead to completely unforeseen consequences.

The engagement of UNPROFOR in BiH had from the outset been confused. Mackenzie makes clear the desire of newly appointed officers of the Force, when briefed in New York (in February 1992) to steer clear of BiH: they had no mandate, and no troops immediately in the vicinity (all the rest of UNPROFOR was initially deployed only in the four UNPAs, which were in Croatia), and there was every indication that civil war was imminent in Bosnia. Not at all, said DPKO (Department of Peacekeeping Operations at UN HQ in New York), Bosnia was peaceful and neutral. So was Ljlubljana, said the officers. Overruled, said DPKO,[2] and so HQ UNPROFOR was established in Sarajevo on 16 March[3] – and driven out on 16 May, after a painful and largely pointless interval, of which MacKenzie later said it was the only time he had been in a headquarters where the troops felt sorry for the staff.[4]

Only much later did the real reason for the location of the headquarters become clear. In late 1991, Itzbegovic had pleaded for a preventive deployment in BiH, but this was refused. According to Warren Zimmerman, then US Ambassador to Yugoslavia, 'Vance and the U.N. leadership in New York took the traditional if puzzling line that peacekeepers are used after a conflict, not before'. As a sop, the Headquarters of UNPROFOR, with some UNMOs (United Nations Military Observers), was located in his capitol as a sort of combination of 'good offices' and deterrent measure.[5] Unfortunately for the soldiers, no one told them of their real role, which they had assumed to be the command and control of a division-sized force. This was made difficult enough by being over 350 kilometres from their nearest units, without becoming directly involved in a different civil war. Nevertheless, less than one month after their arrival, the 'deterrent' having swiftly failed, they of course were.

The involvement of the military with the humanitarian effort deepened with the opening of the Sarajevo airport 'under the exclusive authority of the United Nations' in July 1992, and, in September, the Security Council tasked UNPROFOR 'to provide protection...for UNHCR convoys delivering humanitarian relief throughout Bosnia and Herzegovina'. Eventually the Force also provided road repairs, assisted in medical evacuations, conducted infrastructure needs assessments, loaded and unloaded aircraft, and was responsible for 'support and coordination of airlift and airdrop operations'.[6] From this point on, the military force was in support of a humanitarian operation led by UNHCR. As Sir Michael Rose described the work:

> Daily life for the peacekeepers was a perpetual round of escorting convoys, guarding bases and UN weapons collection points and checkpoints. They were on permanent standby to deploy at short notice to rescue convoys and stop local outbreaks of fighting. They arranged medical evacuation for the sick and wounded, transport for refugees and supervised the exchanges of POWs and other bodies. In everything, they had to deal with local military and civilian authorities who were always looking to turn any humanitarian action to their advantage. The job of the peacekeepers was not just to bring about the conditions of peace, but to assist in the reconstruction of the country when peace arrived.[7]

Wider peacekeeping, indeed. Rose also noted that,

> At the start of the war, some NGOs refused to work with UNPROFOR on the grounds that they did not want to compromise their neutral status by associating with UN peacekeepers. *By 1994*, most NGOs came to see the need to cooperate closely with the UN in order to guarantee the security of their workers, and the arrangement in which the UNHCR became the lead agency coordinating the work of others is likely to remain the model for future humanitarian aid missions in this type of environment.[8]

But why did it take *two years* for the NGOs in Bosnia-Herzegovina to learn that?

But the interface between the military peacekeepers, UNPROFOR, and UNHCR was never simple. For the UNHCR in general, and clearly for Mrs Ogata, the soldiers were to be kept at arms' length. She expresses justifiable pride in UNHCR's leadership of the humanitarian relief operation in Bosnia. Nowhere in her excellent book, *The Turbulent Decade*, however, does she acknowledge that the negotiations to open the airport under UN control were conducted by UNPROFOR, that UNPROFOR was responsible for the security of the airport (cargoes and personnel coming in and going out were inspected by UNPROFOR/ UNCIVPOL) as well as air traffic control, that the aircraft were almost exclusively military, that the flights were planned by an international air operations (military) staff and that, under exceptionally hazardous circumstances, UNPROFOR delivered relief supplies. Mrs Ogata notes, in referring to the arrival in Geneva of seconded air force officers who were to establish an air operations centre, only that 'Traditionally, civilian humanitarian workers kept their distance from military activities. *The arrival of the military on the UNCHCR premises sent out internal shock waves.*'[9]

The United Nations' involvement in Bosnia again deepened with the establishment of the Safe Areas, the first of which was proclaimed in Srebrenica on 16 April 1993, when the Security Council, acting under Chapter VII of the Charter, adopted UNSCR 819. This demanded that 'all parties treat Srebrenica as a "Safe Area," which should be free from any armed attack or other hostile act'. On 21 April, UNPROFOR troops entered Srebrenica,[10] mostly Canadians detached from their parent battalion at Kiseljak (see Chapter 19). On 6 May, with the passage of UNSCR 824, Sarajevo, Tuzla, Sepa, Gorazde and Bihac 'and their surroundings', were added to the list of Safe Areas.[11] On 4 June, that mandate was again expanded to 'deter attacks... monitor the cease fire, to promote the withdrawal of military or paramilitary units other than those of the Bosnian Government and to occupy some key points'. It was at this point that mission creep was born: although the UNPROFOR Force Commander had estimated that 34,000 additional troops would be required 'to obtain deterrence through strength', the Secretary-General

> noted that it was possible to start implementing the resolution under a "light option," with a minimal troop reinforcement of around 7600. That option represented an initial approach and had limited objectives. It assumed the consent and cooperation of the parties and provided a basic level of deterrence.

Despite the sorry experiences of the United Nations with consent, cooperation and deterrence from the outset of the missions in the former Yugoslavia, the Security Council authorized that 'light option' of 7,600 additional troops by the adoption of UNSCR 844 on 18 June. Not having read H.G. Wells on the subject of wars in the air, the Secretary-General informed the Security Council on 18 August that 'the United Nations had the operational capability for the use of airpower in support of UNPROFOR'.[12] The final assault on Srebrenica began on 6 July 1995, and the town fell on 11 July. Zepa fell 14 days later. 'The moral responsibility of the international community is heavy indeed,' the Secretary-General concluded in his report to the Security Council in November.[13] Rose was more to the point: 'It was a cruel deception to suggest that peacekeepers were equipped or mandated to defend territory or offer full protection to civilians caught up in fighting'.[14] He summarized:

> The UN had arrived in Bosnia prepared for a role of traditional peacekeeping in accordance with Chapter VI of the UN Charter, but it was actually required to operate in the more demanding Chapter VII role. Under Chapter VI, the combatants agree to end their conflict and invite the UN to become a mediator to help negotiate and implement the elements of a peace deal. Under Chapter VII, however, it is likely that there will be no prior agreement to end the war and the mission of the UN will be to deliver humanitarian aid and to help create the conditions in which the conflict can be brought to an end. If there is little consent

for the presence of the peacekeepers, as in Bosnia, a great deal of enforcement may be necessary.[15]

Just how much force there might be in enforcement is, for Rose and for others, a moot question. He says:

> it is impossible to draw a clear line between the permissible levels of force in a peacekeeping mission and an act of war. The limit that I termed the 'Mogadishu Line' is defined by the goals being pursued, the levels of force, the strategic imperatives facing the combatants and the political circumstances.

He illustrated the concept of the Mogadishu Line somewhat as in this figure (Figure 17.1).[16]

A military organization must represent a continuum, beginning at the strategic and operational levels with the mandate, traceable through to the tactical level mission and manifest in a balanced force structure which can do, and is believed to be capable of doing, what it has been advertised to do. We must therefore now consider in more detail just what is meant by and entailed in Rules of Engagement, and in force structuring.

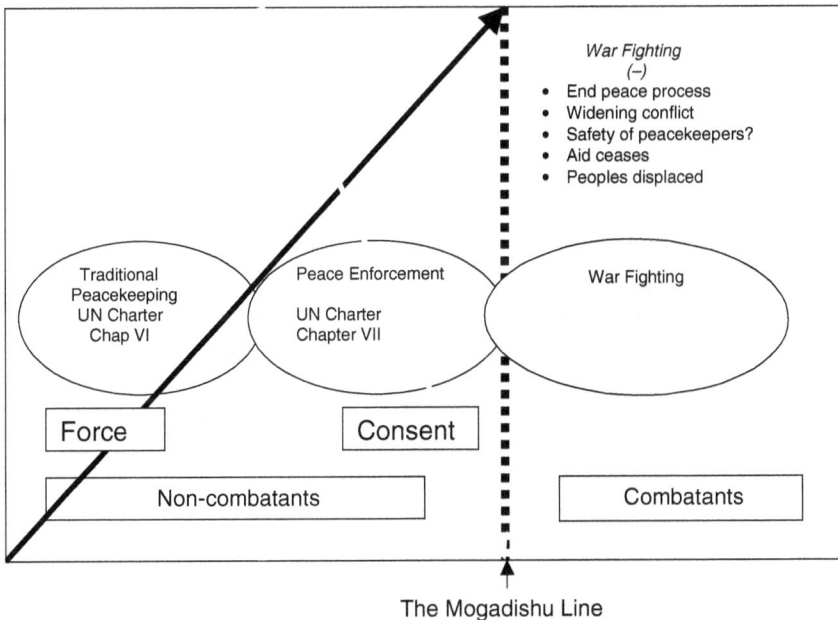

Figure 17.1 The Mogadishu Line.

18

RULES OF ENGAGEMENT

The practice of using Rules of Engagement (ROE) to authorize and to control the application of military force has its modern origins in the Cold War. Heavily armed adversaries were for nearly half a century in very close proximity to each other on land and sea and in the air. It was important that the potentially devastating power of those forces was subject to control at the highest possible level, that neither their intentions nor their capacities could be miscalculated, yet their readiness would not be compromised by inability to react. In the halcyon days of 'traditional peacekeeping', this was for the United Nations a minor matter: with the exception of the Congo operation in 1961, force was no part of the mandate except in the case of a direct threat to the life of a peacekeeper. The definitive reference on 'first generation' peacekeeping operations, 'The Blue Helmets: A Review of United Nations Peacekeeping' (First Edition),[1] does not mention ROE.

In modern peace support operations, however, the threats, and the available responses have escalated to the point where ROE are the most significant and visible expression of the mandate.

There are several fundamental characteristics of ROE for peace support operations. Some of these are:

- Transparency. ROE are authorities for and limitations on the use of force. The use of force by the Force must be absolutely clear to the members of the Force, to the parties to the conflict and, not least, to the governments and the people of the troop contributor nations.
- Restraint, and the Inherent Right of Self Protection (derived from Article 51 of the Charter of the UN), are counter-balancing characteristics of ROE.
- ROE are subject to law, both domestic and international.
- ROE are flexible, and must provide for an orderly and controlled process of escalation and de-escalation, in accordance with changes in the operational situation.
- ROE govern armed force, but that is not just deadly force – it is in fact minimum force, and the use of force must be proportionate to whatever threat prompted its use.

UNPROFOR ROEs were in fact reproduced on a card carried by every member of the Force, and they were translated and widely distributed among the populace. In Somalia, also a peace enforcement operation, the same was done. Leaflets distributed in Somalia warned against interference with relief convoys, and stated clearly that force would be used in response to threats to convoys or personnel. In other words, transparency of the Rules was intended to deter actions that might trigger the use of force; hostile actions could then, within reason, be taken at face value, and the soldiers and their mission adequately and appropriately defended.

In the aftermath of the Somalia mission,[2] eight members of the Canadian Forces were court-martialled, and four were convicted of offences. Following appeals, all convicted were imprisoned. Evidentially central to each of these cases were incidents of misapplication, unauthorized abridgment and/or violations of the ROE.

In the course of the post-Somalia prosecutions, it emerged to the surprise of many Canadians, military and civilian, that ROE are subject to national laws. In the cases of two fatal shootings of Somalis by Canadians that were not prosecuted, it was determined by investigators that the soldiers' ROEs allowed the use of deadly force to protect 'mission essential equipment'. Not at all, noted Canadian military lawyers: the use of deadly force to protect property is illegal under the Criminal Code of Canada, to which Canadian Forces personnel remain subject wherever they may serve and on whatever mission. This national interpretation of, or reservations upon, the ROE thus added another layer to the parallelism of national and multi-national command structures.

To illustrate just a few of the principles of ROE, most notably minimum force and transparency, I relate below two real-life incidents of the application of ROE; I call them:

A tale of two cities

I call this section a tale of two cities because the two examples of the Rules took place in Kyrenia and Ottawa.

Let's then go to the island of Cyprus, and back to the year of 1966, in October. I well recall the beautiful autumn day, my second on the island, and I will never forget the swollen cheekbones, split lips and blackened eyes of the badly beaten young Black Watch Corporal who sat in the Kyrenia District Command Post, fending off the hovering Medical Officer until he had told us his story.

He had been the leader of a two-man vehicle patrol that circled around what was then the northwestern corner of the enclave. It was a routine patrol, they had done it many times over the last six months, and today was their last patrol. Tomorrow they would hand over to us and pack for home. It had to be the last day, when everything that had not happened, nearly happened. Both soldiers were of course armed. Magazines were fully loaded, but were not on the weapons, which had been cleared before the patrol set out.

We never knew just what went wrong. The Canadian soldiers did not recognize the Fighters at the checkpoint. We later surmised that they had recently arrived clandestinely from the mainland. These new arrivals were often a problem: over aggressive, harshly but poorly disciplined and violence prone in a way that more experienced soldiers had outgrown.

The Canadians dismounted and attempted to negotiate to restore their freedom of movement. Suddenly, two Fighters became six, and then eight. They were rude and aggressive, then the Private was on the ground, with a Fighter tugging at his rifle sling. The NCO freed his partner's rifle, and ran to the vehicle. He threw both rifles inside, locked the cab and ran back to rejoin the fray – at about eight-to-one.

There was not much more to tell. We recorded his statement and photographed the bruises, and then the MO led him away. About four days later, I saw him late in the evening as I was leaving work – he was the Security Piquet NCO. He had asked to return to Canada on the last rotation flight, when his bruises would have gone down – he did not want to alarm his family.

I think today we pay people like him about $30,000 per year- plus, of course, that $1.28 per day.

Let's look at how that NCO used his ROE. He first used *minimum force*. This was not a gunfight, it was not likely to become one, and he meant to keep it that way. Short of that, he exercised *self-protection* to the degree possible, and everybody did get out alive – his *restraint* probably saved two lives. He was *flexible*: he stood his ground, and he attempted to negotiate. His intentions were *transparent:* he had every right to be where he was, he did not back down, and the road warriors could be under no misconception that this patrol route would be modified or abandoned; in fact we went back at the regular time the very next day, and every day thereafter for as long as I know.

And that is how a young Corporal, alone and in great danger, got it all right on the very instant when he first confronted such a situation – he knew his ROEs, he knew his mandate, and he knew his job – the peace was kept on that day.

Let's go then to Ottawa, and to a day in February 1995, when things went quite differently.

We are in the area called Lowertown, which includes the locally famous Byward Market. It is a very mixed neighbourhood, and you can find pretty much whatever you are looking for there, from excellent restaurants and fascinating shops, to more trouble than you can imagine.

It was on a stormy late afternoon in the Market, nearly dusk, when two Ottawa Police Constables, a man and a woman, observed a well-dressed middle-aged man park his late model car, quite legally. As he left the car, the female Constable approached him and told him his license was 'unattached'. The civilian, who was black, looked at the firmly screwed-on license plate, smiled and, by *some* accounts, walked on. By *all* accounts he was in seconds face down in the slush and handcuffed. His very expensive suit was ruined and he was cut and bruised.

It subsequently developed that 'unattached' is police jargon for a licence that did not match the car, an error for which the police computer was of course to blame. It further developed that the black man was the very influential leader of the Jamaican-Canadian community in the National Capitol Region, a personal friend of the Police Chief (one of the Constables who took him down was the son of that Chief), and had frequently lectured at the Ontario Police College – on race relations.

What went wrong? Was this *minimum force*, and what of *flexibility*? Could anyone have imagined that smiling at a policewoman could have such a result – is that really *transparent*? Did the police exercise *restraint*? Was their response *proportionate*? The police had a lot of trouble answering those questions, because at that time they had no ROE.

They probably had never heard of ROE.

Thus, a key recommendation of the Brahimi Report concludes that:

> United Nations peacekeepers must be able to carry out their mandates professionally and successfully and be capable of defending themselves, other mission members and the mission's mandate, *with robust rules of engagement*, against those who renege on their commitments to a peace accord or otherwise seek to undermine it by violence.[3]

It is often said of an enforcement mission that it will have 'robust rules of engagement', as though that alone would enable a more determined stance. Of course, ROE in themselves enable nothing and, absent the appropriate force to deliver the enforcement measures implied by this robustness, no one is fooled – not the soldiers themselves, nor those whom the peace enforcers may need from time to time to call to account. We must therefore now look now at the real difference, which is in the force structure.

19

FORCE STRUCTURES

Always use a sledgehammer to crack a walnut

A Chapter VII Enforcement operation differs from a Chapter VI Peacekeeping operation in more than degree. The inverse levels of consent and force will pose significantly greater threats, and the credibility of the Force will depend on its ability to keep pace with, indeed to keep ahead of, escalating violence by the parties in conflict. To the extent that the Force is able to dominate the situation, it may actually less often have to resort to extremes of force, than where it is tempting for the parties to defy or to attempt to intimidate the force. The Peace Enforcers should thus be structurally different from the Peacekeepers. The latter will be mainly light infantry – lightly armed for self-defence only, and lightly protected as well. The Enforcement Force, by contrast, should be capable of using force to induce and to maintain consent, rendering defiance and intimidation unprofitable, and highly risky to any who might try either. It will have firepower, protection and mobility *greater* than any potential antagonists – and will therefore likely have far fewer of them. As MacKenzie said, 'Don't take a knife to a gunfight'.

The seriatim expansions of the UNPROFOR mandate were simply reinforcing failure, advertising missions which had not a shred of credibility, neither for those whom they were intended to protect, nor for those whose actions they were intended to deter – and, indeed, offered precious little comfort to those who served in them. The progression from a Chapter VI operation, which UNPROFOR originally was, to the Enforcement mission it became, should not simply have been a too-little-too-late reinforcement in kind: sending more, inadequately structured forces. The progression should have been to a completely different, more robust force structure, one capable of meeting violence with overwhelming force, and thus ending it – but that had to wait until after Dayton. And for something other than another UN operation.

The Brahimi Report, referred to earlier, has much to say about force structures:

> United Nations military units must be capable of defending themselves, other mission components and the mission's mandate. Rules of Engagement should be sufficiently robust and not force United Nations contingents to cede the initiative to their attackers.

(This) means bigger forces, better equipped and more costly but able to be a credible deterrent threat, in contrast to the symbolic and non-threatening presence that characterizes traditional peacekeeping. United Nations forces for complex operations should be sized and configured so as to leave no doubt in the minds of would-be spoilers as to which of two approaches the Organization has adopted.

To deploy a partial force incapable of solidifying a fragile peace would first raise and then dash the hopes of a population engulfed in conflict or recovering from a war, and damage the credibility of the United Nations as a whole.[1]

And as a recent report commissioned by the United Nations on the use of force in peace operations recommends:

When a peace operation is deployed in the aftermath of conflict, especially when that conflict has seen the partial or total collapse of national security institutions, it should have a robust mandate to protect civilians and restore order. If needed, civilian police should be deployed as quickly as possible. But in the interim, responsibility for law and order falls upon the military or no one. Without security, none of the more complex political tasks that are intended to justify the use of force in the first place can be achieved.[2]

It unfortunately seems *not* to go without saying that the force structure must reflect the mandate – the means must serve the desired ends. Recommending a 'robust mandate' is getting the equation only half right.

As these modern 'complex operations' deploy into a 'fragile peace', or no peace at all, and must restore even a limited security, they must be able to restore the monopoly on force lost by their 'hosts', as governance failed and may have deceased altogether. They will do so only to the extent that they are genuinely able to seize, restore and maintain that monopoly, against any challenges, from any and all 'parties'. To the extent that they are clearly perceived to have that capability, they may be the less called upon actively to exercise it. To the extent that that capability has been denied them, and that falsity in their posture quickly and widely perceived, their lives will be the nightmare of 1990s enforcement operations, and their memories will be of similar humiliations and failure.

20

THE COMMAND AND CONTROL OF JOINT AND COMBINED MILITARY OPERATIONS

The fall of Srebrencia on 11 July 1995 was one of the worst days in UN history, but it need not have happened, at least it need not have happened as it did for the United Nations. It certainly would not have happened *as it did*, had the established norms of command and control of multi-national military forces been followed.

Early in 1993, the 'Safe Area Concept' was proclaimed in respect of Srebrenica, ostensibly in response to heavy Bosnian Serb attacks on several cities in eastern Bosnia, and was eventually expanded to include Sarajevo, Tuzla, Zepa, Gorazde and the Bihac area.[1] It is not my purpose here to relate the Donnybrook that ensued, and the equally distressing aftermath has been well described by Klep and Winslow,[2] as well as in the comprehensive report by the Secretary-General of the United Nations. The origins of the mission have much to say, however, on how not to exercise command under such circumstances, and of seriatim mistakes by people, all of who knew much better.

Despite the measured tones of *The Blue Helmets*, there is evidence that the Safe Area concept was not born in New York, nor was it even a concept for UNPROFOR. As the legend runs, in early 1993 the Commander of UNPROFOR Bosnia-Herzegovina paid an ill-advised visit to Srebrenica, then already under siege and, just as he had been warned might occur, he was prevented from leaving the town by the townspeople.[3] Under what stress can only be imagined, he vowed he would not desert Srebrenica. In remaining, he was of course in great danger; moreover he could not practicably exercise his command in this situation. To answer the first problem, he requested a Canadian platoon from the battalion at Kiseljak near Sarajevo to come to Srebrenica as a security element for his 'advanced' headquarters.[4] A platoon cannot realistically operate for long on its own, so the battalion commander sent a company. As the legend continues, the first the UN DPKO learned that they had a new Bosnian tiger by the tail was when, 'On 21 April, UNPROFOR's FC reported that 170 UNPROFOR troops had been deployed in Srebrenica'.[5] This was likely also the first the Canadian Government, and its Department of National Defence's Joint Staff, learned that a Canadian battalion commander had on UN operations done something that no Canadian NATO commander would ever have done: he had allowed his battalion to be broken up, elements were detached from his command and assigned a very dubious mission; at the same time, his formally assigned mission had been seriously compromised by this dilution of his strength.

There were clearly established procedures for command and control of national forces under foreign command, tried and tested in nearly a half-century of NATO experience, and designed to prevent exactly this sort of frittering away of resources intended for other purposes.[6]

The birthing of the safe area 'concept', and the abrogation of the procedures which, if they would not have prevented it, might have imposed some realism, illustrate by omission two principles of command and control of multi-national forces. These are:

1 there are degrees of and limitations on command and control of national forces under foreign command;
2 there is always a national override on foreign command of national contingents. This is often referred to as 'parallel command'.

To see this in illustration, we shall have to turn to NATO doctrine in this respect. The issues are regrettably less clear in UN practice, where the UN uses the terminology, but often not the underlying doctrine, of NATO.

Modern military forces seldom operate in a single-service environment, and this is also true of peacekeeping forces. For example, air forces provide strategic and sometimes tactical mobility, deliver relief supplies by a variety of methods, provide close air support and enforce no-fly measures. Air forces have also provided medical evacuations, which have saved both civilian and military lives. Naval forces provide strategic lift and logistic support, and participate in sanctions enforcements. Naval personnel have also served as UNMOs, most notably in riverine operations in Latin America and Southeast Asia. These operations, whether in war or in peace, which are co-operatively conducted by different military services, are called *joint operations*.

It is equally unusual that modern military operations are conducted by one nation unilaterally, but are normally multilateral, multi-national coalition undertakings. These are referred to as *combined operations*; again, the terminology is applicable both to war and to peace operations.

Modern peace operations are joint and combined operations. As I have said, the procedures for command and control of such operations are most highly developed in NATO doctrine, the adaptation of which to UN operations is only partial. To understand what should be, and what many troop contributors, and thus the officers and men of those contingents expect should be, we must review the model.

NATO command and control procedures are based on four degrees of authority. These are:

1 *Full command.* This level of command covers all aspects of the employment of forces: their assignment to a theatre of operations, their employment under a

multi-national commander, their detailed logistic support, personnel administration (which includes discipline, promotions and honours and awards) and the termination of the mission. As this is never delegated to a multi-national commander, but is retained exclusively by governments, it is often referred to as 'national command'. The national command chain will usually terminate in theatre with a national contingent commander, who may be a senior appointment in the field force headquarters, or may be the national field force commander, or may be a dedicated appointment with his or her own headquarters. *This is referred to as the strategic level of command and operations.*

2 *Operational command.* This is the highest station in the multi-national force command structure. It will normally be assigned to the most senior international commander having direct responsibility for a given national contingent. That senior commander – in NATO, termed the 'Major NATO Commander (MNC)'; in the United States, normally the FC – has the responsibility to employ the national contingent, *en bloc*, to achieve the assigned and agreed mission. Usually, the area of operations of the national contingent is specified as well. In NATO, the Canadian Brigade was stationed in southern Germany, for operations in the NATO Central Region; in UNPROFOR, the Canadian battalion was initially stationed in Sector West – when that was to be changed, the change was proposed to the Canadian Government for approval. Operational command may not be delegated to a subordinate commander. *This is referred to as the operational level of command and operations.*

3 *Operational control.* The commander having been assigned operational command may place the national force under the operational control of one of his subordinate commands for the purposes of exercising tactical control of operations. There are several limitations on his control: the mission and the area of operations are as specified, and may not be changed by him, and the contingent, of whatever size, will operate continuously under dedicated national command, and all integral national components will remain under their national commander – the units may not be detached, either wholly or partly, for whatever exigencies may arise, without recourse to the entire international chain of command to seek national governmental approval. *This is the tactical level of operations.* In NATO, the Canadian Brigade was earmarked for the operational control of either a German or an American division as a reserve formation and counter-penetration force; the national command terminus was with Canadian Forces Base Europe. In UNPROFOR, the Canadian battalion was initially under the operational control of Sector West; the role of national command representative was first with the Canadian Major General who was the Deputy Force Commander; later a Canadian Contingent Commander with his own staff was established.

4 *Coordinating authority.* This is a temporary measure designed to provide coordination, usually when two formations must occupy the same area, as for example in a passage of lines (of one unit through another), or the crossing of a major obstacle such as a minefield or a river. In peacekeeping operations, this is most often a logistics coordinating mechanism, as for example in controlling

movement on a main supply route. The orders specifying coordinating authority will detail all measures, including the effective timings during which this authority will obtain.

The 'parallel command', so often identified as a weakness in peacekeeping operations, is indeed nothing more than a fact of coalition military operations – and it always has been, at least throughout the previous century. The problem is not that the parallelism exists – it is well known and widely appreciated, but seldom resorted to, in NATO operations.[7] The problem in peacekeeping operations is the frequency with which national command is invoked, which is a function not of a weak doctrine, but is rather a reflection of a lack of trust, of a perceived lack of professionalism, in UN commanders. In the case of the Canadian deployment to Srebrenica, the parallel command system is very much a dog that did not bark when it should have.

There is nothing doctrinally or necessarily inherent in the command and control of peacekeeping operations that has not for long been characteristic of the operations of military coalitions. Gradations of command and control, and parallel structures, both authorize and limit combined operations, just as ROE authorize and limit the application of armed force. Current doctrines governing this have been developing and progressing for the past 50 years, and have been closely derived from the experiences of two world wars in the half-century before that.[8] That the United Nations, and the civilian partners to modern peace operations, have not kept pace with this evolution, is not to fault the doctrine. Unrealistic expectations, demands for seamless structures, are neither helpful nor realistic. The doctrine is not dogma: it consists of guides unto the wise, not laws unto fools. Until replaced with better procedures – which will demand of coalitions, of the practitioners and of the policy-makers, more professionalism – this is probably as good as it gets.[9] For the present state of the art, this is a code worth tackling, and the effort put into the exercise by those concerned to develop real, empathetic partnerships, will be rewarded.

To say, however, that this is as good as it may get, *given current practices*, is not to pronounce the last word, and does not rule out qualitative improvements in the exercise of strategic command and control of forces. To consider this aspect further, we must exhume for re-examination the Military Staff Committee (MSC).

21

THE MILITARY STAFF COMMITTEE
Reveille, or last post?

The Secretary-General of the United Nations has recently estimated that there are in the Secretariat only about 32 military officers. This is fewer than the number of officers normally required for one battalion of about 5–600 soldiers, yet the United Nations in 2005 had about 50,000 peacekeepers in Africa alone. This is approximately the equivalent of two, 20,000-strong divisions, which might be organized into a corps. If so organized, as are nearly all European forces and NATO, each of those two divisions would have a staff of over 100 officers, and there would be nearly 500 officers in the corps headquarters . Thus, by European norms, at least 700 officers would be involved in the operational-level command and control of those 50,000 African peacekeepers. Moreover, those 30-odd officers in New York are not a staff in themselves, but are scattered 'advisors' and 'duty officers', generally of relatively junior rank and scarcely in any position to provide the special expertise so urgently and clearly required of modern peace operations. Thus, as Trevor Findlay has described the results of these omissions, Secretaries-General, 'with the notable exceptions of Dag Hammarskjold and possibly Kofi Annan, have been essentially militarily illiterate'.[1] The Charter has specifically provided that it should be otherwise.

Article 46 of the Charter provides that 'Plans for the application of armed force shall be made by the Security Council with the assistance of the Military Staff Committee', and Article 47.1 provides that:

> There shall be established a Military Staff Committee to advise and assist the Security Council on all questions relating to the Security Council's military requirements for the maintenance of international peace and security, the employment and command of forces placed at its disposal, the regulation of armaments, and possible disarmament.

In accordance with Article 47.2, 'The Military Staff Committee shall consist of the Chiefs of Staff of the permanent members of the Security Council or their representatives'. Accordingly, the MSC was created nearly a half-century ago, and has since remained nearly dormant, not even meeting to inaugurate successive Chairmen, who merely rotate through the office each month in alphabetical order of the five Permanent Members of the Security Council.

There are several reasons why this has been so, but no good ones why this situation need continue to obtain.

Throughout the Cold War, it was common practise that major powers did not participate in peacekeeping operations. Similarly, NATO members were also commonly excluded from such operations. There were exceptions; most notably the Canadians, Danes and Norwegians, and the British provided contingents for UNFICYP principally because that Force could not operate without the support of the British Sovereign Base Areas (SBAs) on Cyprus. The MSC was therefore seen as unable to exercise any command and control of operations in which the nations which they represent took so little part, operations of which they were so little representative. This was especially true as matters of international peace and security were seen as almost entirely of regional significance, and were generally regulated by regional treaties.[2] There were of course no peacekeeping operations in Europe. Thus the largely Euro-Atlantic MSC, quite aside from the East-West split characteristic of a bi-polar world, and a polarized world body, was considered unsuitable even to advise on the very issues and operations it had been created to help oversee. The situation was allowed to drift on like this with little (if any) re-examination, despite indications of changing circumstances as we began to emerge from the Cold War. This drift was likely due in no small part to a generally suspicious attitude towards, when not a distinct hostility to peacekeeping operations, on the part of just those powers who provided the MSC. There was (and there remains) as well an institutional resistance by some of those same members to *any* measures that might have strengthened *any* of the capacities of the United Nations.

This drift must now be brought to an end, and it is now timely and urgent that we re-examine in full what the Charter said over 50 years ago, in founding the MSC.

The drafters of the Charter seem to have anticipated with fair accuracy just the criticisms that have been levelled against the MSC. The same article – 47.2 – which specifies that the MSC be constituted from the permanent five members of the Council, also provided that 'Any member of the United Nations not represented on the Committee shall be invited by the Committee to be associated with it when the efficient discharge of the Committee's responsibilities requires the participation of that member in its work.' That article continues, saying (in 47.4) that 'The Military Staff Committee, with the authorisation of the Security Council and after consultation with appropriate regional agencies, may establish regional sub-committees'.

It therefore seems clear that a re-reading of the Charter provisions, and a re-examination of criticisms become anachronisms, are in order. The major powers, such as remain, are now commonly engaged in peace operations, either as Blue Helmets or as 'regional arrangements or agencies', in the latter case acting in accordance with a UN mandate (as specified in Article 53.1); in 2005 every permanent member of the Council had troops in the field on peace operations. Most NATO member states are now engaged in peace operations, either as out-of-area NATO forces or as Blue Helmets, not infrequently both simultaneously.[3] As the Charter provides, the MSC might (and should) include representatives of troop contributor nations and/or sponsors; as the Charter provides, the MSC might (and should) establish regional sub-committees. Criticisms that the MSC does not represent troop contributors or that it lacks regional representation and authority, are much less true than heretofore, and need not continue to be so at all.

The United Nations lacks an adequate command and control capacity for wide-ranging and robust military operations not by prescription, but by omission. Had the world body anything like the staff resources of any one of its members, not to say anything like any of the European agencies, it would have or could soon develop the required structures and capabilities. When the members agreed, as they did in accordance with Article 43.1 of the Charter, 'to make available to the Security Council...armed forces, assistance and facilities', that could in no way have been intended to exclude the staff function, nor can it retrospectively be implied that such was the case. As Michael C. Williams has written, 'the strategic direction of armed forces at the disposal of the UN cannot be addressed until the Military Staff Committee is resuscitated'.[4] If for whatever reasons – whether hostility towards the United Nations, or to peacekeeping – the MSC cannot be awakened from its long sleep, then it must be replaced by another body which will fulfil the functions that the members, in agreeing to the Charter, have agreed that the United Nations is to have.

Resuscitating the MSC would not solve all the problems of civil-military, international-regional, NGO-management issues bedevilling modern peace operations. Of course, the larger community of organizations and agencies involved in peace-building face analogous problems of coordination, control and direction.[5] Nevertheless, effective strategic command and control of military operations, providing a centre those operations now do not find in the present organization of DPKO would be a good – indeed, an essential – start to ameliorating and eventually helping to resolve present cultural and operational conflicts in the wider community of peace support contributors.

22

REACTION FORCES

'Compulsory and irreproachable idleness'[1]

It is becoming highly stylish in international organizations to develop rapid-reaction forces. The United Nations has been wrangling about them for its entire history. NATO, principally a security organization, has them of course. The EU is doing it, and the OSCE will soon, so they say, have a rapid-reaction capability. There seems ample justification for this: we are constantly being reminded of the importance of rapid reaction, and we are invited to infer that, if only the mission could have been mounted more rapidly, countless lives might have been spared, expenses and mistakes avoided or ameliorated, suffering relieved. This is of course all quite true, but the reasons for delays in mounting missions being misunderstood, the wrong remedies are being proposed.

It is all a matter of getting the questions right: why are missions so slow to materialize? And what are the factors which slow or delay deployment? But, even before we can pose these very important questions, we must ask, what is 'readiness'?

Military forces can be maintained at very high states of readiness for reasonably protracted periods, but there are limitations on the maintenance of extreme readiness states. We will leave aside the matter of mobilization of citizen (conscript) armies; these are seldom if ever the stuff of peace operations. A military unit at a very high state of readiness, however, has only the one task: to be ready. It can do very little else: little maintenance, because critical equipment is often packed, or may even have been moved off to a departure point; it can do little training, for the same reason, and it usually cannot leave its barracks, while the home station may offer little in the way of training facilities. Members cannot usually be spared to go on long career courses, which are how a unit develops its members, and itself. Few can be allowed to go on leave. And what if there is a natural disaster or emergency – is this unit left out, even if they themselves may be living in the effected community?

Eventually, confinement and idleness take their toll, and units must be rotated to another assignment. There then ensues a lengthy and complicated transfer of responsibilities, the new unit must be trained for its new role – which, remember, consists almost solely of waiting – and their equipment must be prepared for deployment, which usually means taking most of it away from them. Ideally, an extra set of gear (costing many millions of dollars) is procured for the rapid reaction force, and that equipment is maintained in readiness (usually at a sea port or at an airhead). If this rotation is done each six months, the sustainment base for this task will be three times the commitment: one unit warned for the task, one on standby and one just off standby. Plus the fourth set of equipment. You really cannot sit on bayonets.

And that is just the military who, as we have said, are never alone. Where then are the civilians who bring the skills and the capacities to counteract the real effects of these complex emergencies, the people who will operate in this security environment the military are to have created? The OSCE has been developing a bold plan to produce very rapidly a panoply of experts in all fields – up to 1,000 persons in two months is one scenario – by a process of pre-mission training in the member states, then using that training as the gateway to a data-base which will provide for the readiness, *and the continuing availability*, of those rostered for rapid deployment.

So, while it may be seen that military units can, at great expense, inconvenience and loss of efficiency, be maintained at a high degree of readiness, and we might or might not be optimistic about the OSCE's' attempt to emulate that readiness with a civilian force – the soldiers are at least getting paid to sit on their bayonets – the effort is, first: unnecessary, and, second: not addressing the real problems of the deployment of a peace force.

The readiness of any military force worthy of the name, to undertake almost any reasonable mission, has never really been a major determining factor in the time it takes to get it operational in a theatre. Nor, unless the mission is a very clear and omnipresent one, such as in the Cold War, is it necessary that forces be dedicated solely to readiness tasks.

NATO has for many years distinguished between *committed* forces and *earmarked*. forces. The former were, as the term implies, committed to a single mission, they were stationed in or adjacent to the operational area and had all their equipment with them. They could balance training and maintenance just as in their home garrison. Nevertheless, leave and out of area courses were strictly controlled, and there were plans for the evacuation of non-combatants. The nearly 30,000 Canadians who lived within 50 kilometres of each other along the Rhine actually represented a relatively large concentration of the Canadian population, and were referred to, even shown on local maps, as 'Klein Kanada'. Nearly 25% of the personnel of these units turned over each year, and units 'rotated' every two-to-three years. However, there was an alternative method.

The Allied Commander's Mobile Forces (Land and Air) (AMF[L] and [A]) were *earmarked* for the reinforcement of the Northern and Southern Regions of NATO. Except for a skeleton headquarters, mostly a plans and training staff, located in Heidelberg, the units remained in home garrisons. In the Canadian case, a battalion group (about 1,200 personnel) was marked for operations in the Northern Region, which was in Norway. Critical equipment was stored in Norway, and a full scale of equipment was with the battalion in its garrison in

Canada. Each second year, the key appointments of the national contingents assembled in the putative area of operations for reconnaissance and a review of plans; each second year the complete units moved to Norway for manoeuvres. Otherwise, they lived a pretty normal, domestic garrison life in Canada: they fought floods and fires, they assisted corrections officials in prison incidents, and they were even sent to Cyprus for service with UNFICYP. Except for a few weeks of each year, when they were either on reconnaissance or on manoeuvres in Norway, they cost NATO nothing, and were available to Canada and to their parent formations in Canada for whatever might from time to time have been the normal tasks of the Canadian Forces. They were, nevertheless, at a very high state of readiness to commence their move to Norway, and the facilities to get them there were, like them, clearly identified and planned – they were *earmarked*.

It is this method of maintaining stand-by forces which the United Nations is now emulating in the formation of the Standby High Readiness Brigade – SHIRBRIG: a brigade-sized, multi-national force, with a dedicated headquarters and staff in Copenhagen, and a data-base of warned – *earmarked* – units domestically garrisoned in troop contributor nations.[2] As with AMF(L), SHIRBRIG's only costs will be for the headquarters, for reconnaissance and, possibly, some exercise concentrations which may be held.

But there is an important difference between forces held in readiness for a specific mission, such as NATO forces during the Cold War, and those forces held in readiness for no specific task, such as SHIRBRIG. For what role, in what area, are peace forces being readied, trained? For what climate? What terrain? What threat? This lack of a specific mission will probably mean no collective training. While individuals may be highly trained, a military unit is like a football team, and it must train as a team, but in this scenario it likely cannot. Who wants to read in their morning paper that a multi-national military force is preparing for operations on their soil?

Parallels to civilians who might be earmarked in the AMF(L)/SHIRBRIG manner for future operations are not clearly apparent. The OSCE believes that training can produce increased readiness, but this needs to be proven. As Hertic, Sapcanin and Woodward have observed, 'The OHR,...required six months to one year after the Dayton signing to set up shop and to establish field offices'; we can assume that those persons who staffed that office were well qualified for their jobs and, given the lengthy Dayton 'process', had in most cases been adequately forewarned of their duties.[3] While one can generalize in forecasting military employment, and individuals and units can be quite flexible as to the specifics of their possible tasks, this is much less true of civilians, and will require a massive data base to ensure the responding populations will provide all the required 'fits' when needs become known. The shelf life of that data base may be cause for some concern – soldiers in units are fairly easy to track, but the availability of individual civilians who have had two weeks training cannot be guaranteed much beyond the last day of the training – if even then. *Readiness* must not be confused with *availability*.[4]

Of course, individuals with aid organizations and NGOs will move quickly to the scene of an emergency, and are often the first on the scene, but not usually in the right numbers, and often not in the right skill-sets. And such critical events as elections seldom fall under the term 'emergency'. This does suggest that, whether or not these are jobs for soldiers, there may be a start-up period during which quite literally only soldiers can do them. Fortunately for OHR, the deployment of IFOR, the military security 'entity', was nearly complete by the end of 1995.

So, much of the discussion on rapid-reaction forces is misdirected and lacking context. Military units need not be singly tasked for readiness, need not be separated from their equipment, they need not even leave home – they need not be *committed* – to become highly effective, very quickly, if they are *earmarked*: warned, trained, prepared. Earmarked forces can deploy quickly, buying time for other agencies, deterring if not entirely preventing the worst-case scenario. Such military readiness is efficient, relatively inexpensive and maximally cost-effective. *But military readiness is not the real issue*, indeed the whole question of response times is not a personnel matter at all. *The real issues are political and diplomatic.*

To deploy an international, or any other mission, the requirements are for the political will to act, the mandate, the logistics to support the deployment and financial support. These must be available for the start-up of the mission, and for its sustainment throughout its life. To the extent that readiness of the mission members or units are or are seen to be the limiting factors on deployment, the international community is being invited to look in the wrong direction – the wrong questions are being asked, and the answers to those readiness-type questions will not materially effect deployment timings.

There has not been a major crisis in the world since the end of the Cold War, which was in any form a surprise. Not Yugoslavia, especially not the civil war in Bosnia-Herzegovina, not Rwanda, not Somalia, not Kosovo. There was throughout the 1990s no lack of information on the clear and (then) present dangers of the situations in Macedonia, in Montenegro and in Vojvodina. There was in those past crises no lack of high-readiness military forces, which might have been made available for an initial intervention. In respect of Montenegro and Vjojvodina, no forces are known to have been placed on any increased states of alert – unless those of Yugoslavia. What was lacking then is what is generally lacking still today: the will to act. Nor was there any consensus, and thus no effective preventive measures planned or even contemplated, on those who thought then still to be below the event horizon – and, against all odds, expected to stay there.

Logistics are much more likely to effect deployment than is commonly realized. Indeed, deployment is an exercise in strategic mobility. There are only three nations in the world with an aviation heavy lift capacity: Russia, the Ukraine and the United States. While the employment of the ground troops of atleast two of those three is fraught with diplomatic and military limitations, many careful observers have suggested that a specialized role for those three nations might be provision of strategic mobility assets for the deployment of a force. However, no such plans exist in any general form. Furthermore, while it seems relatively easy to find the combat forces, principally infantry, it is much more difficult to find the specialized administrative and communications units which are crucial to a well-balanced force. This suggests another specialized role for nations, possibly even smaller nations, which have traditionally had expeditionary force roles which have called up just those types of units in their force structures. Thus, when the Canadian infantry battalion was refused for UNEF (in Gaza) in 1956, possibly a greater contribution was made to the efficacy of the Force by the substitution of logistics elements of the Canadian Army, and for the same reason Canada contributed initially a signals unit for the headquarters of UNAMIR in Rwanda, and later a medical company.

The matter of financial support is too complex to go into here in any detail; suffice it to say that finances are obviously another sine qua non, of starting and sustaining an operation. There are two aspects of this tangled web, which need to be more clearly appreciated and addressed.

The first of these is that, even after the politicians and the diplomats have hammered out a Security Council Resolution, the budget still must be approved in the Fifth Committee of the General Assembly. It is here, away from the public, even from the political, gaze, that dangerous compromises have been made. The Namibia operation (UNTAG – United Nations Transition Assistance Group) offers a case in point:

As early as 1978, the Security Council, in its resolution 435, had approved the so-called Settlement Proposal, which was a detailed peace plan. The plan had been subjected to continuous review and refinement for ten years, until the Brazzaville Protocol in the autumn of 1988 fixed 1 April 1989 as the implementation start date. All parties met at UN HQ on 22 December, a meeting overshadowed by the tragic crash the day before of Pan American Airlines Flight 101, in which one of the delegates had perished.

The plan prepared in this series of meetings was approved by the Security Council in its resolution 629 on 16 January 1989. However, the Security Council, *despite unanimous approval of the plan*, asked for 'cost-saving measures'. In his response, presented to the Security Council on 23 January, the Secretary-General was at pains to stress the importance of the implementation start date of 1 April: if the operation did not start on that date, 'it would not be possible to complete the electoral process before the onset of the rainy season in mid-November, which would make many of the tracks in Northern Namibia impassable'. The Secretary-General 'also stressed that a minimum of six weeks would be needed for the deployment of UNTAG... This could not begin until the General Assembly had approved the budget.' Nevertheless, the Security Council did not approve the Secretary-General's report until 16 February. That same day the Secretary-General had still to face the General Assembly, where he warned that 'the lead times for delivery of many essential items of equipment were already past'.

Notwithstanding the urgency of the situation, the General Assembly did not approve the budget for the operation until 1 March. By the time deployment commenced, six weeks had been lost, the budget had been nearly halved and the military contingent strength reduced from 7,500 to 4,650. *And this was the implementation of a plan approved by the Security Council 10 years previously.*[5]

The second problem is one of sustainment: in order to marshal political support, and this often means domestic political support, short-term mandates are adopted. Partly in a spirit of optimism, partly to disarm the critics who oppose an operation on financial (or other) grounds, pretence is maintained that the intervention is of strictly limited duration. Aside from sending precisely the wrong message about the staying power of the mission, the short-term mandate can actually become self-fulfilling, as the mission runs out of financial resources, is forced into unhealthy compromises and is eventually judged wanting, not on financial grounds, but precisely on the operational grounds it cannot address just because it is under-funded. As the Brahimi Report puts it:

> The Secretariat must tell the Security Council what it needs to know, not what it wants to hear, when recommending force and other resource levels for a new mission, and it must set those levels according to realistic scenarios that take into account likely challenges to implementation. Security Council mandates, in turn, should reflect the clarity that peace-keeping operations require for unity of effort when they deploy into potentially dangerous situations.... The current practice is for the Secretary-General to be given a Security Council Resolution specifying troop levels on paper, not knowing whether he will be given the troops and other personnel that the mission needs to perform effectively, or whether they will be properly equipped.[6]

Admittedly, it will never be a simple matter to align all these requirements, and waiting until the last is in place may be a very long wait. That also is not necessary. Recall the definition, and the use of 'battle procedure', to describe the method by which troops are warned and prepared for operations. The essence of these preparations is concurrent activity: no unit, or part of a unit, ever does nothing, once they have been warned for an operation – *unless it is a UN operation.*

Customarily in UN operations, no preparatory action may be taken until the mandate has been approved in the Security Council, the requests for troops have been formally passed to and accepted by the contributors, and the force structure has been approved. For one example:

Fighting began in Croatia in June 1991, and UNSCR 713 of 25 September signalled the United Nations involvement in the crisis – the EU and the CSCE (Conference on Security and Cooperation in Europe – which became the OSCE on 1 January 1995) were already engaged. Mr Vance, acting as the Personal Envoy of the Secretary-General, convened talks with the Presidents of Serbia and Croatia and the EU in Geneva on 23 November. An agreement on a cease-fire was quickly achieved and was endorsed by the Security Council in UNSCR 721 of

27 November. UNSCR 724 approved the Secretary-General's plan for a peace force on 15 December. The Implementing Accord on the Cease Fire was signed in Sarajevo on 2 January 1992. On 21 February UNSCR 743 established UNPROFOR, and full deployment of the Force was authorized on 7 April.[7]

By April, more than six months had gone by since the initial involvement of the United Nations, four months since a cease-fire had been agreed, two months since the mandate had been approved. Fighting had continued during this period, the cease-fire was in danger of unravelling altogether, and all the devastations of civil war were continuing. The deployment was becoming increasingly urgent and difficult. However, and despite the fact that from the autumn of 1991 it had been widely believed that there would eventually be a peacekeeping force in Yugoslavia, prior to the approval of the Force mandate in February there had been absolutely no preparations authorized in any form among the very high-readiness NATO units stationed – committed – in Germany. This was despite the fact that substantial elements of those NATO forces had already been declared redundant to their former missions, and were in many cases expecting repatriation to their home countries in the course of 1992.

Of course, they began to study the potential mission, and to prepare themselves as well as they could. However, in the case at least of the Canadians, the troops were forbidden to take any preparatory measures of any kind. Vehicles could not be painted UN-white, no UN insignia were even held anywhere in Canadian Forces Europe, no personnel measures, not even medical, could be authorized. No plans were developed with German railways for the move. No staff tables were drafted. Every German Auto Club map of Yugoslavia disappeared from the garages and bookstores all around Klein Kanada (the first topographical maps of Bosnia-Herzegovina to be received by the Canadians in HQ UNPROFOR, were purchased for them from the JNA by the Canadian Embassy in Belgrade, and were dated 1943). However, beyond briefing each other almost daily on events, absolutely nothing was done – until all the New York ducks were lined up. The forces were then committed, precipitously, to do in days what they had been forbidden for four months even to plan.

In the event, the Russian and Canadian rail moves were a shambles. The 'NATO' Canadian trains were held at the border with 'neutral' Austria until clearances could be arranged, and the main body of the Russian contingent, which we once feared might have taken Mannheim in four days, took 40 days to reach Belgrade. Canadian combat engineers began demining in Croatia in green berets, on the very day on which the Bosnia Muslim Territorial Defence Forces adopted the green beret as their headdress. It eventually took nearly three months to complete the UNPROFOR deployment, well over half of which consisted of European-based contingents, which took place over routes now driven by tourists in one or two days.

Nearly all of that deployment time could have been saved if sensible and prudent military preparations had been allowed to run concurrently with the diplomatic process.

To be sure, there will always and for good reason be limitations on preparations, on reconnaissance, especially if sensitive negotiations are being conducted at the time. There will be restrictions on the taking into use of UN insignia before the force has been approved and its formation authorized. These restrictions must, however, be set against the time lost when concurrent activity is prohibited.

It must be asked why Canadian NATO troops who had trained for years to clear their barracks on alert in less than two hours, took several weeks to get to Croatia – just ahead of the Russians, whose own readiness had for fifty years caused the NATO troops to remain at such a high degree of alertness. It was not military readiness or mobility, which failed here; neither was the issue in the spring of 1992. The international community, which was so anxious to see UNPROFOR arrive in Croatia, and still cannot understand why they were not there sooner, is looking in the wrong direction when increased *military* readiness is discussed.

Romeo Dallaire, the Canadian FC of the UNAMIR in 1994, provides another and much more tragic example of the affects of non-military factors on a military deployment:

UNAMIR had been established by the Security Council on 24 September 1993, with an authorized strength of 2,500 troops. Due to the failure of the Arusha Accords, which it had been the Force mission to oversee, the Security Council on 21 April 1994 reduced the Force to a strength of 250. In response to the genocide, which had been foretold by UNAMIR as early as 11 January 1994, the Security Council on 17 May approved Resolution 918 which *inter alia* increased the strength of Dallaire's force and authorized the deployment of 5,500 personnel over the next thirty days. Nevertheless, thirty-one days later on 19 June Dallaire had a troop strength of only 503, all ranks. On that day, the Secretary-General informed the Security Council that the new force, called UNAMIR 2, would in fact not be fully operational for another three months. When Dallaire left the mission in August, three months after the authorization of 5,500 troops, the Force strength had reached barely 1,000.

However the nearly-simultaneous French intervention in Rwanda, Operation Turquoise, shows in stark contrast what military forces can do, when the will and the support exist.

Dallaire was informed of the operation on 18 June. The French forces began to arrive in Rwanda on 22 June, even before the Security Council had approved their deployment. By 30 June, France had assembled in Rwanda a force of 2,500 soldiers, equipped with sophisticated command and control systems, over 100 armoured vehicles, heavy mortars, reconnaissance and medium troop-lift helicopters, even ground-attack and reconnaissance jet aircraft. The French deployment had been supported by an international air armada of at least four nations. That entire process of mounting and deployment had for the French taken just twelve days. Dallaire, who had in three months received only about 750 reinforcements, wryly concluded, 'So much for the argument that the international community did not have the means to rapidly deploy UNAMIR 2.'[8]

Far more time could be saved by the judicious conduct of troop preparations concurrently with political preparations, than can be gained by a host of inconvenient, uncomfortable and very expensive 'readiness' measures. As Nash puts it, albeit in the slightly different context of overall mission structure, 'we spend far too much time talking about the military issues and too little time analyzing the political, economic, social and broader security problems that must be resolved'[9]; his comment is equally appropriate to the mounting of the mission.

The political will to act, an achievable mandate, a mission adequately supported logistically and financially, are the requirements for the launch of a mission. The sustainment of these factors will equal the sustainment of the mission. Whipping up military forces to go somewhere and do something may be good for public consumption, but it is not good peacekeeping. Getting them out there and leaving them to shift for themselves is not either.

It is not faster reactions that are needed, it is better grounding in the first place, and then 'remaining seized of the matter'. The answer to faster deployment times is not military reactions, which are or can be quite fast enough. The delays are in the political processes. The effects of these delays can be greatly if not almost entirely offset by concurrent activity: 'the essence of battle procedure'.

Part IV

TRAINING AND EDUCATION
A part of the main

23

GENERAL

It may seem simplistic to say that the gaps between the military and the civilians may be sutured up by better training and education. Yet, if that is so, then why have the comprehensive international, regional and national efforts to do just that, left the problems unsolved? The answer to this is not quantitative – there are lots of training opportunities out there – rather the problems are qualitative, and there are four qualitative aspects of current training methods and offerings which are critical. These are:

- Is this training, or is it education? What is the difference?
- Where is the training/education being offered, and by who?
- Who participates in the training/education?
- How and why is participation in training opportunities limited or wasted?

These issues will be addressed in the next chapters of this part.

24

TRAINING VS. EDUCATION

According to *Fowler*, 'education is a drawing out and not a putting in'. The analogy is a useful illustration of the difference between education and training. *The Concise Oxford* says that to train is to 'bring a person...to a desired state or standard of efficiency'; to educate is to 'give intellectual and moral training'; education refers *inter alia* to the 'development of character or moral powers'. We may allow these distinctions to become blurred, as they often are in practice, but they have something important to tell us, and they must not be completely ignored.

Trainers refer to the intended results of their work as *responses*, and these are described as *motor, verbal* and *attitudinal*:

- *Motor* responses refer to skills which can be performed to prescribed standards.
- *Verbal* responses demonstrate knowledge, as for example of procedures, policies, organizations, *cultures*.
- *Attitudinal* responses refer principally to perceptions, and may be a combination of all three types of response – for example, even a beginner's *skill* in the use of an equipment may reduce aversion to the equipment (such as a four-wheel drive vehicle); *knowledge* of an organization's history may facilitate a healthier and more participative response to the organization; these should combine to produce a positive *attitudinal* response.

Training generally imparts skills and knowledge non-judgementally, thus trainers will usually be comfortable with programmes for motor and verbal responses. They are often extremely uneasy with attitudinal responses, which are indeed more properly the subject of *education*. In training, the subject, so long as it is within the competence of the trainer and appropriate to the trainee, is less important than the method. In education, the subject is all-important, the method, so long as it produces the desired response, is less important. Nevertheless, trainers and educators alike are very uncomfortable with any attempt to influence what learners may think, and educators will only gingerly approach *how* they may think.

One important result of this is that attitudinal responses are seldom if ever directly the subject either of training or of education. Attitudes are of course *influenced* by training and education, but that is almost never *the intention*. However, if it is attitudes which most influence cross-cultural responses, then this is a vital aspect of training and education which is not receiving the emphasis it deserves.

Most cross-cultural training never refers to organizational problems, and I have seldom heard a trainer refer to an organization as a culture. Cross-cultural trainers usually describe a general problem in general terms: religion, language, customs, history; it is then up to individuals to decide what they make of that, and how they might apply that very general description of a potential problem to their own specific situation and experience. Moreover, cross-cultural training is almost always aimed to prepare a mission member for encountering the *host nation* culture; such training is almost never aimed at preparing one to encounter the culture of the *other organizations* in the mission area, but that is where the most critical and problematic relationships will be built – or will not.

We can now allow the blurring to resume, and will henceforth refer to both training and education generally as 'training'. The distinctions are not to be ignored, however, and we may return to them as we find it useful or necessary to do so.

25

TRAINING ESTABLISHMENTS

Where and by who?

The International Association of Peacekeeping Training Centres was founded in Canada in 1995 at the Pearson Peacekeeping Training Centre. The aim of the Association is 'to facilitate communication and exchange of information between the various peacekeeping training centres and/or among people responsible for, and interested in, peacekeeping training'.[1] In addition to annual meetings, the Association maintains a data-base of training centres and resources world-wide, and the list of such centres and resources, governmental and non-governmental, civilian and military, is over thirty-five pages long.

So there are a lot of opportunities out there, but the complete picture of capacity building through training is not good. This is not the place to describe them all in any detail, but a review of some of the more prominent training organizations will reveal a pattern of under-use, under-funding, and generally dubious sustainability and effect. Another major issue for training is the extent to which it forms a part of the mainstream of an organization, in other words, is or is not an integral component of the culture of a given agency or body. I will examine these two aspects: the resources, and how they are used, in the following sections of this chapter.

Peacekeeping Training at the United Nations

The United Nations is not in a position directly to conduct training for most of those allocated to a peace mission, as the military and police components are provided by member states; civilians come from the Secretariat, from other UN missions or may be hired directly for the mission. There being no effective standby system, deployments are usually in emergencies, and training generally forms little or no part of a mission deployment. Through such agencies as the United Nations Institute for Training and Research (UNITAR) and the Training and Evaluation Service (TES), the United Nation provides standards, packages, documents and advice which it can only hope will be followed in preparing contingents for deployments. There is not much the United Nations can do about non-compliance with its suggestions, thus there are really no mandatory standards at all, and of course practice has too often tended to reflect this omission.

The United Nations actually does not do much better with training its own Secretariat personnel, than it does in recommending how others train theirs. Despite the power and authority of mission Chief Administrative Officers (CAOs), and after two generations of steady complaints about CAOs from Heads of Missions, and especially from Force Commanders, the United Nations introduced formal training for CAOs only in the last two years – most of the incumbents have thus likely had no training for their posts. A recent review of UN information operations found that:

> the major personnel problem is insufficient training for information operations. ... Training for specific public information issues has a role, but there is no training for the nuts and bolts of public information... Some fifty percent of staff are not adequately trained or prepared for missions in the field.[2]

Training and capacity building at the Organization for Security and Cooperation in Europe

Since its inception the OSCE has been marked by an appreciation of training and capacity building as essential components of the culture of the Organization. Because the OSCE is staffed mostly by individuals seconded from other bodies and governments and who therefore spend a relatively short time with the Organization, it was early appreciated that some sense of corporate identity would be essential to generally transient members. Thus the OSCE was also from the outset concerned with that very ticklish aspect of training, that of the attitudinal response.

This matter of attitudes was made more urgent in the course of reviewing the conduct of the Kosovo Verification Mission (KVM), which was the first large-scale deployment for the Organization. Fielded in late 1998 to verify compliance by Yugoslavia with the Rambouillet agreements (which had been formalized by United Nations Security Council Resolution 1199), the Mission was assembled and deployed in great haste, only to be equally hastily withdrawn as the situation there deteriorated in the spring of 1999. It detracts not in the slightest from the bravery and the ingenuity of those men and women who pursued an almost impossible mission, to say that administratively and in many other ways that Mission dealt the OSCE some experiences it did not wish to repeat. Therefore, as it appeared that 1999 would in fact see an even larger role for the OSCE in Kosovo, many of the lessons learned from the KVM formed the core of a very deliberate training programme for members to be employed with the new OSCE Mission in Kosovo (OMiK).

An extremely important aspect of that training was considered to be the implanting of a sense of corporate identity in these highly qualified and experienced new members, who nevertheless were essentially without any knowledge of the history, organization or culture of the OSCE, nor of the highly sensitive and critical role the Organization was assuming in Kosovo. The results of those omissions had been seen before, and so this training programme addressed deliberately the attitudes of these new members. For just one example of organizational culture, the OSCE is the only European security organization to have declared itself (at the 1992 Helsinki Summit) 'a regional arrangement in the sense of Chapter VIII of the Charter of the United Nations'. This self-definition was central to defining for the OSCE a working relationship with the United Nations, which in turn did much to enable the architecture of the Kosovo mission to be designed as it was.

In addition to the culture of the OSCE, efforts were also made to address the cultural and organizational aspects of the other 'pillars' of the UNMIK as well as the 'international security presence' (KFOR), as this was to be one of the most ambitious multi-dimensional missions yet undertaken, with the most advanced inter-agency structure yet seen in modern peace operations.

There was another, more subtle challenge facing the OSCE as it prepared for the OMiK mission: the OSCE is not as well known in Europe as it should be, and it is nearly unknown in the United States. Nevertheless, the OSCE was from the outset of the Kosovo mission the one organization with the most experience in a very tough neighbourhood. Thus it was anticipated that members of OMiK would be the subject of some curiosity, and it was vital that the experiences of the Organization – many of the original OMiK deployment were returning ex-KVM – should be of value to the international and regional community, and not just in Kosovo. It was appreciated that the best representative of any organization is a thoroughly knowledgeable member, therefore no effort was spared to educate the new members (and some not so new) as to the history and structures of the Organization and of its new mission.

In the event, this training programme was so successful that in January 2000 it was expanded to include all new members of the OSCE: all missions and new Secretariat members. That the training had slowed deployment somewhat, was seen to have been more than offset by the rapidity with which well-informed and well-oriented members became effective in very demanding circumstances. The initial sessions in Vienna were soon being supplemented by more mission-specific training in the mission area, and training sections were soon thereafter created in most missions, to take fullest advantage of the induction sessions in Vienna. Eventually, the Training and Capacity Building Section of the Secretariat in Vienna was taking further training to missions in the field; by 2002 the field mission training sections were fully independent of Vienna and were actually offering training to each other.

The OSCE then has always seen training as capacity building, and this is a mainstream function of recruiting and staffing for the Organization. The time and other resources to conduct this training have never been seriously challenged, and there can be few members who will need to be convinced that this is time and effort well spent. The OSCE has a reputation for being a training organization, and the reputation is well deserved.

144

NATO

The importance of the OSCE's emphasis on corporate knowledge and identity is demonstrated in its contrast to NATO.

NATO officers will generally deny a Chapter VIII relationship with the United Nations. They will state that NATO is a purely security alliance, that its right of self-protection cannot be dependant on the United Nations and that only the North Atlantic Council can determine the security situation of the Alliance. They add that NATO may be from time to time and in certain circumstances influenced by the Charter, but never limited by it. (NATO also generally shuns any UN control of their forces in the field, probably because they know so little of the role or the evolution of the office of the SRSG.)

Notwithstanding those reservations, however, the North Atlantic Treaty (Washington, DC, 4 April 1949) refers in Article 2 to the elimination of 'conflict in...international economic policies' and encourages 'economic cooperation'; in Article 5 it provides for 'collective self-defence recognised by Article 51 of the Charter of the United Nations'; Article 7 reaffirms 'the primary responsibility of the Security Council for the maintenance of international peace and security'.

Given this lack of knowledge of the organizational culture of the United Nations, *and of their own*, the NATO attitudes towards soft power issues, the Charter of the United Nations and the office of the SRSG, are predictably negative. However, if NATO is to continue to lead peace operations coalitions as in Bosnia and in Kosovo, quite a few of its officers will need some broader organizational and cultural awareness training – they might start with some knowledge of their own charter.

The Lester B. Pearson Canadian International Peacekeeping Training Centre: an example of an academic NGO

The Pearson Peacekeeping Centre (PPC) opened in Cornwallis, Nova Scotia in April 1995. It was intended to be an entirely civilian NGO, designed to present a range of course training and education packages for 'The New Peacekeeping Partnership'. This was at the time two novel concepts: (1) that there was a de facto *partnership* among a range of military, police and civilian agencies, including among the latter such diverse functions as democratization, relief, development, human rights and governance; and (2) that an NGO with an academic mandate was the best way to conduct the largely educative process of further nurturing and developing the partnership. Indeed both were ideas whose time had come – the dawning of an era of post-Cold War peacekeeping coincided with an outbreak of complex humanitarian emergencies which urgently needed the 'New Peacekeeping Partnership' to be effective, and the replacement of wars between states with internal conflicts demanded a re-examination of the legal and doctrinal bases of intervention strategies. Barely two years after its founding, the PPC was recognized by the United Nations as an accredited academic NGO.

The range of courses offered by the PPC was extensive, and the quality of the training and of the trainees was very high. Canada had created a world-class institute entirely in keeping with the nation's reputation at the UN and in international peacekeeping. It was clearly recognized that a good deal of learning is from other trainees, and the direction of the training was highly participative, with only the minimum of direction from the faculty. Scales fell from eyes, shibboleths were demolished, attitudes were changed. Among the many lessons learned were tolerance and cultural awareness, and a degree of inter-agency, inter-organizational empathy was instilled. The only drawback to this was that such a climate existed almost nowhere in the real world of field operations.

But all was not well, and the survival of the PPC is now seriously jeopardized.

In the first place, it was to be a civilian organization, and it was hoped that the majority of the participants would be civilian. Neither developed as had been foreseen. The faculty members were nearly all serving or ex-military, and so were the participants. This was unavoidable from the outset, when gratis military contributions to the faculty, and serving officers financed from military unit training and temporary duty budgets (and these nearly all Canadian) got the Centre going and helped it grow. However, the expedient became over time a norm which the Centre could not shake off, and the civilian identity of the Centre has always been questioned. One participant observed that the Centre seemed more Canadian than International, and there were many reservations about the military influence. Partly as a result of this perception of the Centre as a quasi-military activity, it has been further mis-appreciated as duplicating and/or competing with Canadian Forces activities and establishments – and the Department of National Defence is one of the co-sponsors of the PPC.

The second problem was that the Centre was at first entirely financed by the Canadian Government. However, it had always been foreseen that the Centre would eventually become financially independent – it was initially estimated that this would occur over the first five years, or by 2000. By 1998 it was clear that nothing of the sort would be possible, not then nor likely ever. The government then extended the subsidy, but began to tighten the screws. In 2004 it was announced that the Centre would locate its training and operations, and all seconded military faculty, in Ottawa, and that the PPC would virtually abandon an infrastructure, the refurbishment and maintenance of which had had much to do with the continuing poverty of the Centre.

It is far from clear what the future of this Centre may be. It has never been realistic to expect it to become self-supporting, nor is government support of such a facility in any way improper or inappropriate. The PPC has proven to the world that training and education are critical to the New Peacekeeping Partnership, and that the sort of training offered there these past nine years makes great strides in fostering and maintaining the empathetic relationships so crucial to modern peace operations.

The United States Army Peacekeeping Institute

The difficulties of the US Army Peacekeeping Institute have already been very briefly referred to (see Chapter 12). A colleague who has been on the faculties of both that institute and of the PPC has shared with me his observations.

The Army-Air Force Center for Low Intensity Conflict had already been closed in 1995. Then, in the summer of 2002, the US Army, despite its desperate need for expertise in peacekeeping and stability operations, moved to disband the US Army Peacekeeping Institute. This was the only organization in the US forces which could provide the Army with access to resources, information, context, civilian agency contacts, concepts and doctrine, to prepare the Army for peace operations. Nevertheless, the Institute was scheduled to close effective 1 October 2003.

Apparently, the leadership of the US Army wanted the Institute closed, simply because peacekeeping had come to equate nation building, and nation building necessarily implies a long-term intervention. Not only does this not meet the military's criteria for declaring early success and going home, it clearly suits neither the Secretary of Defence, nor almost anyone else in the US government.

However, in early 2004 it became obvious to the US Congress that the United States had won the war in Iraq but was in serious danger of losing the peace, and the US Army Peacekeeping Institute was granted a reprieve. It was nearly too late: staff and resources had been dispersed (the library was nearly entirely given away, and all files were dispersed or destroyed). What can be saved remains to be seen, but the prestige of the Institute has been dealt a nearly-mortal blow. Even the terms 'peace' and 'peacekeeping' may not be used: the newspeak is 'stability' – in a report I was provided by my colleague, the phrase 'peace, now stability operations' recurs, *in full*, fourteen times in one paragraph.

It is ironic that, notwithstanding that a strong characteristic of the military culture is training and education, this training institution should have been so short-lived, and that it exists today so precariously. Or, on the other hand, perhaps it is only natural that, if you want to do something, you train for it; if you don't, you don't, and if you are by chance doing so anyway, you stop – immediately. It is a further irony that the Congress, in correctly assessing the importance of training, seems to be telling the US government and Defence Department something it very much wants them to hear, and is using the US military's own language to say it. And, as we have seen, no one needs to hear this more than does the US military.

Out of Africa always something new: the Kofi Annan International Peacekeeping Training Centre, Ghana[3]

The Kofi Annan International Peacekeeping Training Centre (KAIPTC) was conceived as a regional centre of excellence for sub-Saharan Africa as early as 1997, but it did not open its doors and commence training until early 2004. Initially located on the premises of the Ghana Staff College, it is now in its own facilities. It now offers training covering a full spectrum of civil, military and police functions at the operational level. Some of the courses already conducted have used trainers and training materials from Canada's PPC. The KAIPTC aims to train at least 1,000 persons per year. In addition, it will host, organize and support several regional and international conferences and seminars.

While aiming to foster and maintain regional and international understanding and cooperation, the KAIPTC is itself an example of cooperation. In addition to the training support from the PPC, Canada has donated over $2 million over three years, France has donated staff officers and helped design courses and other training materials, Germany has assisted in the construction of the training facil- ities, and the United Kingdom and the Netherlands have assisted in training development. Other contributors and supporters include Denmark, Norway, the EU, India, Japan, Switzerland and the United States.

This is an imaginative and widely supported effort to improve regional peace operations capacities in the most efficient and cost-effective manner: by training, *in situ*, the people who are needed, to do the jobs they are needed to do. It is to be hoped that the Kofi Annan Centre will serve as a model of *international* cooperation for *regional* capacity building.

26

TRAINING FOR WHOM?

An important aspect of the military organizational culture is training: if you want to do something, you train for it. There is individual training, which imparts the skills and the knowledge to do the job. Collective training builds the attitudes, skills and knowledge required to assemble an effective team. In professional advancement training, individual potential is built and tested, not for the present job but for future employment, thereby building collective capacities on the enhanced potential of individuals. Refresher training is designed to maintain skill levels especially where they may have been unused for a period. There is also lateral training, in which new equipments and techniques are introduced to experienced practitioners: a pilot changing aircraft types may undergo up to a year of cross-training to the new type.

The process is constant throughout a military career; training is the peace-time or garrison equivalent of war, and the training staff is normally a component of the operations staff. Officers and NCOs undergo course training, and testing, at every rank level and often at every employment station. Career progression in peace-time militaries is often largely based on course training performance. In any unit budget, training is probably the major financial commitment, and will include funds for travel and accommodations for courses outside the unit. In my 36-year career, I spent nearly five years on courses, plus one year of self-study for promotion examinations.

In 1994, as the crisis in Rwanda was peaking and refugees were fleeing in thousands, refugee camps, especially at Goma in Zaire, were flooded with people in very desperate straits. The combined populations of the camps was many thousands, supplies and the supply system were totally inadequate, security was non-existent and the political situation, especially in regard to the government of Zaire, was extremely delicate. Dallaire described the situation in Goma as 'truly desperate'.[1] The person in charge of one of the largest of these camps, whom I later came to know well, was brave and resourceful far beyond any norm, and was thirty years old and had a baccalaureate degree in English.

A major problem at the PPC was and has remained an inability to attract sufficient civilian participation on its courses. Absent the required civilian enrolment, the courses tended to fill up with military officers. As I have indicated, the military recognized their need, saw these courses as the natural fulfilment of the need and had funds for just this sort of training in their budgets. The PPC could not turn away fee-paying participants, but this overload of military participants was not quite what *they* needed.

In the first place, students learn at least as much from each other as from the faculty. However, this group was skewed far too far towards a military population, which was not at all representative of the community that is really out there in the missions. The military and the civilians were not meeting and were not training together, and this had to have an effect on the quality of the mutual learning experience.

Second, it was clear that it was really the civilians who needed this training the most – the military were the most experienced and the best trained at their own jobs, and the best of them would eventually learn most of what they needed to know about other organizations. The training simply was not reaching the civilian members of that New Peacekeeping Partnership, and it was urgent to find out why.

The answer turned out to be as simple as it was confounding: money, and, to a lesser extent, time. And, as might have been expected, the NGOs expressed it most clearly. They existed, so they said, almost entirely on donor funding. Donor funding was often earmarked, and donors commonly expected that all or nearly all their contributions would go directly to a target beneficiary population. That expectation was usually around 90%, which must reach the beneficiaries. There was almost no funding for personnel support, and usually none at all for training, travel or accommodations outside the mission area. Moreover, mission members were contracted only for the duration of their assignment to a specific mission; in between assignments they were usually unemployed. Those few NGOs who made it to the PPC almost always did so at their own expense, and too often left the courses when called to the next mission – they of course had no choice in this. Nor was it clear that, having undergone this training, their employability was in any way enhanced – the few senior members of NGOs to whom I have spoken of this were generally dismissive of the value of this training.

But more than numbers have been changing for NGOs, and many if not most are today far from the shoe-string affairs they traditionally have been, notwithstanding that this is an image they usually like to maintain.

There are two common sources of NGO funding which are not directly from donors.

The first is an increasing practice of 'implementing partnerships': of smaller with larger NGOs, and the larger NGOs with specialized agencies of the United Nations (such as UNHCR), and with regional organizations (such as the EU), or with international organizations (such as the International Committee of the Red Cross (ICRC)). By 1994, the EU was distributing 67% of its relief aid through NGOs, and the ICRC estimated that NGOs had in 1999 disbursed more money than had the World Bank.

The second source of NGO funds is from governments themselves: one-fourth of Oxfam's funding in 1999 was from the British Government and the EU.

World Vision US received U$55 million from the US government in 1998, and MSF gets 46% of its funding from government sources. There were 120 new NGOs founded between 1993 and 1997; all but 9 were funded entirely by governments.[2]

Nor are donors that parsimonious in good causes. According to the OECD, NGOs raised U$5.5 billion from private donors in 1997,[3] and in 2001, US corporations and corporate donors gave over U$9 billion to 'non-profits'.[4] In 1999, one corporate donor gave U$25 million to one NGO.[5]

So we see that NGOs are not the bow-and-arrow outfits of legend: they are often more like big businesses, with big budgets, capabilities and responsibilities, and they are changing accordingly. One of the major climatic changes for NGOs is that they are being required to conform to the accountability standards of the governmental, corporate, international and regional organizations with whom they form partnerships, and from whom they derive assignments and funding. The EU recently imposed its auditors on some of its tributary NGOs; one of the results of this was a scramble for hiring of accountants and bookkeepers – in organizations which had prided themselves on their avoidance of bureaucracy. Is operational training for NGO staff any less affordable, or desirable, or necessary, than accounting?

There is resistance to training, especially in the case of short-term employees, whose contracts are more often measured in months than in years. There is simply no slack time in the employment of a given member.

Both problems – time and money – must be overcome. They are not truly functions of structure nor of necessary practice, but of attitudes and priorities. The money required for training is not large – most courses at the PPC are two weeks, and cost about U$2,000, including full board. The time for this training could be built into contracts, and might even be an incentive at the beginning of a contract, and/or a reward upon completion of a contract. The NGO community is constantly exchanging and recycling employees, and it should not be beyond the imagination of the managers of NGOs to see an advantage to the entire community to be derived from better trained and prepared individuals. Funds could easily be earmarked, for example, two weeks of course training per person year, plus travel expenses. The cost-effectiveness of such a modest outlay for training is hard to deny.

Civilians need to learn from the military in this matter, and the civilian organizational culture must adapt to the increasing complexity and importance of their roles by providing for training as an important component of personnel resource management, as well as building and maintaining their capacities to organize and manage projects and missions. The money and the time are not major impositions, and the rewards will be out of all proportion to the effort. The urgency of an emergency deployment is not addressed by sending ill-prepared and untrained people into the field. When there is no alternative and deployment cannot be slowed, training for replacement personnel must begin immediately. There may be some reasons for less well-prepared workers in an emergency deployment; there is no excuse whatsoever when their replacements are no better prepared.

27

SO WHAT?

Whether we speak of the purpose of training or of education, we really mean the desired motor, verbal and attitudinal responses which prepare the subjects for their duties, measure their performance and ensure that they can perform as expected *before* they encounter the operational environment. Most trainers and trainees are comfortable with the demands of motor and verbal responses – skills and knowledge – they are usually embedded in job descriptions, and there are proven techniques for teaching and testing in these areas. Almost no trainers are at all comfortable with attitudinal responses – what people think, and how that should be influenced or changed. Yet it is precisely in attitudes that culture resides, and it is attitudes which determine whether culture will be a barrier or a window, an obstacle or an opportunity. This is the challenge of education – and almost no one is doing anything about it.

Our relationship to our culture, and our encounters with other cultures, are largely a function of attitudes. Prejudice is generally a function of a negative attitude: fear, envy, anger, resentment – the FEAR reaction. The best counter to this will be education. A particularly important aspect of this education will be information about the organizational cultures we may encounter: the history, doctrines and structures of other organizations. The aim will be to replace ignorance with knowledge, and thereby replace antipathy with empathy. These organizational cultures then should be at the centre of cross-cultural training – but this is almost never the case.

The military culture has training thoroughly embedded in the mainstream of the organizations – skill and knowledge training for the jobs at hand, and for those which might arise either as contingencies of further employment or of career advancement. But as we have seen, peacekeeping training is in some jeopardy in two countries which are major contributors to military forces in peace operations: the United States and Canada. These two examples are especially unfortunate, as the Canadians have much to offer, while the US forces have much to learn. Of particular concern are lost opportunities for concurrent civilian and military learning, about each other and about themselves in relation to each other. The military, being culturally oriented towards the study of their profession, will probably suffer least from this, and will learn on the job what they need to know – if they acknowledge that they need to know it. The civilians, especially the NGOs, believe that they do not have the resources to undergo training, and have little or no place in their culture for continuing training and education.

The requirement, then, is for civilians and the military to train together as they expect to work together. The mutual learning experience inherent in such training and education will go far in achieving the desired attitudinal responses – it is nearly impossible for people who have successfully trained together *not* to work together successfully.

Part V

CONCLUSION

Peacekeeping is a 50-year old enterprise that has evolved rapidly in the past decade from a traditional, primarily military model of observing cease fires and force separations after inter-state wars, to incorporate a complex model of many elements, military and civilian, working together to build peace in the dangerous aftermath of civil wars.

(The Brahimi Report)[1]

28

TO SAVE SUCCEEDING
GENERATIONS . . .

It seems that the surest way to create divisions among the international agencies, who are supposed to be cooperating, and who must co-operate, is to have similar organizations pursuing similar goals – we lose no time in running Occam's Razor down nearly invisible lines, separating from each other elements more alike than different. Is the similarity of roles itself a threat, making competition a perceived imperative, like the territorial behaviour of humans (as well as other animals)? Is it, on the other hand, a basic dissimilarity in goals, which, despite the similarity in means, is the fundamental conflict? Do we *need* conflict with other agencies to maintain the cohesion of *our* group? Perhaps our most serious differences will indeed arise when we do the same or nearly the same things for different reasons. Where we may be unsure of our aims, we may not be able to clearly identify the sources of our differences. Thus the peacekeeper who wants mines cleared to maintain tactical mobility may be fated to clash with the Mine Action Centre which wants to restore agriculture; the Convoy Escort Commander who insists on freedom of movement, with the humanitarian worker who wants to feed and cloth the needy; the soldiers who restored the hospital with a view to stopping the fighting, with those who wanted only to run a medical facility.

Perhaps the most basic conflict may be between those who, on the one hand, will link assistance to results which contribute to a restoration of a peaceful society and the resolution of the conflict and, on the other hand, those whose mission is disinterested aid for its own sake, relieving suffering without conditions. The former will see the latter as contributing little to resolution, possibly prolonging conflict; the reverse view will be of an occupying force, imposing stereotyped solutions as the price of assistance, caring more for the mission than for those in danger. Stewart Patrick, quoting Johnson's observation that the road to Hell is certainly paved with good intentions, has noted these mixed views of conditionality as a characteristic of aid organizations and agencies:

> Since post-conflict recovery is a political as well as an economic undertaking, donors need to reconcile their support for peace implementation with their assistance programmes for reconstruction and self-sustaining growth. In practice, this does not always occur. Rather, the two strategies may be

designed, pursued, and supervised along two independent tracks. One result has been a clash between an 'economic' approach to conditionality, which makes aid contingent on economic performance, and a 'political' approach, which makes it contingent on peace-building objectives.[2]

Bell put it even more starkly:

> First, a merely victim-based strategy doesn't work, and probably prolongs the war. It is misdirected in practice, because it tends to feed the front-line troops. And it is morally objectionable, because it stands impartially between good and evil...and unwittingly helps the aggressor by acting as his welfare agency.[3]

However and whenever the soldiers and 'the Humans' may act together to resolve these fundamental differences, it is certainly true that much needs to be done to define military roles in support of humanitarian operations. The uses of force, the importance of consent in enforcement operations, and the inter-relationship of these two factors, will continue to cause unease, but that is an unease the military shares with their civilian partners. The presence of the military forces of major powers, the role of major regional organizations and the inter-relationships of international, regional, governmental and NGOs – all these issues are connected, and need to be resolved in a coherent body of doctrine before it can be expected that cohesive, effective joint practices will emerge.

As affairs now stand, *ad hoc* developments at the tactical level are outpacing the development of reasoned principles at the strategic level. The risks of these *ad hoc* developments are not just for *post facto* and unhelpful criticisms, but real damage is done to the development of joint practices when fragmented policies are seen at 'senior levels' to have been contravened at working levels. It takes very little experience of Monday Morning coaching for wariness to replace whatever trust may have been emerging; finger-pointing easily and quickly displaces cooperation; the game of credit-and-blame becomes the only game in town. Prudent managers will find it more congenial and re-assuring to rely only on their own organizations for whatever is vital to their own role; concern for duplications and omissions will be 'something for another day'. What the media will make of these conflicts among those attempting to 'manage' the 'real' conflict, will usually be little helpful.

Cooperation carries risks, as does building confidence, and these risks can easily be made to seem unacceptable. Someone, somehow, somewhere has to take the first steps to building empathetic relationships, concentrating on the mission as a whole rather than on one's own organizational contribution, image and recognition. As John C. Cockell has written in his excellent article, 'Civil-Military Responses to Security Challenges':

> While NATO has taken some steps to institutionalize aspects of civil-military interaction in the field, these have generally been only to the

extent of formalized *cooperation*. Military and civilian actors are, however, increasingly having to address security sector issues in an overlapping and interdependent manner. In this context, a growing strategic interest is to apply comparative advantage in mission roles, a goal that implies the *coordination* of joint operational and tactical action to achieve shared objectives in the field. Coordination of joint action, in turn, requires a qualitative shift in civil-military interaction toward integrated planning and shared operations, *with all the compromises implicit in loss of autonomy on both sides*.[4]

It seems that the military may be the best positioned to take these first steps. The militaries are attempting to do this by learning about the other partners; their next and urgent measures will be to present themselves better, as the better partners they are attempting to become. They must reform their language, and they must reach out to those who may not welcome their initiative, who may indeed resent their presence and will not welcome being reminded how important the military presence is to 'their' operation. The challenge, of avoiding that FEAR-reaction is one of some delicacy. The best time to address these problems is before deployment on a mission, and the best way to do this is by programmes of mutual and concurrent training for civilian and military members. A vital component of such training will be cross-cultural training, where the putative partner agencies and individuals are introduced to each other as cultures.

But of course the military acting alone – even to the extent of inviting civilians to participate in military training and mission preparations – will achieve little more than they already have. The civilians, for their part, need to stop wishing the military away on one day and complaining of lack of cooperation on the next. Civilians need first to accept that the military presence will often be a *sine qua non* of an effective international response to a humanitarian emergency. As Michael Williams describes the situation:

> The reluctance of civilians and NGOs to engage with the military must also be addressed. ... these groups have relied on the military for their security. The military's ability to protect movement, communications and logistics should encourage more active partnerships to strengthen humanitarian and post-conflict operations. ... NGOs should strive for greater understanding of the military mindset. This would help to avoid many of the culture clashes that marred the complex emergency operations of the 1990s.[5]

In other words, civilians must learn to use the tools and the capabilities which the military will afford them intelligently and actively. Civilians thus would clearly benefit from a culture of training but, as we have seen, most receive little or none.

In the long run, however, it is abundantly clear that building real interoperability at the working levels cannot be solely a bottom-up process.

It is imperative that cooperation among agencies and organizations be initiated at the highest levels – mandated specifically from the outset, and thereafter maintained as a central goal of management at all levels. Bottom-up cooperation is fragile and episodic, depending almost entirely on personalities and having little corporate longevity. 'Grass roots' learning is seldom transportable to a new or another mission, even where the new mission may be – it usually is – staffed with experienced persons. It is common that cooperation in a new mission, despite the collective experience levels of the members of the various organizations and agencies, is very slow to develop: as Sir Michael Rose observed, it took those two years before the NGO community learned to trust and to work with the military in Bosnia-Herzegovina. It has nevertheless been reliably reported that, despite hard-won local achievements, cooperation, especially between the military and the NGOs, reverted to near zero with the arrival of the NATO-led IFOR in Bosnia. Those start-up periods are simply not available to be wasted re-learning lessons so expensively, often so tragically, already learnt elsewhere – but gone missing in transit. The record so far in this regard, is one of lessons *not* learnt.[6] This must change. Again, John Cockell has summarized the challenges:

> Most structured civil-military interaction in the Balkans has been at the middle, or operational, level. Tactical coordination is increasingly common but is more subject to ad hoc arrangements and variations. Least explored to date has been strategic coordination between head-quarters in New York/Genevea, Brussels/Mons, and Vienna.[7]

I conclude with reference to a conference, 'Interagency Cooperation in Peace Operations', held at the US Army Command and General Staff College in October 1994, and this quote from the forward to the Conference Record:

> Is it a soldier's job to feed starving babies, to rebuild sewers, to hand out bags of flour, or run refugee camps? The short answer is no. Soldiers are remarkably versatile, but they can do none of these things as well as their civilian counterparts. They become involved because these tasks are often fraught with danger. Soldiers can sometimes achieve what civilians cannot. This should not blind either to the contributions of each. Getting the balance right . . . is the challenge of interagency cooperation.

Anachronistic stereotypes, prejudices, cultural conflicts, historical apocrypha – these are usually central to the conflicts the international community has intervened to treat, to resolve. Importing similar conflicts of our own is neither professional nor workable. If the military are to function as well as they can, *as well as they must*, in humanitarian operations, their capabilities and their limitations must be clearly understood by their potential partners. I have suggested that this will be most effectively accomplished, and enduring and trusting relationships built, by training and education. This is the best, if not the only way for us to move beyond the Freudian narcissism of minor differences, to a point where not minor differences but close similarities are the common perception, and these similarities are perceived as enabling cooperation, not productive of competition. No one would deny that tribalism, authoritarianism, association with violence are a part of the military culture. The military are for their part too often guilty of chauvinism, which can indeed arise in any community as a short cut to cohesiveness, but that will be a cohesiveness formed at the expense of any useful external relationships.

Any attempt to get beyond these stereotypes should quickly reveal groups and groupings of institutions which have evolved further and more rapidly than is commonly perceived. The ICRC has been rethinking its relationship to the military, and the practice of NGOs forming implementing partnerships with international and regional organizations is reforming their attitude towards accountability. Creating and sustaining empathetic relationships among agencies, and replacing the ill-informed, adversarial relationships which have seemed up to now to dominate the scene, clearly must be a mutual affair. Nevertheless, it seems now both opportune and urgent for the military to take the lead in building understanding of their roles, their limitations, their capacities for partnership – that is, by transparent and frank dissemination of the military organizational culture. The people we say we have gone out to help are usually in urgent need of our help, and there is no time for the pettiness which has informed too many of our experiences, still less are their emergencies our learning opportunities – any longer. We have now been at this for over fifty years, and it is time to act like it. We must put disinformation, ignorance and prejudice – FEAR – behind us – or stay home.

NOTES

1 PREFACE

1 Winston Churchill, *My Early Life*, Chapter 26.
2 *Foreign Affairs* January/February 2000, 'Campaign 2000: Promoting the National Interest', by Condaleeza Rice, p. 53.
3 *International Herald Tribune*, 19 June 2002.
4 *International Herald Tribune*, 'American General Calls for More Afghanistan Aid', 10 July 2003.

2 INTRODUCTION

1 Williams, Michael C., *Civil-Military Relations and Peacekeeping*, The International Institute for Strategic Studies, Adelphi Paper 321, Oxford University Press, London, 1998 (p. 37).
2 *The Responsibility to Protect: Report of the International Commission on Intervention and State Sovereignty*, p. 9 (italics added). The International Development Research Centre, Ottawa, 2001 (see also http://www.idrc.ca).
3 United States Institute for Peace, *Special Report: Balkans Returns*, Washington, DC, 21 December 1999.
4 *The Economist*, 'Sins of the Secular Missionaries', 27 January 2000.
5 Weiss, Thomas G., 'The United Nations in Civil Wars', in *The New Peacekeeping Partnership*, Alex Morrisson (ed.), The Lester B. Pearson Canadian International Peacekeeping Training Centre, Cornwallis, NS, 1995, p. 78.
6 Williams, *Civil-Military Relations and Peacekeeping*, Oxford University Press, London, 1998, pp. 38–40.
7 Hobsbawm, Eric, *Age of Extremes: The Short Twentieth Century, 1914–1991*, Abacus, London, 1995, p. x.
8 The so-called Hartford Experiments were a series of studies, conducted in the United States in the 1920s, which were intended to measure the effects on workers' output of various factors such as structures and environment. Curiously, however, *all* experiments resulted in improved performance, apparently proving only that workers who know themselves to be the subjects of an experiment will *always* improve their performances.
9 Lew MacKenzie has described a briefing in Sarajevo for Cyrus Vance on 16 April 1992, 'to the background noise of mortar fire a few hundred yards from our building'. Mr Vance later described this with characteristic good humour as 'the Vance Effect'; it had in fact been relatively quiet in Sarajevo up to his arrival. (See MacKenzie, Lewis, *Peacekeeper: The Road to Sarajevo*, Harper Collins, Toronto, 1993, pp. 226–7.)

10 Dana Priest, in her excellent book, *The Mission*, of which I have made much use, describes an Indonesian officer as having earned 'the Special Forces' coveted parachute insignia for mastering a risky high-altitude, low opening jump' (p. 220). There is no such thing as a Special Forces parachute insignia, and many thousands of civilians manage just this sort of descent every weekend. Elsewhere, she describes how an American ambassador in Indonesia 'proudly carried a well-worn 7th Special Forces Group commemorative coin in his pocket' (p. 236) – which is just why they have those things. Military leg-pulls are a sort of an art.

11 In fact, when a Canadian colleague who had been a Military Attache' in Moscow warned me that my Russians were almost certainly KGB, I was able to reply in paraphrase of Lincoln's response on being warned that Grant drank.

3 TOWARDS A CONCEPTUAL FRAMEWORK FOR PEACE OPERATIONS

1 We now are to have a chance to reassess the degree of American responsibility for the delayed response to genocide in Rwanda in 1994. On 9 September 2004 Secretary of State Colin Powell told the Security Council that 'the United States viewed the killings, rapes and destruction of homes in the Darfur region of western Sudan as genocide, and he called on the United Nations Security Council to recognize that the situation required urgent action'. The spokesman for the Secretary-General said that 'the declaration has no immediate effect on the role or the obligations of the United Nations', but admitted that it could be an invocation of Article 8 of the 1948 Convention on the Prevention of the Crime of Genocide, for the first time calling on the United Nations to take action. *Could be?* That convention, which *might* have been invoked, and *might* be calling for action, is 56 years old. Meanwhile, Pakistan opposed calls for action, if that is indeed what was called for on 9 September – we are not sure – preferring to continue to 'engage'with the government of Sudan, and the Chinese ambassador suggested that China might veto a Security Council resolution. See *The New York Times*, 'Powell Says Rapes and Killings in Sudan Are Genocide', by Steven R. Weisman, 10 September 2004.

2 Phjlip Gourevitch, 'Never Againism', in *Granta*, 87, Autumn 2004, London, p. 116.

3 See Gita Katarina Swamy, 'Humanitarian Assistance', in *A Concise Encyclopedia of the United Nations*, Helmut Volger (ed.), Kluwer Law International, The Hague, 2002.

4 Duffield, Mark, *Global Governance and the New Wars: The Merging of Development and Security*, Zed Books, London, 2002, pp. 11, 18.

5 'Peacekeeping and Critical Theory', by Michael Pugh, in *International Peacekeeping*, Vol. 11, Spring 2004, pp. 39–58 (see especially p. 47).

6 *The Blue Helmets: A Review of UN Peacekeeping Operations*, 2nd edn, UN Department of Information, New York, 1990, p. 5.

7 May, Terry M., *Historical Dictionary of Multi-national Peacekeeping*, The Scarecrow Press, Lanham, MD, 1996, p. 139.

8 *Blue Helmets, A Review of UN Peacekeeping Operations* p. 4: 'as United Nations practice has evolved over the years, a peacekeeping operation has come to be defined as *an operation involving military personnel*' (italics added).

9 Pugh, Ibid.

10 May, *Historical Dictionary of Multi-national Peacekeeping*, The Scarecrow Press, Lanham, MD, p. 2 (italics added).

11 Pugh, p. 48.

12 Ibid., p. 41.

13 'Media images of a humanitarian emergency and their (often negative) effect on the perceptions of the conflict among public and policy-makers alike, can impact the entire peace process.' See Lehmann, Ingrid, *Peacekeeping and Public Information: Caught in the Crossfire*, Frank Cass, London, 1998, p. 2. See also Figure 1, p. 17.

14 Boutros Boutros-Ghali, *An Agenda for Peace: Preventive Diplomacy, Peacemaking and Peace-keeping*, The United Nations, New York, 1992.

15 See Schmidl, Ernst, 'Agenda for Peace', in *A Concise Encyclopedia of the United Nations*, Helmut Volger (ed.), Kluwer Law International, The Hague, 2002.

16 *Supplement to an Agenda for Peace: Position Paper of the Secretary-General on the Occasion of the Fiftieth Anniversary of the United Nations*, A/5060/; S/1995/1, 3 January 1995.

17 See Martin Shaw, 'The Contemporary Mode of Warfare?' in *Review of International Political Economy*, Vol. 7, No. 1, 2000, pp. 171–80; and Mary Kaldor, *New and Old Wars: Organized Violence in a Global Era*, Stanford University Press, Stanford, 1999, pp. 90–111.

18 Kaldor, *New and Old Wars: Organized Violence in a Global Era*, p. 11.

19 Rose, General Sir Michael, *Fighting for Peace: Lessons from Bosnia*, Harvill Press, Great Britain, 1998, p. xviii. Sir Michael was Commander, UNPROFOR Bosnia-Herzegovina from January 1994 to January 1995.

20 Pugh, pp. 39–58.

21 Ibid., p. 41.

22 Duffield, *Global Governance and the New Wars*, p. 11. Duffield regards war 'as a given' (p. 13), and 'violence is seen as creating a level playing field on which the possibilities of development have been renewed and invigorated'. This is what Douglas Hurd meant when he called it 'the level killing field'. Thus Duffield is able to refer to the efforts of Military Professional Resources Incorporated, and their Democracy Transition Assistance Programme in Croatia in 1995 as simply 'a training programme for officers, NCOs and civilians... in such areas as leadership, management and civil-military operations' (pp. 66–7). In fact, that 'assistance' enabled the Croatian Army to expel from Western Slavonia and the Krajine the Serbs who had lived there since the late seventeenth century, which is nearly as long as White Europeans have been in North America. See Arbuckle, James, *The Level Killing Fields of Yugoslavia: An Observer Returns*, The Pearson Press, Cornwallis, 1998, pp. 2–3. This was done not only with the full knowledge (not the approval) of the US government, but with the active advice of the US State Department – see Holbrooke, Richard, *To End a War*, The Modern Library, New York, 1998, pp. 62–3, 72–3, 238.

23 Neoliberalism and neorealism 'are concerned with maintaining a status quo because they take the prevailing international framework as uncontestable', therefore conflict resolution theories characteristically undertake 'problem-solving to smooth the functioning of the system'. Pugh, 'Peacekeeping and Critical Theory', p. 40.

24 Paris, Roland, *At War's End: Building Peace After Civil Conflict*, Cambridge University Press, Cambridge, 2004, pp. 6–7.

25 Ibid., pp. 40–51.

26 *The OSCE Magazine*, May 2004, No. 2, 'Soul Searching in Kosovo: March Violence Poses Challenge to International Community', by Bryan Hopkinson.

27 Glendon, Mary Ann, *A World Made New: Eleanor Roosevelt and the Universal Declaration of Human Rights*, Random House Trade Paperbacks, New York, 2001, p. xvi.

28 Ibid., pp. 166, 176.

29 Ibid., p. 170.

30 Ibid., p. 228.

31 *Foreign Affairs*, November/December 2001, 'The Attack on Human Rights', by Michael Ignatieff, pp. 102–16.

32 Ignatieff, pp. 104–5.

4 INTRODUCTION

1 *The Economist*, 'More Dangerous Work Than Ever: Aid Agencies', 20 November 2004 (US edition).
2 The probable original of this was the reference by Lord Erskine (1750–1823) to 'The uncontrolled licentiousness of a brutal and insolent soldier'. The Prime Minister, Edmund Burke, in 1783 referred to the East India Company as 'a rapacious and licentious soldiery'. The Duke of Wellington (1769–1852) would have agreed with them: 'I don't know what effect these men will have upon the enemy, but, by God, they terrify me.' Small wonder that George Bernard Shaw said 'The British soldier can stand up to anything except the British War Office.'
3 The US Army's Joint Readiness Training Centre exercises are 'designed to replicate the myriad...political, military and humanitarian challenges posed by modern peace enforcement operations...(and) include...NGO workers'. See 'PVOs Help US Military Train for Humanitarian Action', from *Monday Developments*, 5 September 1994.
4 From *Crosslines*, The Independent News Journal on Humanitarian Action, Development and World Trends, January 1996.
5 Extract from 'Working Paper, Council of Delegates, 1995', ICRC and International Federation, Council of Delegates, Geneva, 1–2 December 1995 (see http://www.icrc. org/unicc/icrcnew).
6 *The Atlantic Monthly*, 'Peace is Hell', by William Langewiesche, October 2001.
7 Quoted in Dandeker and Gow, 'Military Culture and Strategic Peacekeeping', by Christopher Dandeker and James Gow, in *Peace Operations Between War and Peace*, Erwin A. Schmidl (ed.), Frank Cass, London, 2000.
8 Ibid.
9 *International Herald Tribune*, 'A Human Security Doctrine for Europe, and Beyond: A Force for Intervention', by Mary Kaldor, 30 October 2004, http://iht.com/ articles/541120.html
10 Gabriel, Richard A. and Savage, Paul L., *Crisis in Command: Mismanagement in the Army*, Hill and Wang, New York, 1978, p. 32.

5 THE ROLE AND INFLUENCE OF CULTURES

1 Handy, Charles, *Understanding Organizations: How Understanding the Ways Organizations Actually Work Can Be Used to Manage Them Better*, Oxford University Press, Oxford, 1993, pp. 180–3.
2 Dandeker and Gow, 'Military Culture and Strategic Peacekeeping' by Christopher Dandekar and James Gow, in *Peace Operations Between War and Peace*, Erwin A. Schmidl (ed.), Frank Cass, London, 2000.
3 From *The World as I See It*, by Albert Einstein.
4 Murray, Nicholas, *Aldous Huxley – An English Intellectual*, Little, Brown London, 2002, p. 63.
5 Huxley, Aldous, Brave *New World Revisited*, Harper and Brothers, 1958.
6 Address by the Secretary-General of the United Nations to the Stockholm International Forum for Combating Intolerance, Stockholm, 29 January 2001.

6 COHESION AND CONTINUITY: 'THE CLANGOUR OF THEIR SHIELDS'

1 From *Bugles and a Tiger: A Personal Adventure*, by John Masters, quoted in *The Penguin Book of War – Great Military Writings*, John Keegan (ed.), Penguin, London, 1999.

2 Roberts, Kenneth, *Northwest Passage, Random* House Canada, Toronto, 1964 (originally published 1940).

3 Keegan, John, *The Face of Battle: A Study of Agincourt, Waterloo and the Somme*, Penguin Books, London, 1976, p. 33.

4 Ironically, the term 'tabbed' seems to have originated with the First World War British Army's use of red collar gorgets, 'tabs', to identify General Staff Officers. R.H. Mottram, author of *The Spanish Farm Trilogy*, in describing life in a head-quarters, wrote that 'soon the non-regular, untabbed personnel of the staff outnum-bered the brass hats'. Quoted in Holmes, Richard, *Tommy: The British Soldier on the Western Front 1914–1918*, Harper Collins, London, 2004, p. 238.

5 Stephen Brumwell's excellent book on the raid on St Francis, *White Devil* (Orion Publishing Group, London, 2004), includes as an appendix 'Rogers' "rules to be observed in Ranging Service"'; the version given there makes no reference to the 'code' described by Roberts (and used probably unwittingly by today's US Rangers). Nevertheless, Brumwell is undoubtedly correct when he says that 'Rogers is regarded as the founding father of the American Army's Special Forces units'.

6 Omer Bartov, 'Trauma and Absence: France and Germany 1914–1945', in Paul Addison and Angus Calder (eds) *Time to Kill: The Soldier's Experience of War in the West 1939–45*, London 1997. Quoted in Holmes, *Tommy*, Harper Collins, London, 2004, p. xviii.

7 Fussell, Paul, *The Great War and Modern Memory*, Oxford University Press, Oxford, 1975, p. 12.

8 Ropp, Theodore, *War in the Modern World*, Duke University Press, 1962, p. 180.

9 Fussell, *The Great War and Modern Memory*, pp. 155–9. Fussell considered giving this book the sub-title *An Inquiry into the Curious Literariness of Real Life*. Although Private John Ball is the fictional central character of the epic poem *In Parentheses*, the author of that work, David Jones, who before the war had trained as a draughtsman, served as a Private in the Royal Welch Fusiliers in Flanders from December 1915 to March 1918. On the first day of the Battle of the Somme, on 1 July 1916, the British Army suffered 60,000 casualties, nearly two-thirds of the troops committed to that Battle. The *Oxford Book of English Verse* was 'compact and printed on onion-skin paper, . . . easily carried by men on the move and . . . exercised some influence on the . . . way . . . soldiers described their war'. See *The Times literary Supplement*, 'Ecstasy in the desert', by Robert Irwin, 2 April 2004.

10 Eksteins, Modris, *Rites of Spring: The Great War and the Birth of the Modern Age*, Lester & Orpen Denys, Toronto 1989, p. 71. Although most of Europe did not have leg-islation governing elementary schooling until the 1870s, Prussia had had such legisla-tion since the sixteenth century. In the 1860s, Prussian school enrolment was nearly 100%; in Saxony at the same time the figure was over 100% because so many foreign students were enrolled there. Of course, conscription also tends to spread military culture into the general population, just as it first enrols a broader – and thus better educated – spectrum of the population, and then (at least in peacetime) usually fairly shortly releases them back into the mainstream.

11 Remarque, Erich Maria, *All Quiet on the Western Front*, Ullstein A.G., Berlin, 1928.

12 Ford Maddox Ford, *The Good Soldier*, A. & C. Boni, New York, 1927 (from the Foreword). Ford (1873–1939) served with the Welch Regiment in France, from June 1916 to March 1917, even though he was already 43 years old when he went out.

13 Maurois, Andre, *Proust: Portrait of a Genius*, Carroll and Graf, New York, 1950, pp. 160–6. Proust related how 'the whole of Combray and its surroundings, taking shape and solidity, sprang into being, town and gardens alike, from my cup of tea'. (*Remembrance of Things Past: Swann's Way, Overture.*)

7 A CLOSER LOOK AT MILITARY ORGANIZATIONAL CULTURE

1 A USMC fighter pilot told me that, when flying missions over Bosnia-Herzegovina in 1995, he carried in his cockpit four sets of ROEs: over the Adriatic, entering the target area, engaging a target and exiting the target area (see section on ROE below).

2 See Dallaire, Romeo, *Shake Hands with the Devil: The Failure of Humanity in Rwanda*, Random House Canada, 2003.

3 See *Report of the Independent Inquiry into the Actions of the United Nations During the 1994 Genocide in Rwanda*, 15 December 1999, at http://www.un.org/News/ossg/rwanda_report.htm

4 Respectively: Kofi Annan (UN Secretary-General), Iqbal Riza (Chef-de-Cabinet to the Secretary-General), Jaques-Roger Booh Booh (now said to be writing a book to confound Dallaire, as if he had not already done so) and General Maurice Baril (former Canadian Chief of the Defence Staff).

5 See 'Clinton in Short Visit to Rwanda', All-Africa News Agency, 6 April 1998, at http://www.africanews.org/usaf/stories/19980406_feat1.html: 'We did not immediately call these crimes by their rightful name: genocide'. The observances of the tenth anniversary of the genocide in Rwanda, and several recent books and at least one film, may have served to raise the contemporary consciousness of the omissions of 1994 – if so, then that alone is a good reason for such observances.

6 *Rwanda: The Preventable Genocide*, see: http://www.africanews.org/east/rwanda/stories/20000710/20000710_feat2.html

7 See http://www.ottawacitizen.com/national/000708/4411479.html. Romeo Dallaire was appointed by the Prime Minister of Canada to the Canadian Senate in May 2005.

8 That this perception by America's political and military leaders may have been inaccurate or incomplete has been brilliantly exposed by Krull, Ramsay and Warf: 'The Myth of American Rejectonism', in *Global Dialogue*, Spring 2000. It matters little, in fact, whether or not the perceptions on which the policy was grounded were then or are now accurate: the policy, and its effects, were as described.

9 *The Atlantic Monthly*, 'Peace is Hell', by William Langewiesche, October 2001.

10 Langewiesche, 'Peace is Hell,' October 2001.

11 There were from the outset indications that a British-led force in Afghanistan would interpret its security requirements quite differently: speaking of the current discussions on force planning, an analyst for the Royal United Services Institute said, 'They are prepared to take risks and send small forces into built-up areas, rather than intimidate citizens by sending in large forces in big vehicles, concerned about self-protection.' It was also noted that 'In Bosnia, British peacekeepers are known for going out in T-shirts and playing football with the local people, in contrast to US forces, which are always well-protected. ... But this approach would not be effective unless UK soldiers also had a reputation for discipline and ability in high intensity warfare.' *The Financial Times (London)*, 'A theatre where nobody wants a long run: defence chiefs warn of "overstretch" as talks continue on a peacekeeping force for Afghanistan', by Brian Groom and Alexander Nicoll, 13 December 2001.

12 'In Bosnia and Herzegovina, ... 14 accused have been delivered by SFOR since July 1997. Four of these were delivered this year.' See 'Remarks to the Security Council' by Mme. Carla del Ponte, Prosecutor, the International Criminal Tribunal for the former Yugoslavia, 10 November 1999.

13 *The International Herald Tribune*, 'Stopping Kosovo Attacks on Serbia is a Mission for NATO', by William Pfaff, 1 February 2001.

14 William Nash, in 'Can Soldiers be Peacekeepers and Warriors?', in *NATO Review*, Summer 2001.

15 While it may be fair to accuse the military of a certain cultural myopia, this is not entirely a military characteristic. I once listened to some civilians in OMIK head-quarters in Pristina bewailing the state of the apartments they had found in a devastated capital – they could not even get their laundry done properly, and these people seem never to have *heard* of air conditioning. After several minutes of this, our KFOR liaison officer smilingly excused himself – he had to tidy up his tent, and try to find a wash-board so he could do his laundry. He also had to find a changing room in our building, as the Head of OMIK would not allow him to wear uniform on the premises.

16 Bell, Martin, *In Harm's Way: Reflections of a War-Zone Thug*, Penguin, London, 1996, p. 297.

17 Rose, *Fighting for Peace*, Harvill Press, Great Britain, 1998, p. 57.

18 Bell, *In Harm's Way*, Penguin, London, 1996, p. 127.

19 Ibid, p. 76. Italics added.

20 'Upside-Down Policy', in *The Use of Force After the Cold War*, H.W. Burnes (ed.), Texas, A&M Press, College Station, 2003, p. 127.

21 *The International Herald Tribune*, 'For EU and NATO, Snags Over Intelligence', by Judy Dempsey, 13 November 2004.

8 CULTURE AND CHANGE: A BARRIER OR A WINDOW?

1 In the first fifty years of the UN's history, the veto was cast in the Security Council nearly 300 times (about 120 were cast by the USSR); since the end of the Cold War, there have been only seven vetoes cast in the Security Council. During the Cold War, Chapter VII, the 'enforcement' chapter of the Charter of the United Nations, was used only three times (Korea, the Congo and the 1991 Gulf War); in 1993, there were eleven Security Council Resolutions passed under Chapter VII of the Charter in respect of Bosnia-Herzegovina alone, and 'enforcement mandates' had become the norm.

2 See Lehmann, Ingrid, *Peacekeeping and Public Information: Caught in the Crossfire*, and Arbuckle, *The Level Killing Fields of Yugoslavia*, The Pearson Press, Cornwallis, 1998.

3 However, the issue of force protection and its effects on US operations has not gone away: after US soldiers were called upon to assist Italian and French soldiers in con-taining violent disturbances on the bridge at Mitrovica (Kosovo) in February of 2000, The Washington Post reported that 'US troops will stick to their own turf under orders announced by the Pentagon. . . that sharply limit missions to assist the peacekeepers of other nationalities'. This reflected concerns 'over a violent encounter last week between a Serbian [*sic*] mob and American soldiers' (OSCE Situation Centre Report for 1 March 2000). A previous NY Times report had indicated that 'snowballs, stones and bricks' had been thrown, and that US forces had withdrawn. A recent article in Foreign Affairs has suggested that 'Washington must fully commit to the mission and stop alienating its allies by refusing to endanger U.S. troops.' See *Foreign Affairs*, 'Kosovo Seething', by David Rhode, May/June 2000.

4 The UNMIK/KFOR CMOCC was disbanded in early 2000, it having been judged that it had done its job so well that a formal organization for that purpose was no longer required.

5 *The Penguin Book of War: Great Military Writings*, John Keegan (ed.), Viking, London, 1999, p. 205. There were, according to a British observer, Lt Col. John Fremantle, both Prussian and Austrian observers with him in the Confederate lines during the Battle of Gettysburg. Fremantle, seems to have seen nothing remarkable in that the entire Army of the Potomac (Shaara in *The Killer Angels* – estimates its strength at approximately 80,000 men) was, as the battle opened, 'concentrated into a space apparently not more than a couple of miles in length' (p. 207). Robert Kaplan has estimated

that 'the average engagement during the Civil War featured 26,000 men per square mile of battle front' (see Kaplan, *Warrior Politics*, Randam House, New York and Toronto, 2002, p. 120). At the battle of Neuve Chapelle in March 1915, the British First Army, then consisting of thirteen infantry divisions and five cavalry divisions, attacked on a frontage of kilometres (see Liddell-Hart, Sir Basil H., *History of the First World War*, Pan Books, London, 1972, p. 141).

6 *Makers of Modern Strategy*, E.M. Earle (ed.), 'Engels and Marx: Military Concepts of the Social Revolutionaries', Atheneum, by Sigmund Neumann, New York, 1966, p. 166.

7 Churchill, Winston, *The History of the English Speaking Peoples: The Great Democracies*, Dodd, Mead and Co., New York, 1958, p. 76.

8 Chamberlain, Muriel, *Pax Britannica: British Foreign Policy 1789–1914*, Longman, London & New York, 1988, p. 9.

9 Churchill, *The History of English Speaking Peoples*, Dodd, Mead and Co., New York, 1958.

10 Morris, James, Heaven's *Command: An Imperial Progress*, Penguin, Harmondsworth, 1979, p. 408 (italics added).

11 Catton, Bruce, *The Army of the Potomac: Mr. Lincoln's Army*, Doubleday, Garden City, 1951, p. 186. Of 124 references cited by Catton for this volume of his (three-volume) history of the Civil War, ninety-seven were published prior to the First World War.

12 By 1918, 'the cavalry had become a Cinderella force…Included in every major offensive plan since 1915…Time after time, the cavalry would move up to the front only to be sent back when no breakthrough was achieved. … So the cavalry remained in the rear areas, training with the hope that someday they might fight on open ground.' See Grodsinski, Capt. John R., *The Battle of Moreuil Wood*, Kingston, Ont., 1993, p. 5.

13 Wells, H.G., *The War in the Air*, Penguin, Harmondsmith, 1908 and 1941, p. 165. Elsewhere, in the chapter 'How War Came to New York', Wells says of air forces (long before air forces), 'From above they could inflict immense damage; they could reduce any organized Government to…capitulation…but they could not disarm, still less could they occupy, the surrendered area below' (p. 136).

14 See *Online NewsHour: A Conversation with Tim Judah and Michael Ignatieff*, 31 May 2000, http://www.pbs.org/newshour/gergen/jan-juneoo/kosovo_5-31.html

15 *Frankfurter Allgemeine Zeitung* (English edition), 'Learning to Lead: School Shapes Ranks of Future Officers', by Peter Carstens, 26 June 2000 (No. 67).

16 When, in 1992, I took my leave of the Bundeswehr to proceed on peacekeeping duties in Bosnia-Herzegovina, one of my German colleagues said to me, 'We would like so much to go with you, but for us the history is still too young.'

9 CIVIL-MILITARY CULTURES IN COLLISION: *FESTINA LENTE*

1 Williams, 'Peace is Hell', p. 37.

2 See http://www.cdnpeacekeeping.ns.ca/iaptc.htm, and Chapter 25.

3 Quoted in the Challenges Project, *Challenges of Peace Operations: Into the 21st Century: Concluding Report 1997–2002*, Elanders Gotab, Stockholm, 2002, p. 144.

10 UNIT ROTATIONS: *LES ABSENTS SE TROMPENT*

1 In 1992, as a Lieutenant-Colonel in HQ UNPROFOR, I was paid by the UN USD1.28 per day, and lodged in one of the worst hotels, with the worst food, of my life. My civilian colleagues, for whom this was inadequate, received (untaxed) subsistence allowances totalling USD188 per day. That sum × 365 days, far exceeded my gross annual pay. Perhaps I was fortunate – in the Congo in 1962, the soldiers' UN pay was

only USD01.25 per day – UN pay for peacekeepers having actually risen by USD0.03 per day in thirty years. The subsistence per diem in UNMIK in 2002 was USD95.
2 Gabriel and Savage, *Crisis in Command*, Hill and Wang, New York, 1978, p. 41.
3 Marshall, Colonel S.L.A., *Men Against Fire*, William Morrow & Co., New York, 1947, p. 161.
4 Ibid.
5 Gabriel and Savage, *Crisis in Command*, Hill and Wang, New York, 1978, p. 35.
6 Ibid.
7 Hedges, Chris, *War is a Force That Gives Us Meaning*, Anchor Books, New York, 2002, p. 38.
8 Nash, *NATO Review*, 'Can Soldiers be Peacekeepers and Warriors?' Summer 2001.

11 THE US FORCES: THE MILITARY ANTIPODEANS

1 As quoted by Jackson Diehl, in 'Another Balkan Alarm, and Again Washington Is Napping', in *The International Herald Tribune*, 28 May 2001.
2 Kissinger, Henry, *Diplomacy*, Touchstone, New York, 1994, p. 809.
3 'Washington, George', Microsoft® Encarta® Online Encyclopedia 2003 http://encarta.msn.com © 1997–2003 Microsoft Corporation.
4 Priest, Dana, *The Mission – Waging War and Keeping Peace with America's Military*, Norton, New York, 2003.
5 See http://store.yahoo.com/expandnato/anybut.html
6 Priest, *The Mission*, Norton, New York, 2003, p. 97.
7 Nye, Joseph, *The Paradox of American Power: Why the World's Only Superpower Can't Go It Alone*, Oxford University Press, New York, 2002, p. 143.
8 Priest, *The Mission*, Norton, New York, 2003, p. 53.
9 Lipsky, David, *Absolutely American: Four Years at West Point*, Houghton Mifflin Company, Boston and New York, 2003, p. 48.
10 *The New York Times*, 'Making Sense of the Mission', by James Traub, 11 April 2004.
11 Dobbins, James, Jones, Seth G., Crane, Keith, Rathmell, Andrew, Steele, Brett, Teltschik, Richard and Timilsina, Anga, *The UN's Role in Nation-Building: From the Congo to Iraq*, The Rand Corporation, Santa Monica, 2005, p. xxxv.
12 *Der Spiegel*, 'Recipe for a Disaster', interview by Siegesmund von Ilseman, No. 34, 18 August 2003 (translation by this author).
13 Priest, *The Mission*, Norton, New York, 2003, p. 46.
14 Ibid., p. 256.
15 Ibid.
16 Ibid., p. 392.
17 Ibid., p. 390. (Emphasis added.)
18 Woodward, Bob, *Plan of Attack*, Simon & Schuster, New York, 2004, p. 150.
19 Quoted in Holbrooke, Richard, *To End a War*, The Modern Library, New York, 1999, p. 217.
20 Ibid.
21 Priest, *The Mission*, Norton, New York, 2003, p. 52.
22 *The International Herald Tribune*, 'Nominee's Initial Talk Relies on Broad Strokes', by Steven Erlanger, 18 December 2000.
23 *The New York Times*, 'A Doctrine Left Behind', by Mark Danner, 21 November 2004.
24 Nye, *The Paradox of American Power*, Oxford University Press, New York, 2002, pp. 8–9.
25 *The New York Times*, 'Powell Backs U.S. Role to Aid Liberia', 24 July 2003.
26 *The International Herald Tribune*, 'Pentagon Leaders Warn of Dangers for U.S. in Liberia', by Christopher Marquis and Thom Shanker, 25 July 2003. It certainly speaks volumes for the confidence these two officers had in opposing the views of their

Secretary of State, and in his own words, that they were speaking at their own Senate confirmation hearings – and both were speedily confirmed in their appointments. General Peter Pace's self-confidence has proven to have been especially well placed – he has now (2005) been nominated to succeed General Meyers and will himself become Chairman.

27 Janowitz, Morris, *The Professional Soldier: A Social and Political Portrait*, The Free Press, New York, 1971, pp. 417–18 (italics added).

28 Susan L. Woodward, *Plan of Attack*, Simon & Schuster, New York, 2004, p. 113.

29 *Global Governance*, 'What UN Principles? A U.S. Debate on Iraq', by Leon Gordenker, Vol. 9, No. 3, July–September 2003, p. 283.

30 *The New York Times*, 11 January 2004, 'Challenge for Bootstrap General is Winning Over the Wary Iraqis' (italics added).

31 Bacevich, Andrew J., *The New American Militarism: How Americans are Seduced by War*, Oxford University Press, Oxford, 2005. See especially Chapter 7: 'Blood for Oil'.

32 Steven Miller corroborates the emergence of this interpretation: 'To the policy-dominant coalition in the United States, the attacks of September 11th had one clear meaning: WWIV is at hand.' See *Global Governance*, 'Terrifying Thoughts', Vol. 11, No. 2, April–June 2005.

33 'A Conversation with Peter Pace', The Council on Foreign Relations, Washington, DC, 17 February 2004 (italics added).

34 William Pfaff, who wasn't there, did know what to call it: 'a kind of postmodern parody of a world war'. See *The Bullet's Song: Romantic Violence and Utopia*, Simon & Schuster, New York, 2004, p. 128.

35 Burns, John F., in *The New York Times*, 'Violence Surges Across Iraq with 30 New Deaths Reported', New York, 29 May 2005.

36 Ibid., 'When the Joneses Wear Jeans', by Jennifer Steinhauer.

12 PRIDE AND PREJUDICE: YOU NEVER GET A SECOND CHANCE TO MAKE A FIRST IMPRESSION

1 Austen, Jane, *Pride and Prejudice*, Penguin Classics, 1996 (from the 1972 Introduction, by Toby Tanner).

2 Christopher Bellamy, 'Combining Combat Readiness and Compassion', in *NATO Review*, Summer 2001. Bellamy also commented on the US forces 'strong emphasis on force protection and intimidating appearance', and observed that 'their remoteness from the locals may reduce their effectiveness in the peacekeeping role'.

3 Marshall, Colonel S.L.A., *Men Against Fire*, William Morrow & Co., New York, 1947, p. 173.

4 Chalfont, Alun, *Montgomery of Alamein*, Atheneum, New York, 1976, p. 144.

5 Hamilton, Nigel, *Monty: The Making of a General (1887–1942)*, Hamish Hamilton, Great Britain, 1981, p. 469.

6 The aged helicopters of the Canadian Navy lack 'particle separators', which are designed to prevent the ingestion of foreign objects by the jet intakes. This was 1993 – two years later, in 1995, these aircraft had become so unreliable that the naval helicopter fleet in Canada was averaging one forced landing per week; eventually they were grounded – temporarily. Those helicopters remain in service in the twenty-first century.

7 'CIMIC in East Timor: An Account of Civil-Military Co-operation, Co-ordination and Collaboration in the Early Phases of the East Timor Relief Operation', UN Office for the Coordination of Humanitarian Affairs, Geneva (italics added).

8 Salignon, Pierre, 'Violence Intensifies in Port au Prince, Haiti' (trans. Nina Freidman), in *Doctors Without Borders Emergency Alert*, newsletter_msf@newyork.msf.org 30 June 2005.

9 'The Changing Role of the United Nations', by Margaret P. Karns and Karen Mingst, p. 231, in Thakur and Schnabel (eds), 'UN Peacekeeping Operations in Yugoslavia'.

10 Arbuckle, James V., *The Level Killing Fields of Yugoslavia: An Observer Returns*, The Canadian Peacekeeping Press, Cornwallis, 1998, p. 20.

11 *The Times Literary Supplement*, 'Police and thieves', by Andrew Lambert, 5 September 2003 (italics added).

12 Bell, *In Harm's Way*, Penguin, London, 1996, p. 161 (italics in original).

13 Lipsky, *Absolute American*, Houghton Mifflin Company, Boston and New York, 2003, p. 7.

14 Short-service conscripts spend their entire enrolment in basic training, do no collective training, and cannot be deployed on peacekeeping tours of duty (which would usually exceed their period of service). It requires most of the efforts of most of the rest of the force to train and administer them. The Bundeswehr, with its present strength of just under 300,000, includes about 100,000 who are either basic trainees or their trainers and administrators, thus nearly one-third of the entire force is unavailable for operational tasking. When a German Combat Engineer Company was recently deployed to Bosnia, the 137 members of the Company were assembled from longer-serving volunteers of 18 different units. See *Der Speigel*: 'Stempeln in der Etappe', by Ralf Beste, Issue No. 34, 18 September 2003.

   Given the paucity of their training and the complexities of modern armies, draftees have almost no 'shelf life', that is, the ex-conscripts have no potential to form a reserve force, without such extensive re-training as to almost obviate their ever having been conscripted in the first place.

15 *United Nations Peacekeeping Operations: Ad Hoc Missions, Permanent Engagement*, Ramesh Thakur and Albrecht Schnabel (eds), 'UN Peacekeeping Operations in Yugoslavia', by Satish Nambiar, p. 168. (The United Nations University Press, Tokyo, 2001.)

16 Thakur and Schnabel, *United Nations Peacekeeping Operations*, 'Cascading Generations of Peacekeeping', p. 21.

17 Submitted to the Security Council and to the General Assembly of the United Nations by the Secretary-General under A/55/305 – S/2000/809, dated 21 August 2000 (p. ix). Hereinafter referred to as 'The Brahimi Report'.

18 *The Atlantic Monthly*, 'The Coming Anarchy', by Robert Kaplan, February 1994, p. 72.

19 Hersh, Seymour, *Chain of Command: The Road from 9/11 to Abu Ghraib*, Harper Collins, New York, 2004, p. 147.

20 From 'Civil-Military Communications in Complex Emergencies', in *PeaceWatch*, The United States Institute of Peace, Vol. VI, No. 4, Washington, DC, June 2000. The reference reports on a conference held in San Antonio, Texas, 6–9 April 2000, 'to discuss information sharing in complex interventions internationally', and attended by 'some 170 representatives of U.S. and European civil affairs units, NGOs and IOs and the U.S. government'.

21 *Global Governance: A Review of Multilateralism and International Organizations*, Vol. 7, No. 2: 'Intervention and State Sovereignty: Breaking New Ground,' by Gareth Evans and Mohamed Sahnoun, Lynne Riener, Boulder, CO, April–June 2001 (italics added).

22 Ibid., 'Protecting the People', by Charles T. Call and William Stanley (italics added).

23 Bell, *In Harm's Way*, Penguin, London, 1996, p. 133.

14 WAR AND PEACE: MATTERS OF PRINCIPLE

1 Tuchman, Barbara, *The Guns of August*, The Macmillan Company, New York, 1962, p. 20, and Ropp, Theodore, *War in the Modern World*, Collier Books, New York, 1959, p. 224.

2 *Introduction to the Study of Military History for Canadian Students*, Colonel C.P. Stacey, O.C., O.B.E., C.D. (ed.) 6th edn, 4th Rev., Directorate of Training, Canadian Forces Headquarters, Appendix A. Hereinafter, in this section, referred to as 'text'.

3 Italics added.

4 *The United Nations and Somalia, 1992–1996*, The United Nations Blue Book Series, Vol. VIII, United Nations Department of Public Information, New York, 1996: Document 52, p. 262.

5 Ibid., Document 55, p. 268.

6 Bowden, Mark, *Black Hawk Down*, Corgi Books, London, 1999, pp. 139–41.

7 Ibid., p. 116.

8 Ibid., p. 145.

9 Woodward, Susan, *Balkan Tragedy: Chaos and Dissolution After the Cold War*, The Brookings Institution, Washington, DC, 1995, p. 128. Woodward in this case was describing the confusion which arose when NATO contended that air strikes in Bosnia were peace enforcing, while the United Nations considered them justified only in defence of the peacekeepers.

10 Boothby, Derek, 'Application of Leverage in Eastern Slavonia', in *Leveraging for Success in United Nations Peace Operations*, Jean Krasno, Bradd C. Hayes and Donald C.F. Daniel (eds), Praeger, Westchester, 2003, p. 131.

11 See also Chapter 26.

12 *The International Herald Tribune*, 'Nation-building: The UN has been learning how it's done', by Dennis McNamara, 29 October 2002.

13 See also Chapter 14.

14 Liddell-Hart, *History of the First World War*, Pan Books, London, 1972, p. 24.

15 Shara, Jeff, *Rise to Rebellion*, Ballantine, New York, 2001, p. xviii. Adams might well have recorded these thoughts while he was preparing to defend the British officer accused of ordering the Boston 'Massacre' on 5 March 1770.

16 Lehmann, Ingrid, *Peacekeeping and Public Information: Caught in the Cross-fire*, Frank Cass, London, 1999.

17 See *The International Herald Tribune*, 'U.S. and UN at odds on leeway for Iraq', by Colum Lynch, 18 November 2002. The relationship between the *two* missions was not simplified by the fact that Blix was in 1998 the Director General of the IAEA; Elbaradei was his successor at the Agency. A CNN interview with Richard Butler, who was the Chief Weapons Inspector of UNSCOM when Blix headed the IAEA, displayed in its condescending tone towards Blix, strong indications of the type of tensions which can exist when there are too many chiefs, and too many missions (see CNN Transcript #111811CN.V73, 18 November 2002).

15 THE MILITARY ROLES IN SUPPORT OF HUMANITARIAN OPERATIONS

1 I use here the current (since 1974) terminology; up to then, the position was styled Force Economics Officer (Operations 'E').

2 This was and remains the only amendment to the UNFICYP mandate in forty years.

3 At year-end 1998, UNHCR listed 265,210 'persons of concern', nearly all IDPs who, it must be said, were probably displaced twenty-six years previously. The UNCHR budget for Cyprus was then just over USD 250k (see http://www.unhcr.ch/world/euro/cyprus.htm).

4 Although MacKenzie greeted the agreement negotiated by Cedric Thornbury and John Wilson as 'a coup', it seems that, typically, little thought had been given to the availability of the 1,000-man force required for airport security. It was three months since UNPROFOR had begun to deploy, the deployment was not yet complete, and it

was unlikely that additional forces could be available in less than a month. Therefore, MacKenzie reasoned, only a force currently in-theatre could be used, and only the French and Canadian battalions were up to the job at such short notice. In the event, the Canadian battalion was re-deployed (with Canadian Government approval) from Sector West in Croatia. (See MacKenzie, *Peacekeeper*, pp. 299–306.) MacKenzie was right: it was late September before additional forces began to arrive for the new Sector Sarajevo.

5 The juxtaposition of an enforcement mission with a humanitarian operation arises from the phrasing of Article 2.7 of the UN Charter: 'Nothing contained in the... Charter shall authorise the United Nations to intervene in matters which are essentially within the domestic jurisdiction of any state... *but this principle shall not prejudice the application of enforcement measures under Chapter VII*' (italics added). It can also be inferred that while the humanitarian intervention may be a consensual operation, the necessarily accompanying security force might not be consensual, or may not require the 'hosts' consent to deploy.

6 The mission of 'the international security presence' in Kosovo, as specified by the UN Security Council in Resolution 1244 (12 July 1999), includes deterring renewed hostilities, enforcing a cease fire, preventing the return of the 'Federal and Republic military, police and paramilitary forces', demilitarization, establishing a secure environment for refugee return, for 'the international civil presence' and for the delivery of humanitarian aid, ensuring public safety and order, supervising demining, supporting and coordinating closely with the international civil presence.

7 Von Horn, Karl, *Soldiering for Peace*, David McKay, New York, 1966, pp. 162–3.

8 The Bundeswehr, forbidden by the Constitution of the Federal Republic from 'internal security' tasks in Germany, was most uneasy effecting arrests of civilians in Kosovo.

9 In Bosnia in 1994, Rose did order convoys to 'force their passage through' one notorious checkpoint 'if they were blocked'. On one occasion, passage was forced by a British Infantry Fighting Vehicle (Warrior) Company, with four NATO aircraft directly overhead. See Rose, *Fighting for Peace*, Harvill Press, Great Britain, 1998, pp. 57–8. This local superiority is highly unusual in peace operations. In the long term, the principle that military force is deterrent and defensive in nature, will be the norm. Elsewhere, Rose makes it clear that he generally accepted such limitations on armed force, for example: '(UNPROFR) was a peacekeeping force that could use only a limited degree of military force *to deter attacks*' (p. 167; italics added).

10 *Revival: The Newsletter of the Post-War Reconstruction and Development Unit at the University of York*, 'Power Politics in Southern Itraq', by Lt Col. Richard Brown, Issue 19, February 2004, p. 10.

16 FIRST-GENERATION PEACEKEEPING: THE AGE OF CONSENT

1 See Urquhart, Sir Brian, *Hammarskjold*, Harper and Row, New York, 1972, pp. 159–94.

2 The Uniting for Peace Resolution is also referred to as 'The Acheson Plan', after its originator, who intended to strengthen the provisions of Articles 10, 11, 14 and 20 of the Charter. This resolution provides that 'if the Security Council, because of a lack of unanimity of the permanent members, fails to exercise its primary responsibility for the maintenance of international peace and security... the General Assembly shall consider the matter immediately' (see *Basic Facts About the United Nations*, Department of Public Information, New York, 1998, p. 7 [footnote]). Urquhart (*Hammarskjold*, Harper and Row, New York, 1972, note p. 175) notes that 'The constitutionality of this device... had always been challenged by the U.S.S.R.' Article 18.2

of the Charter of the United Nations specifies that 'Decisions of the General Assembly on important questions shall be made by a two-thirds majority of the members *present and voting*' (italics added). Thus, given a quorum, absences and abstentions would have no effect.

3 Italics added.

4 This was, in effect, an enforcement action without Security Council authorization: 'no enforcement action shall be taken by regional arrangements or by regional agencies without the authorisation of the Security Council (Article 53.1)', and is thus, despite the Soviet pretence of Hungarian 'consent', quite similar to the NATO action in Yugoslavia in 1999. The subsidiary issue which might be raised today would concern the legitimacy of the Hungarian government of that day, and thus of the validity of their 'consent' to the Soviet action.

5 Urquhart, *Hammarskjold*, Harper and Row, New York, 1972, p. 171.

6 Urquhart, *Hammarskjold*, Harper and Row, New York, 1972, pp. 232–4.

7 From 28 October to 5 November, the Security Council and the General Assembly met fifteen times: nine times on the Suez issue; five times on Hungary.

8 Urquhart, *Hammarskjold*, Harper and Row, New York, 1972, p. 180.

9 Urquhart, *Hammarskjold*, Harper and Row, New York, 1972, p. 187. Several years later, in 1964, Archbishop Makarios' objection to black troops for UNFICYP was, very quietly, allowed to stand. Makarios, who might have had much in common with Nasser, did not object to a Canadian battalion from the 'Royal Vingt-dousieme Regiment du Canada', which was later followed by the same Queen's Own Rifles of Canada, to whose inclusion in UNEF Nasser had objected.

10 Urquhart, ibid.

11 Urquhart, *Hammarskjold*, Harper and Row, New York, 1972, p. 205 (italics added).

12 *The Blue Helmets: A Review of United Nations Peacekeeping*, 3rd edn, Department of Public Information, New York, 1996, pp. 41, 54.

13 *Blue Helmets III*, pp. 54–5.

14 And so with UNPROFOR: 'On 22 March, 1995, the Secretary-General informed the Security Council that, in Croatia, the retention of UNPROFOR in its existing form and...mandate would not enjoy the consent of the Government of Croatia.' *Blue Helmets III*, p. 540. The UN force in Croatia was 'restructured' and re-titled United Nations Confidence Restoration Operation in Croatia (UNCRO) (UNSCR 981, 31 March 1995). One month later, Croatian forces overran Western Slavonia; three months after that, their attacks in the Krajina resulted in the deaths of four peacekeepers and injuries to 16. By August 1995, an estimated 170,000 Serb Croatians had been expelled from the Krajina, apparently 'with the usual brutality'. (Arbuckle, James, *The Level Killing Fields of Yugoslavia: An Observer Returns*, Occasional Paper No. 1, The Pearson Press, Cornwallis, Nova Scotia, 1998, pp. 2–3.)

15 *Canadian Defence Quarterly*, Vol. 25, No. 2, Baxter Publications, Toronto, December 1995, 'Peacekeeping, Public Perceptions and the Need for Consent', by Ingrid A. Lehmann (p. 18).

16 *The Fletcher Forum of World Affairs*, Vol. 19, No. 1, 1995, 'Public Perceptions of U.N. Peacekeeping', by Ingrid A. Lehmann (p. 115). Lehmann has written more extensively on the issue of the information component of peace operations in her book *Peacekeeping and Public Information: Caught in the Cross-fire*, Frank Cass, London, 1998.

17 'Peace Operations and the United Nations: Preparing for the Next Century', by Secretary-General of the United Nations Kofi Annan, in *Conflict Resolution Monitor*, Issue 1, Summer 1997, Bradford University (see http://www.brad.ac.uk/acad/confres/crm1.html#comment). Italics added.

18 Ibid.

19 Ibid.

20 Arbuckle, *The Level Killing Fields of Yugoslavia*, The Pearson Press, Cornwallis, 1998, pp. 16–17.

21 *Study Report: The Development of Indigenous Mine Action Capabilities*, by Robert Eaton, Chris Horwood and Norah Niland, Lessons Learned Unit, Policy and Analysis Division, Department of Humanitarian Affairs, New York (italics added).

17 SECOND-GENERATION PEACEKEEPING: CROSSING THE MOGADISHU

1 *Blue Helmets*, 3rd edn, p. 514.

2 Mackenzie, *Peacekeeper*, Harper Collins, Toronto, 1993, p. 160, with additional input from conversations with the author. Note that the same arguments against placing the headquarters in Sarajevo were successful in preventing the administrative base from being placed in Banja Luka (ibid., p. 161).

3 'At least', my Bundeswehr colleagues said to me as I left for Belgrade on 13 March, 'you aren't going to Sarajevo'.

4 Martin Bell confirms this: 'It was the only known case in military history where a headquarters staff received messages of sympathy and concern from the front-line troops in the field.' (*In Harm's Way*, p. 24.)

5 The refusal of the United Nations to sponsor a preventive deployment in BiH, followed by the ill-advised decision to place HQ UNPROFOR in Sarajevo, is reported by Warren Zimmerman in his article in Foreign Affairs, March/April 1995: *The Last Ambassador* (p. 16). Other references may be found in Susan Woodward, *Balkan Tragedy: Chaos and Dissolution After the Cold War*, Brookings Institution Press, Washington, 1995 (p. 193); in Bell, *In Harm's Way* (pp. 186–7); in Ivo Daalder, *Getting to Dayton*, Brookings Institution Press, Washington, 2000 (p. 2); in Henryk J. Sokalski, *An Ounce of Prevention: Macedonia and the UN Experience in Preventive Diplomacy*, The United States Institute of Peace Press, Washington, 2003 (p. 18); and in MacKenzie, *Peacekeeper* (pp. xix, 160–1, 170, 232, 485). It may well have been a tacit acknowledgement of the failure to respond to Itzbegovic's request in 1991, that spurred the United Nations to react so uncharacteristically swiftly to the Macedonian request. Alice Ackermann says as much in her book, *Making Peace Prevail: Preventing Violent Conflict in Macedonia*, Syracuse Studies on Peace and Conflict Resolution, Syracuse University Press, 1999, p. 3: 'Itzetbegovic's plea was rejected... on the grounds that it was not established practice to send peacekeepers to an area before the outbreak of hostilities.' In the case of Macedonia, which made the same request thirteen months later, she notes that, 'Within less than a month, the Security Council authorized the first preventive deployment of peacekeepers in U.N. history.'

6 *The Blue Helmets III, A Review of United Nations Peacekeeping*, p. 500.

7 Rose, *Fighting for Peace*, Harvill Press, Great Britain, 1998, p. 317.

8 Ibid., p. 365. Italics added.

9 Ogata, Sadako, *The Turbulent Decade: Confronting the Refugee Crises of the 1990s*, W.W. Norton, London and New York, 2005. See especially p. 57 (italics added).

10 *The Blue Helmets III, A Review of United Nations Peacekeeping*, p. 525.

11 Ibid.

12 Ibid., p. 526. Rose had estimated a battalion (over 500 soldiers) for each Safe Area, which would have been a fairly effective deterrent, as well as having some capability to occupy the 'surroundings' (whatever that might have meant in New York, it meant little in the mountains of Bosnia). What he got was a company for each (about 120), which was actually worse than nothing. The wording of the referenced passage in *The Blue Helmets III* is revealing of the New York mentation, then and later (when the book was written): 'The Security Council... further expanded the mandate of UNPROFOR

to enable it to' (italics added). A mandate alone enables nothing, but the phraseology is indicative of a legislative, pedantic mindset that seemed to imply a degree of UN authority that had long since ceased to have any reality in Bosnia-Herzegovina.

13 Rose, p. 559.

14 Ibid., p. 314.

15 Ibid., p. 362.

16 This diagramme adapted from Rose, *Fighting for Peace*, p. 355. The phrase was actually coined by de la Presle, in respect of the NATO bombing of the Ubdina airfield in Croatia, and the pressure to strike at Bosnian Serb air defences, in November 1994.

18 RULES OF ENGAGEMENT

1 Department of Public Information, United Nations, New York, 1990.

2 A very concise review of the Canadian operation in Somalia and its aftermath, with a comparison with the Dutch experience in Srebrenica, is contained in *Peace Operations Between War and Peace*, Erwin A. Schmidl (ed.), 'Lessons Learned the Hard Way: Somalia and Srebrenica Compared', by Chris Klep and Donna Winslow, Frank Cass, London, 2000. The authors note, *inter alia*, how successive layers of changes to the mission led to layers of confusion about the ROE as the missions in both cases 'crept' from their original Chapter VI mandates, to Chapter VII Enforcement Missions.

3 Report submitted to the Security Council and to the General Assembly of the United Nations under A/55/305 – S/2000/809, dated 21 August 2000, p. 10 (italics added). Hereinafter referred to as *Brahimi*.

19 FORCE STRUCTURES: *ALWAYS* USE A SLEDGEHAMMER TO CRACK A WALNUT

1 *Brahimi*, op.cit., pp. 9, 11.

2 Chesterton, Simon, *The Use of Force in UN Peace Operations*, The United Nations Department of Peacekeeping Operations, Best Practices Unit, 31 August 2004, p. 3.

20 THE COMMAND AND CONTROL OF JOINT AND COMBINED MILITARY OPERATIONS

1 UNSCRs 819 and 824 (1993) (respectively); see *The Blue Helmets: A Review of United Nations Peacekeeping*, 3rd edn, UN Department of Public Information, New York, 1996, p. 523.

2 Ibid.

3 See Ogata, *The Turbulent Decade*, W.W. Norton, London and New York, 2005, p. 86, and MacKenzie, Lewis, 'The real story behind Srberencia; the massacre in the UN "safe haven" was not a black and white event', *The Globe and Mail*, Toronto, 14 July 2005: 'Morillon had – against the advice of his UN masters – bullied his way into Srebrenica...and told its citizens they were now under the protection of the UN. The folks at the UN were furious with Gen. Morillon but, with the media on his side, the were forced to introduce the "safe haven" concept'; this was eventually extended to five other towns and cities in Bosnia.

4 To answer the second problem, he adopted a Napoleonic measure: shortly after the troops he had requested arrived in Srebrenica, he left Srebrenica.

5 *The Blue Helmets III, A Review of United Nation Peacekeeping*, p. 525. Although UNSCR 819 had proclaimed Srebrenica a Safe Area on 16 April, DPKO seems to have been taken by surprise when the town was actually occupied by UN troops.

6 From 1993 to 1995 I tried to find out how this could have happened. It should not have happened without the consent of the Canadian Deputy FC, a Major General who was

also the Canadian Contingent Commander, and who could have stopped it, or referred the matter to the Canadian Government in time for them to have objected. The battalion commander, whom I asked about this two years after the fact, stated that he had the permission of the Canadian Contingent Commander, but this might have been difficult – on that day, the outgoing Deputy-Force/Canadian Contingent Commander was at the airport in Zagreb, being seen off by his replacement, whose first day in office that was. It is my surmise that the decision had been taken by the battalion commander, apparently in the space of one phone call (which was, it must be remembered, a call from a Lieutenant-General to a Lieutenant-Colonel). It seems, to continue the legend, that both the United Nations and the Canadian Government, seeing too much toothpaste to put back in the tube, could only squeeze on more. So with the Dutch government: on 10 March 1994, a Dutch battalion (about 600 men and women) replaced the Canadian company. Sixteen months later, Srebrenica fell – on, in addition to the luckless Srebrenicans, the Dutch. In fact, according to Martin Bell, the Dutch mission in Srebrenica was terminated 'by order of their Chief of Staff in Holland'. The previous year, Rose, who was also the British Contingent Commander, was over-ruled by his own Government when he ordered British troops to Gorazde. (See Bell, *In Harm's Way*, p. 182.)

7 It was often my lot, as a Canadian liaison officer to a major Bundeswehr formation, to diplomatically remind a German general that he could not detach the Canadian artillery or combat engineers from their parent brigade for 'some little job', that the Canadian commander would never allow it, but if he did, he would be on his way home, so let's don't even think about it, Sir. It always worked; the system and the doctrine were quite clear to us all.

8 As a good example of what may occur when command is too inflexibly interpreted, or where the doctrine is itself not well developed, in 1944 the 'Battle of the Bulge' resulted in Omar Bradley's 12th Army Group being split. Patton's Third Army remained south of the Bulge, the US First Army was split by the point of the Bulge, and the US Ninth Army was north of the Bulge in the area of Montgomery's 21st Army Group. The perfectly logical suggestion to transfer command of all US elements north of the Bulge to the British 21st Army Group was delayed until 20 December, four days after the initial German attacks, and by which time Bradley had been out of touch with his northern Armies for nearly 72 hours. Before being forced by Eisenhower to accede to the transfer, Bradley threatened to resign rather than 'turn over to Monty your two armies on the north' – forces over which Bradley in fact had no control. (See *Eisenhower – A Soldier's Life*, by Carlo d'Este, pp. 641–8.) It was likely the collective memory of such contretemps that lead the post-war SHAPE, on its way to becoming NATO, to begin to develop a more flexible and graded doctrine of command and control of combined forces.

9 It may indeed be inferred from considerable evidence that the paralleling national command systems have had the quite unintended consequence of protecting DPKO from itself – had it been entirely up to DPKO to command what, by 1995, amounted to a Corps in the field, they might have suffered a record of mutinies not seen, at least in European armies, since 1917.

21 THE MILITARY STAFF COMMITTEE: REVEILLE, OR LAST POST?

1 Findlay, Trevor, *The Use of Force in United Nations Peace Operations*, Oxford: SIPRI and the Oxford University Press.

2 Which is why Chapter 8 of the Charter provides that 'Members...shall make every effort to achieve pacific settlement of disputes through regional arrangements

or... agencies *before* referring them to the Security Council' (Article 52.2; italics added).

3 For example, Canada in the 1990s had troops simultaneously on UN Peacekeeping Forces, with the NATO-led I/S/KFORs, with the ECM Mission in Yugoslavia and with the Multi-national Force Observers in the Sinai.

4 Williams, *Civil-Military Relations and Peacekeeping*, Oxford University Press, London, 1998, p. 69.

5 For an excellent description of the requirement for formal peace-building policies and structures, see Paris, *At War's End*, Cambridge University Press, Cambridge, 2004, pp. 228–33. See also: Brahimi, 'Summary of Recommendations (Peace-building Strategy, and Peace-building Support in DHA); Security Council Press Release SC 6948 of 13 November 2000' and Annex thereto (S/2000/1085), especially Section VI; and Report of the Secretary-General's High Level Panel on Threats, Challenges and Security: *A More Secure World: Our Shared Responsibility*, Executive Summary, pp. 5–6.

22 REACTION FORCES: 'COMPULSORY AND IRREPROACHABLE IDLENESS'

1 Tolstoy, Leo, *War and Peace*: 'The chief attraction of military service has consisted and will consist in this compulsory and irreproachable idleness.' (VII. Ch. 1.)

2 I have not referred specifically to the UN Standby Arrangements System (UNSAS) for peacekeeping operations. This system, in which 88 member states participate, is said to have a total of 147,500 troops, which are however mainly infantry, from which no balanced force structure can be derived, it has no strategic mobility, it can conduct no collective training and would take three to four months to 'put troops on the ground'. See *Press Briefing by Head of Standby Arrangements Unit*, 14 March 2000, at http://www.un.org/peace/. In other words, in the context of an enforcement operation, merely a re-statement of Article 43 of the Charter. *Brahimi*, op. cit., admits that 'The Standby Arrangements System... has yet to become a dependable supply of resources' (P. 14).

3 Hertic, Zlatko, Sapcanin, Amelia and Woodward, Susan L., 'Bosnia and Herzegovina', in *Good Intentions: Pledges of Aid for Postconflict Recovery*, Shepard Forman and Stewart Patrick (eds), Lynne Riener, Boulder and London, 2000, p. 344.

4 NATO has always differentiated between readiness and availability. Reinforcements 'earmarked' for operations are reported as under 'readiness' and 'availability': the former refers to target strengths of forces; the latter is a measure of the time in which they could be deployed.

5 *The Blue Helmets III*, Chapter 11, pp. 205–9.

6 *Brahimi*, op.cit., p. x.

7 *The Blue Helmets III*, p. 488.

8 See Dallaire, *Shake Hands with the Devil*, Random House, Canada, 2003, pp. 374, 427, 432, 449.

9 Nash, *NATO Review*, 'Can Soldiers be Peacekeepers and Warriors?', 2001.

25 TRAINING ESTABLISHMENTS: WHERE AND BY WHO?

1 See http://www.iaptc.org

2 *International Peacekeeping*, 'Untapped Power? The Status of UN Information Operations', by Dan Lindley, Vol 11, No. 4, Winter 2004, pp. 617–18.

3 See http://www.kaiptc.org/kaiptc/cse2005a.htm

26 TRAINING FOR WHOM?

1 Dallaire, Romeo, *Shake Hands with the Devil: The Failure of Humanity in Rwanda*, Random House Canada, Toronto, 2003, p. 477.
2 *The Economist*, 'More dangerous work than ever'.
3 Ibid.
4 Riggs, David and Huberty, Robert, 'NGO Accountability: What the U.S. Can Teach the U.N.', paper presented to a conference 'We're Not From the Government But We're Here to Help You', sponsored by the American Enterprise Institute, Washington, DC, 11 June 2003.
5 *The Economist*, 'More dangerous work than ever'.

28 TO SAVE SUCCEEDING GENERATIONS...

1 *Brahimi*, op.cit., p. 3.
2 Patrick, Stewart, 'The Donor Community and the Challenge to Postconflict Recovery', in *Good Intentions*, op. cit., p. 47. Patrick concludes, optimistically, that 'the past decade has witnessed the emergence of a "second generation" of aid conditionality focussed on democratic governance, human rights, administrative accountability, and excessive military expenditures'. On the other hand, he notes, 'It is not clear...that any combination of carrots or sticks will induce the Bosnian Serbs to agree to refugee returns in Republika Srpska', James K. Boyce sums up: 'the central issue is not *whether* aid will have political impacts, but *what* these will be'. ('Beyond Good Intentions: External Assistance and Peace Building', in *Good Intentions*, op. cit., p. 380.)
3 Bell, *In Harm's Way*, p. 201.
4 *Global Governance: A Review of Multilateralism and International Organizations*, Vol. 8, No. 4, Oct.–Dec. 2002, 'Civil-Military Responses to Security Challenges', by John C. Cockell, p. 484 (final italics added).
5 Williams, *Civil-Military Relations and Peacekeeping*, Oxford University Press, London, 1998, p. 71.
6 There are some possible exceptions to this apparent rule that 'what we learn is that we do not learn': it seems that UNTAES did learn from UNPROFOR (but it seems that OHR, the OSCE and IFOR *et al.* in post-Dayton Bosnia did not); UNMIK appears to have learned from UNTAES. Just how and, more often why not, missions learn is an area requiring further research: why does individual knowledge, experience, learning, seem to have collectively so little and infrequent effect on the performance of subsequent similar missions? One possible, partial explanation is the lack of institutionalized professional education, indeed the lack of any concept *or culture* of collective professionalism, for international aid and care workers. This is an important component of the military culture – the officer factories, the staff colleges, the promotion examinations – manifest a culture of learning, even if, at least until recently, the military scholar would have been more directly concerned with studying war, than peace.
7 Cockell, *Global Governance*, p. 485.

BIBLIOGRAPHY

Books

Aal, Pamela, Miltenberger, Lt Col. Daniel and Weiss, Thomas G., *Guide to IGOs, NGOs and the Military in Peace and Relief Operations*, United States Institute of Peace Press, Washington, DC, 2000

Ackermann, Alice, *Making Peace Prevail: Preventing Violent Conflict in Macedonia*, Syracuse Studies on Peace and Conflict Resolution, Syracuse University Press, 1999

Addison, Paul and Calder, Angus (eds), *Time to Kill: The Soldier's Experience of War in the West 1939–45*, Pimlico, London, 1997

Arbuckle, James, *The Level Killing Fields of Yugoslavia: An Observer Returns*, The Canadian Peacekeeping Press, Cornwallis, NS, 1998

Austen, Jane, *Pride and Prejudice*, Penguin Classics, London, 1996 (novel)

Bacevich, Andrew J., *The New American Militarism: How Americans are Seduced by War*, Oxford University Press, Oxford, 2005

Bell, Martin, *In Harm's Way: Reflections of a War-Zone Thug*, Penguin, London, 1996

Boothby, Derek, 'Application of Leverage in Eastern Slavonia', in *Leveraging for Success in United Nations Peace Operations*, Jean Krasno, Bradd C. Hayes and Donald C.F. Daniel (eds), Praeger, Westchester, 2003

Bowden, Mark, *Black Hawk Down*, Corgi Books, London, 1999

Brumwell, Stephen, *White Devil*, Orion Publishing Group, London, 2004

Burnes, H.W. (ed), *The Use of Force After the Cold War*, Texas A&M Press, College Station, 2003

Catton, Bruce, *The Army of the Potomac: Mr. Lincoln's Army*, Doubleday, Garden City, 1951

Chalfont, Alun, *Montgomery of Alamein*, Atheneum, New York, 1976

Chamberlain, Muriel, *Pax Britannica: British Foreign Policy 1789–1914*, Longman, London and New York, 1988

Churchill, Winston, *The History of the English Speaking Peoples: The Great Democracies*, Dodd, Mead and Co., New York, 1958

Churchill, Winston, *My Early Life*, Eland, London, 2002

Daalder, Ivo, *Getting to Dayton*, Brookings Institution Press, Washington, 2000

Dallaire, Romeo, *Shake Hands with the Devil: The Failure of Humanity in Rwanda*, Random House Canada, 2003

Dandeker, Christopher and Gow, James, 'Military Culture and Strategic Peacekeeping', in *Peace Operations Between War and Peace*, Erwin A. Schmidl (ed.), Frank Cass, London, 2000 d'Este, Carlo, *Eisenhower – A Soldier's Life*, Holt, New York, 2002

Dobbins, James, Jones, Seth G., Crane, Keith, Rathmell, Andrew, Steele, Brett, Teltschik, Richard and Timilsina, Anga, *The UN's Role in Nation-Building: From the Congo to Iraq*, The Rand Corporation, Santa Monica, 2005

Duffield, Mark, *Global Governance and the New Wars: The Merging of Development and Security*, Zed Books, London, 2002

Durch, William J. (ed.) *The Evolution of UN Peacekeeping – Case Studies and Comparative Analyses*, St. Martin's Press, New York, 1993

Earle, E.M. (ed.), *Makers of Modern Strategy*, Atheneum, by Sigmund Neumann, New York, 1966

Einstein, Albert, *The World as I See It*, Citadel Press, New York, 1986

Eksteins, Modris, *Rites of Spring: The Great War and the Birth of the Modern Age*, Lester & Orpen Denys, Toronto, 1989

Findlay, Trevor, *The Use of Force in United Nations Peace Operations*, SIPRI and the Oxford University Press, 2002

Ford, Ford Maddox, *The Good Soldier*, A. & C. Boni, New York, 1927

Fussell, Paul, *The Great War and Modern Memory*, Oxford University Press, Oxford, 1975

Gabriel, Richard A. and Savage, Paul L., *Crisis in Command: Mismanagement in the Army*, Hill and Wang, New York, 1978

Glendon, Mary Ann, *A World Made New: Eleanor Roosevelt and the Universal Declaration of Human Rights*, Random House Trade Paperbacks, New York, 2001

Goulding, Sir Marrach, *Peacemonger*, Murray, London, 2002

Grodsinski, Capt. John R., *The Battle of Moreuil Wood*, Kingston, Ont., 1999

Hamilton, Nigel, *Monty: The Making of a General (1887–1942)*, Hamish Hamilton, Great Britain, 1981

Handy, Charles, *Understanding Organizations: How Understanding the Ways Organizations Actually Work Can Be Used to Manage Them Better*, Oxford University Press, Oxford, 1993

Hedges, Chris, *War is a Force That Gives Us Meaning*, Anchor Books, New York, 2002

Hersh, Seymour, *Chain of Command: The Road from 9/11 to Abu Ghraib*, Harper Collins, New York, 2004

Hobsbawm, Eric, *Age of Extremes: The Short Twentieth Century, 1914–1991*, Abacus, London, 1995

Holbrooke, Richard, *To End a War*, The Modern Library, New York, 1999

Holmes, Richard, *Tommy: The British Soldier on the Western Front 1914–1918*, Harper Collins, London, 2004

Huxley, Aldous, *Brave New World Revisited*, Harper and Brothers, New York, 1958

Janowitz, Morris, *The Professional Soldier: A Social and Political Portrait*, The Free Press, New York, 1971

Kaldor, Mary, *New and Old Wars: Organized Violence in a Global Era*, Stanford University Press, Stanford, 1999

Kaplan, Robert, *Warrior Politics*, Randam House, New York and Toronto, 2002

Keegan, John, *The Face of Battle: A Study of Agincourt, Waterloo and the Somme*, Penguin Books, London, 1976

Keegan, John (ed.) *The Penguin Book of War – Great Military Writings*, Penguin, London, 1999

Kissinger, Henry, *Diplomacy*, Touchstone, New York, 1994

Klep, Chris and Winslow, Donna, 'Lessons Learned the Hard Way: Somalia and Srebrenica Compared', in *Peace Operations Between War and Peace*, Erwin Schmidl (ed.), Frank Cass, London, 2000

Last, David M., *Theory, Doctrine and Practice of Conflict De-Escalation in Peacekeeping Operations*, The Canadian Peacekeeping Press, Cornwallis, NS, 1997

Lehmann, Ingrid, *Peacekeeping and Public Information: Caught in the Crossfire*, Frank Cass, London, 1999

Liddell-Hart, Sir Basil H., *History of the First World War*, Pan Books, London, 1972

Lipsky, David, *Absolutely American: Four Years at West Point*, Houghton Mifflin Company, Boston and New York, 2003

MacKenzie, Lewis, *Peacekeeper: The Road to Sarajevo*, Harper Collins, Toronto, 1993

Mackinlay, John (ed.), *A Guide to Peace Support Operations, The Thomas J. Watson Jr. Institute for International Studies*, Brown University, Providence, 1996

Marshall, Colonel S.L.A., *Men Against Fire*, William Morrow & Co., New York, 1947

Maurois, Andre, *Proust: Portrait of a Genius*, Carroll and Graf, New York, 1950

May, Terry M., *Historical Dictionary of Multi-national Peacekeeping*, The Scarecrow Press, Lanham, MD, 1996

Morrison, Alex (ed.), *The Changing Face of Peacekeeping*, The Canadian Institute of Strategic Studies, Toronto, 1993

Murray, Nicholas, *Aldous Huxley – An English Intellectual*, Little, Brown London, 2002

Nye, Joseph, *The Paradox of American Power: Why the World's Only Superpower Can't Go It Alone*, Oxford University Press, New York, 2002

Ogata, Sadako, *The Turbulent Decade: Confronting the Refugee Crises of the 1990s*, W.W. Norton, London and New York, 2005

Paris, Roland, *At War's End: Building Peace After Civil Conflict*, Cambridge University Press, Cambridge, 2004

Pfaff, William, *The Bullet's Song: Romantic Violence and Utopia*, Simon and Schuster, New York, 2004

Priest, Dana, *The Mission – Waging War and Keeping Peace with America's Military*, Norton, New York, 2003

Remarque, Erich Maria, *All Quiet on the Western Front*, Ullstein A.G., Berlin, 1928

Roberts, Kenneth, *Northwest Passage*, Random House Canada, Toronto, 1964 (originally published 1940)

Ropp, Theodore, *War in the Modern World*, Duke University Press, Collier Books, New York, 1962

Rose, General Sir Michael, *Fighting for Peace: Lessons from Bosnia*, Harvill Press, Great Britain, 1998

Shara, Jeff, *Rise to Rebellion*, Ballantine, New York, 2001 (novel)

Sokalski, Henryk J., *An Ounce of Prevention: Macedonia and the UN Experience in Preventive Diplomacy*, The United States Institute of Peace Press, Washington, 2003

Stacey, Colonel C.P., O.C., O.B.E., C.D., *Introduction to the Study of Military History for Canadian Students*, 6th edn, 4th Rev., Directorate of Training, Canadian Forces Headquarters, Ottawa

Thakur, Ramesh and Schnabel, Albrecht (eds), *United Nations Peacekeeping Operations: Ad Hoc Missions, Permanent Engagement*, The United Nations University Press, Tokyo, 2001

Tuchman, Barbara, *The Guns of August*, The Macmillan Company, New York, 1962

Urquhart, Sir Brian, *Hammarskjold*, Harper and Row, New York, 1972

Volger, Helmut (ed.), *A Concise Encyclopedia of the United Nations*, Kluwer Law International, The Hague, 2002

von Horn, Karl, *Soldiering for Peace*, David McKay, New York, 1966

Weiss, Thomas G., 'The United Nations in Civil Wars', in *The New Peacekeeping Partnership*, Alex Morrisson (ed.), The Lester B. Pearson Canadian International Peacekeeping Training Centre, Cornwallis, NS, 1995

Weiss, Thomas G. and Gordenker, Leon (eds), *NGOs, the UN, & Global Governance*, Lynne Rienner, Boulder, CO, 1996

Wells, H.G., *The War in the Air*, Penguin, Harmondsmith, 1908 and 1941

Williams, Michael C., *Civil-Military Relations and Peacekeeping*, The International Institute for Strategic Studies, Adelphi Paper 321, Oxford University Press, London, 1998

Woodward, Bob, *Plan of Attack*, Simon & Schuster, New York, 2004

Woodward, Susan, *Balkan Tragedy: Chaos and Dissolution After the Cold War*, Brookings Institution Press, Washington, 1995

Zartman, I. William (ed.), *Elusive Peace – Negotiating an End to Civil Wars*, The Brookings Institution, Washington, DC, 1995

Articles

Beste, Ralf, 'Stempeln in der Etappe', in *Der Spiegel*, Issue No. 34, 18 September 2003

Burns, John F., in *The New York Times*, 'Violence Surges Across Iraq with 30 New Deaths Reported', New York, 29 May 2005

Carstens, Peter, 'Learning to Lead: School Shapes Ranks of Future Officers', in *Frankfurter Allgemeine Zeitung* (English edition), 26 June 2000 (No. 67)

Danner, Mark, 'A Doctrine Left Behind', in *The New York Times*, 21 November 2004

Dempsey, Judy, 'For EU and NATO, Snags Over Intelligence', in *The International Herald Tribune*, 13 November 2004

Diehl, Jackson, in 'Another Balkan Alarm, and Again Washington Is Napping', in *The International Herald Tribune*, 28 May 2001

The Economist, 'Sins of the Secular Missionaries', 27 January 2000

The Economist, 'More Dangerous Work than Ever: Aid Agencies in Dangerous Places', 20 November 2004 (US Edition)

Erlanger, Steven, 'Nominee's Initial Talk Relies on Broad Strokes', in *The International Herald Tribune*, 18 December 2000

Groom, Brian and Nicoll, Alexander, 'A Theatre Where Nobody Wants A Long Run: Defence Chiefs Warn of "overstretch" as Talks Continue on a Peacekeeping Force for Afghanistan', in *The Financial Times (London)*, 13 December 2001

International Herald Tribune, 'American General Calls for more Afghanistan Aid', 10 July 2003

Kaplan, Robert, 'The Coming Anarchy', in *The Atlantic Monthly*, February 1994

Lambert, Andrew, 'Police and Thieves', in *The Times Literary Supplement*, 5 September 2003

Langewiesche, William, 'Peace is Hell', in *The Atlantic Monthly*, October 2001

Lynch, Colum, 'U.S. and UN at Odds on Leeway for Iraq', in *The International Herald Tribune*, 18 November 2002

MacKenzie, Lewis, 'The Real Story Behind Srberencia; The Massacre in the UN "Safe Haven" was not a Black and White Event', in *The Globe and Mail*, Toronto, 14 July 2005

McNamara, Dennis, 'Nation-building: The UN Has Been Learning How it's Done', in *The International Herald Tribune*, 29 October 2002

Marquis, Christopher and Shanker, Thom, 'Pentagon Leaders Warn of Dangers for U.S. in Liberia', in *The International Herald Tribune*, 25 July 2003

The New York Times, 'Powell Backs U.S. Role to Aid Liberia', 24 July 2003

The New York Times, 'Challenge for Bootstrap General is Winning Over the Wary Iraqis', 11 January 2004

Pfaff, William, 'Stopping Kosovo Attacks on Serbia is a Mission for NATO', in *The International Herald Tribune*, 1 February 2001

Phjlip Gourevitch, 'Never Againism', in *Granta*, 87, London, Autumn 2004

Pugh, Michael, 'Peacekeeping and Critical Theory', in *International Peacekeeping*, Vol. 11, Spring 2004

'PVOs Help US Military Train for Humanitarian Action', from *Monday Developments*, 5 September 1994

Rhode, David, 'Kosovo Seething', in *Foreign Affairs*, May/June 2000

Rice, Condaleeza, 'Campaign 2000: Promoting the National Interest', in *Foreign Affairs* January/February 2000

Salignon, Pierre, 'Violence Intensifies in Port au Prince, Haiti' (trans. Nina Freidman), in *Doctors Without Borders Emergency Alert* (newsletter_msf@newyork.msf.org) 30 June 2005

Steinhauer, Jennifer, 'When the Joneses Wear Jeans', in *The New York Times*, 29 May 2005

Traub, James, 'Making Sense of the Mission', in *The New York Times*, 11 April 2004

von Ilseman, Siegesmund, 'Recipe for a Disaster', in *Der Spiegel*, No. 34, 18 August 2003

Washington, George, Microsoft® Encarta® Online Encyclopedia 2003

Weisman, Steven R., 'Powell Says Rapes and Killings in Sudan Are Genocide', in *The New York Times*, 10 September 2004

Zimmerman, Warren, 'The Last Ambassador', in *Foreign Affairs*, March/April 1995

http://encarta.msn.com © 1997–2003 Microsoft Corporation

Journals

Annan, Kofi (Secretary-General of the United Nations), 'Peace Operations and the United Nations: Preparing for the Next Century', in *Conflict Resolution Monitor*, Issue 1, Summer 1997, Bradford University

Bellamy, Christopher, 'Combining Combat Readiness and Compassion', in *NATO Review*, Summer 2001

Brown, Lt Col. Richard, 'Power Politics in Southern Itraq', in *Revival: The Newsletter of the Post-War Reconstruction and Development Unit at the University of York*, Issue 19, February 2004

Call, Charles T. and Stanley, William, 'Protecting the People', in *Global Governance: A Review of Multilateralism and International Organizations*, Vol. 7, No. 2

'Civil-Military Communications in Complex Emergencies', in *PeaceWatch*, The United States Institute of Peace, Vol. VI, No. 4, Washington, DC, June 2000

Cockell, John C., 'Civil-Military Responses to Security Challenges', in *Global Governance: A Review of Multilateralism and International Organizations*, Vol. 8, No. 4, October–December 2002

Crosslines, The Independent News Journal on Humanitarian Action, Development and World Trends, January 1996

Evans, Gareth and Sahnoun, Mohamed, 'Intervention and State Sovereignty: Breaking New Ground', in *Global Governance: A Review of Multilateralism and International Organizations*, Vol. 7, No. 2, April–June 2001

Gordenker, Leon, 'What UN Principles? A U.S. Debate on Iraq', in *Global Governance*, Vol. 9, No. 3, July–September 2003

Hopkinson, Bryan, 'Soul Searching in Kosovo: March Violence Poses Challenge to International Community', in *The OSCE Magazine*, Vol. 1, No. 2, May 2004

Ignatieff, Michael, 'The Attack on Human Rights', in *Foreign Affairs*, November/December 2001

Lehmann, Ingrid A. 'Peacekeeping, Public Perceptions and the Need for Consent', in *Canadian Defence Quarterly*, Vol. 25, No. 2, Baxter Publications, Toronto, December 1995a

Lehmann, Ingrid A., 'Public Perceptions of U.N. Peacekeeping', in *The Fletcher Forum of World Affairs*, Vol. 19, No. 1, 1995b

Miller, Steven, 'Terrifying Thoughts', in *Global Governance*, Vol. 11, No. 2, April–June 2005

Nash, William, 'Can Soldiers be Peacekeepers and Warriors?', in *NATO Review*, Summer 2001

Riggs, David and Huberty, Robert, 'NGO Accountability: What the U.S. Can Teach the U.N.', Paper presented to a conference 'We're Not From the Government But We're Here to Help You', The American Enterprise Institute, Washington, DC, 11 June 2003

Shaw, Martin, 'The Contemporary Mode of Warfare?' in *Review of International Political Economy*, Vol. 7, No. 1, 2000

United States Institute for Peace, *Special Report: Balkans Returns*, Washington, DC, 21 December 1999

Documents

Address by the Secretary-General of the United Nations to the Stockholm International Forum for Combating Intolerance, Stockholm, 29 January 2001

Annan, Kofi (Secretary-General of the United Nations), *The Question of Intervention*, The United Nations Department of Public Information, New York, 1999

Basic Facts About the United Nations, Department of Public Information, New York, 1998

The Blue Helmets: A Review of UN Peacekeeping Operations, 2nd edn, UN Department of Information, New York, 1990

The Blue Helmets: A Review of United Nations Peacekeeping, 3rd edn, Department of Public Information, New York, 1996

Boutros Boutros-Ghali, *An Agenda for Peace: Preventive Diplomacy, Peacemaking and Peace-keeping*, The United Nations, New York, 1992

Chesterton, Simon, *The Use of Force in UN Peace Operations*, The United Nations Department of Peacekeeping Operations, Best Practices Unit, 31 August 2004

CIMIC in East Timor: An Account of Civil-Military Co-operation, Co-ordination and Collaboration in the Early Phases of the East Timor Relief Operation, UN Office for the Co-ordination of Humanitarian Affairs, Geneva

'Clinton in Short Visit to Rwanda', All-Africa News Agency, at http://www.africanews.org/usaf/stories/19980406_feat1.htm 1, 6 April 1998

del Ponte, Mme. Carla, 'Remarks to the Security Council', Prosecutor, the International Criminal Tribunal for the former Yugoslavia, 10 November 1999

Eaton, Robert, Horwood, Chris and Niland, Norah, *Study Report: The Development of Indigenous Mine Action Capabilities*, Lessons Learned Unit, Policy and Analysis Division, Department of Humanitarian Affairs, New York, 1997

Gotab, Elanders, *Challenges of Peace Operations: Into the 21st Century: Concluding Report 1997–2002*, Stockholm, 2002

Report of the Independent Inquiry into the Actions of the United Nations During the 1994 Genocide in Rwanda, at http://www.un.org/News/ossg/rwanda_report.htm, 15 December 1999

The Responsibility to Protect: Report of the International Commission on Intervention and State Sovereignty, The International Development Research Centre, Ottawa, 2001 (see also http://www.idrc.ca)

Rwanda: The Preventable Genocide, http://www.africanews.org/east/rwanda/stories/20000710/20000710_feat2.html

Submitted to the Security Council and to the General Assembly of the United Nations by the Secretary-General under A/55/305 – S/2000/809, dated 21 August 2000 ('The Brahimi Report')

Supplement to an Agenda for Peace: Position Paper of the Secretary-General on the Occasion of the Fiftieth Anniversary of the United Nations, A/5060/; S/1995/1, 3 January 1995

The United Nations and Somalia, 1992–1996, The United Nations Blue Book Series, Vol. VIII, United Nations Department of Public Information, New York, 1996: Document 52

'Working Paper, Council of Delegates, 1995', ICRC and International Federation, Council of Delegates, Geneva, 1–2 December 1995 (see http://www.icrc.org/unicc/icrcnews)

Interviews

'A Conversation with Peter Pace', The Council on Foreign Relations, Washington, DC, 17 February 2004

Online NewsHour: A Conversation with Tim Judah and Michael Ignatieff, http://www.pbs.org/newshour/gergen/jan-juneoo/kosovo_5–31.html, 31 May 2000

INDEX

For Product Safety Concerns and Information please contact our EU
representative GPSR@taylorandfrancis.com
Taylor & Francis Verlag GmbH, Kaufingerstraße 24, 80331 München, Germany

www.ingramcontent.com/pod-product-compliance
Lightning Source LLC
Chambersburg PA
CBHW050442280326
41932CB00013BA/2208